ISBN 978-1-4400-9882-6
PIBN 10184445

This book is a reproduction of an important historical work. Forgotten Books uses
state-of-the-art technology to digitally reconstruct the work, preserving the original format
whilst repairing imperfections present in the aged copy. In rare cases, an imperfection in
the original, such as a blemish or missing page, may be replicated in our edition. We do,
however, repair the vast majority of imperfections successfully; any imperfections that
remain are intentionally left to preserve the state of such historical works.

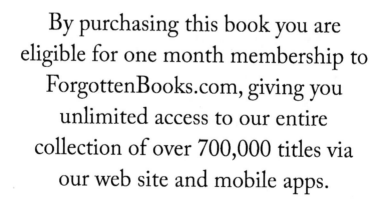

'AT THE CROW'S NEST'   *page 273*

EXPERIENCES
OF · A · DUG-OUT
1914-1918
BY MAJOR-GENERAL SIR
C. E. CALLWELL, K.C.B.

WITH A
FRONTISPIECE

16086

19 4

LONDON : CONSTABLE
& COMPANY LIMITED 1920

CROW'S NEST

EXPERIENCES OF·A·DUG OUT
1914-1918

BY MAJOR-GENERAL SIR
C. E. CALLWELL, K.C.B.

WITH A
FRONTISPIECE

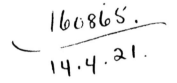

LONDON : CONSTABLE
& COMPANY LIMITED   1920

NOTE

SOME passages in this Volume have already appeared in *Blackwood's Magazine*. The Author has to express his acknowledgements to the Editor for permission to reproduce them.

Had Lord Fisher's death occurred before the proofs were finally passed for press, certain references to that great servant of the State would have been somewhat modified.

CONTENTS

CHAPTER I

CHAPTER II

CHAPTER III

nition of the magnitude of the contest—He makes things
hum in the War Office—His differences of opinion with
G.H.Q.—The inability of G.H.Q. to realize that a vast
expansion of the military forces was the matter of primary
importance—Lord K.'s relations with Sir J. French—The
despatch of Sir H. Smith-Dorrien to command the Second
Corps—Sir J. French not well treated at the time of the
Antwerp affair—The relegation of the General Staff at
the War Office to the background in the early days—
Question whether this was entirely due to its having
suffered in efficiency by the withdrawals which took place
on mobilization—The General Staff only eliminated in respect to operations.

CHAPTER IV

The munitions question and the Dardanelles to be dealt
with later—The Alexandretta project of the winter of
1914–15—Such an operation presented little difficulty then
—H.M.S. *Doris'* doings—The scheme abandoned—I am
sent to Paris about the Italian conventions just after the
Dardanelles landings—Concern at the situation after the
troops had got ashore at Helles and Anzac—A talk with
Lord K. and Sir E. Grey—Its consequences—Lord K.
seemed to have lost some of his confidence in his own
judgement with regard to operations questions—The
question of the withdrawal of the *Queen Elizabeth* from
the Aegean—The discussion about it at the Admiralty—
Lord K.'s inability to take some of his colleagues at their
own valuation—Does not know some of their names—
Another officer of distinction gets them mixed up in his
mind—Lord K.'s disappointment at the early failures of
the New Army divisions—His impatience when he wanted
anything in a hurry—My own experiences—Typists'
idiosyncrasies aggravate the trouble—Lord K. in an unreasonable mood—His knowledge of French—His skilful
handling of a Portuguese mission—His readiness to see
foreign officers when asked to do so—How he handled
them—The Serbian Military Attaché asks for approval
of an attack by his country upon Bulgaria at the time
of Bulgarian mobilization—A dramatic interview with Lord
K.—Confidence placed in him with regard to munitions
by the Russians—His speeches in the House of Lords—
The heat of his room—His preoccupation about the
safety of Egypt—He disapproves of the General Staff
plan with regard to its defence—His attitude with regard
to national service—His difficulties in this matter—His
anxiety to have a reserve in hand for delivering the
decisive blow in the war—My last meeting with him—His
pleasure in going to Russia—His failure to accomplish

his mission, a great disaster to the Entente cause—A final word about him—He did more than any man on the side of the Allies to win the war—Fitz.

CHAPTER V

The Tabah incident—The Dardanelles memorandum of 1906—Special steps taken with regard to it by Sir H. Campbell-Bannerman—Mr. Churchill first raises the question—My conference with him in October 1914—The naval project against the Straits—Its fundamental errors—Would never have been carried into effect had there been a conference between the Naval War Staff and the General Staff—The bad start—The causes of the final failure on the 18th of March—Lord K.'s instructions to Sir I. Hamilton—The question of the packing of the transports—Sir I. Hamilton's complaint as to there being no plan prepared—The 1906 memorandum—Sir Ian's complaint about insufficient information—How the 1906 memorandum affected this question—Misunderstanding as to the difficulty of obtaining information—The information not in reality so defective—My anxiety at the time of the first landing—The plan, a failure by early in May—Impossibility of sending reinforcements then—Question whether the delay in sending out reinforcements greatly affected the result in August 1915—The Dardanelles Committee—Its anxiety—Sir E. Carson and Mr. Churchill, allies—The question of clearing out—My disinclination to accept the principle before September—Sir C. Monro sent out—The delay of the Government in deciding—Lord K. proceeds to the Aegean—My own experiences—A trip to Paris with a special message to the French Government—Sent on a fool's errand, thanks to the Cabinet—A notable State paper on the subject—Mr. Lloyd George and the " sanhedrin "—Decision to evacuate only Anzac and Suvla—Sir W. Robertson arrives and orders sent to evacuate Helles—I give up the appointment of D.M.O.

CHAPTER VI

A reversion to earlier dates—The statisticians in the winter of 1914-15—The efforts to prove that German man-power would shortly give out—Lack of the necessary premises upon which to found such calculations—Views on the maritime blockade—The projects for operations against

CHAPTER VII

CHAPTER VIII

CHAPTER IX

CHAPTER X

CHAPTER XI

CHAPTER XII

CHAPTER XIII

CHAPTER XV

The Russian Revolution the worst disaster which befell
the Entente during the Great War—The political situation in Russia before that event much less difficult to
deal with than had been the political situation in the
Near East in 1915—The Allies' over-estimate of Russian
strength in the early months of the war—We hear about
the ammunition shortage first from Japan—Presumable
cause of the breakdown—The Grand Duke Nicholas'
difficulties in the early months—Great improvement
effected in respect to munitions subsequent to the summer
of 1915—Figures—Satisfactory outlook for the campaign
of 1917—Political situation goes from bad to worse—
Russian mission to London ; no steps taken by our Government—Our representatives in Russia—Situation at the end
of 1916—A private letter to Mr. Lloyd George—The Milner
Mission to Russia—Its failure to interpret the portents
—Had Lord Kitchener got out it might have made all the
difference—Some excuse for our blundering subsequent
to the Revolution—The delay in respect to action in
Siberia and at Vladivostok.

CHAPTER XVI

The appointment of Colonel Ellershaw to look after
Russian munition supplies—His remarkable success—I
take over his branch after his death—Gradual alteration
of its functions—The Commission Internationale de
Ravitaillement—Its efficiency—The despatch of goods to
Russia—Russian technical abilities in advance of their
organizing power—The flame projector and the Stokes
mortar—Drawings and specifications of Tanks—An early
contretemps in dealing with a Russian military delegate—
Misadventure in connection with a 9·2-inch howitzer—
Difficulties at the northern Russian ports—The American
contracts—The Russian Revolution—This transforms the
whole position as to supplies—Roumania—Statesmen in
conflict—Dealings with the Allies' delegates in general—
Occasional difficulties—Helpfulness of the United States
representatives—The Greek muddle—Getting it disen-
tangled—Great delays in this country and in France in
fitting out the Greeks, and their consequences—Serbian
supplies—The command in Macedonia ought on administrative grounds to have been in British hands.

CHAPTER XVII

CHAPTER XVIII

CHAPTER I

THE OUTBREAK OF WAR

Unfair disparagement of the War Office during the war—Difficulties under which it suffered owing to pre-war misconduct of the Government—The army prepared, the Government and the country unprepared—My visit to German districts on the Belgian and Luxemburg frontiers in June 1914—The German railway preparations—The plan of the Great General Staff indicated by these—The Aldershot Command at exercise—I am summoned to London by General H. Wilson—Informed of contemplated appointment to be D.M.O.—The unsatisfactory organization of the Military Operations Directorate—An illustration of this from pre-war days—G.H.Q. rather a nuisance until they proceeded to France—The scare about a hostile maritime descent—Conference at the Admiralty—The depletion of my Directorate to build up G.H.Q.—Inconvenience of this in the case of the section dealing with special Intelligence services—An example of the trouble that arose at the very start—This points to a misunderstanding of the relative importance of the War Office and of G.H.Q.—Sir J. French's responsibility for this, Sir C. Douglas not really responsible—Colonel Dallas enumerates the great numerical resources of Germany—Lord Kitchener's immediate recognition of the realities of the situation—Sir J. French's suggestion that Lord Kitchener should be Commander-in-Chief of the Expeditionary Force indicated misconception of the position of affairs.

IN a record of experiences during the Great War that were for the most part undergone within the War Office itself, it is impossible to overcome the temptation to draw attention at the start to the unreasonably disparaging attitude towards that institution which has been adopted so generally throughout the country. Nobody will contend that hideous blunders were not committed by some departments of the central administration of the Army in Whitehall during the progress of the struggle. It has to be admitted that

considerable sums of money were from time to time
wasted—it could hardly be otherwise in such strenuous
times. A regrettable lack of foresight was undoubtedly
displayed in some particulars. But tremendous difficulties, difficulties for the existence of which the military
authorities were nowise to blame, had on the other
hand to be overcome—and they were overcome. Nor
can the War Office be robbed of its claim to have borne
the chief share in performing what was the greatest
miracle of all the miracles performed during the course
of the contest. Within the space of less than two years
the United Kingdom was, mainly by the exertions of
the War Office, transformed into a Great Military Power.
That achievement covers up many transgressions.

It has to be remembered that in this matter the
detractors had it all their own way during the struggle.
Anybody harbouring a grievance, real or imaginary,
was at liberty to air his wrongs, whereas the mouths of
soldiers in a position to reply had perforce to remain
closed and have to a great extent still to remain closed.
The disgruntled had the field pretty well to themselves.
Ridiculous stories for which there was not one atom of
foundation have gained currency, either because those
who knew the truth were precluded by their official
status from revealing the facts or because no one took
the trouble to contradict the absurdities. Some of these
yarns saw the light in the newspapers, and the credulity
of the public in accepting everything that happens to
appear in the Press is one of the curiosities of the age.
Not, however, that many of the criticisms of which the
War Office was the subject during the protracted broil
were not fully warranted. Some of them were indeed
most helpful. But others were based on a positively
grovelling ignorance of the circumstances governing the
subject at issue. Surely it is an odd thing that, whereas
your layman will shy at committing himself in regard
to legal problems, will not dream of debating medical
questions, will shrink from expressing opinions on

matters involving acquaintance with technical science, will even be somewhat guarded in his utterances concerning the organization and handling of fleets, everybody is eager to lay the law down respecting the conduct of war on land.

A reference has been made above to the extraordinary difficulties under which the War Office laboured during the war. The greatest of these, at all events during the early days, was the total misconception of the international situation of which H.M. Government had been guilty—or had apparently been guilty—during the years immediately preceding the outbreak of hostilities. No intelligible and satisfactory explanation of this has ever been put forward. Their conduct in this connection had been the conduct of fools, or of knaves, or of liars. They had been acting as fools if they had failed to interpret auguries which presented no difficulty whatever to people of ordinary intelligence who took the trouble to watch events. They had been acting as knaves if they had been drawing their salaries and had not earned them by making themselves acquainted with facts which it was their bounden duty to know. They had been acting as liars if, when fully aware of the German preparations for aggressive war and of what these portended, they had deliberately deceived and hoodwinked the countrymen who trusted them. (Personally, I should be disposed to acquit them of having been fools or knaves —but I may be wrong.) Several Ministers had indeed deliberately stated in their places in Parliament that the nation's military arrangements were not framed to meet anything beyond the despatch to an oversea theatre of war of four out of the six divisions of our Expeditionary Force ! One of the gang had even been unable " to conceive circumstances in which continental operations by our troops would not be a crime against the people of this country."

Much has been said and written since 1914 concerning the unpreparedness of the army for war. But the truth is that the army was not unprepared for that limited-liability, pill-to-stop-an-earthquake theory of making war which represented the programme of Mr. Asquith and his colleagues before the blow fell. Take it all round, the Expeditionary Force was as efficient as any allied or hostile army which took the field. It was almost as well prepared for the supreme test in respect to equipment as it was in respect to leadership and training. The country and the Government, not the army, were unprepared. There was little wrong with the military forces except that they represented merely a drop in the ocean, that they constituted no more than an advanced guard to legions which did not exist. Still one must acknowledge that (as will be pointed out further on) even some of our highest military authorities did not realize what an insignificant asset our splendid little Expeditionary Force would stand for in a great European war, nor to have grasped when the crash came that the matter of paramount importance in connection with the conduct of the struggle on land was the creation of a host of fighting men reaching such dimensions as to render it competent to play a really vital rôle in achieving victory for the Entente.

As it happened, I had proceeded as a private individual in the month of June 1914 to inspect the German railway developments directed towards the frontiers of Belgium and of Luxemburg. This was an illuminating, indeed an ominous, experience. Entering the Kaiser's dominions by the route from the town of Luxemburg to Trèves, one came of a sudden upon a colossal detraining station that was not quite completed, fulfilling no conceivable peaceful object and dumped down on the very frontier—anything more barefaced it would be difficult to conceive. Trèves itself, three or four miles on, constituted a vast railway centre, and three miles or so yet farther along there was its counterpart in another great railway centre where there was no town at all. You got Euston, Liverpool Street, and Waterloo—only the lines and sidings, of course—grown up like mushrooms in a non-populous and non-industrial region, and at the very gates of a little State of which Germany had guaranteed the neutrality.

Traversing the region to the north of the Moselle along the western German border-line, this proved to be a somewhat barren, partly woodland, partly moorland, tract, sparsely inhabited as Radnor and Strathspey; and yet this unproductive district had become a network of railway communications. Elaborate detraining stations were passed every few miles. One constantly came upon those costly overhead cross-over places, where one set of lines is carried right over the top of another set at a junction, so that continuous traffic going one way shall not be checked by traffic coming in from the side and proceeding in the opposite direction—a plan seldom adopted at our most important railway centres. On one stretch of perhaps half-a-dozen miles connecting two insignificant townships were to be seen eight lines running parallel to each other. Twopenny-halfpenny little trains doddered along, occasionally taking up or putting down a single passenger at some halting-place that was large enough to serve a Coventry or a Croydon. The slopes of the cuttings and sidings were destitute of herbage; the bricks of the culverts and bridges showed them by the colour to be brand-new; all this construction had taken place within the previous half-dozen years. Everything seemed to be absolutely ready except that one place on the Luxemburg frontier mentioned above, and that obviously could be completed in a few hours of smart work, if required.

One had heard a good deal about the Belgians having filled in a gap on their side of the frontier so as to join up Malmedy with their internal railway system, and thus to establish a fresh through-connection between the Rhine-land and the Meuse, so I travelled along this on my way back. But it was unimpressive. The drop from the rolling uplands about the camp of Elsenborn down to Malmedy gave rise to very steep gradients on the German side, and the single line of rail was so dilapidated and was so badly laid that, as we ran down with steam off, it hardly seemed safe for a short train of about half-a-dozen coaches. That the Great General Staff had no intention of making this a main line of advance appeared to be pretty clear. They meant the hosts that they would dispose of when the moment came, to sweep round by communications lying farther to the north, starting from about Aix-la-Chapelle and heading for the gap south of the Dutch enclave about Maestricht. The impression acquired during this flying visit was that for all practical purposes the Germans had everything ready for an immediate invasion of Belgium and Luxemburg when the crisis arrived, that they were simply awaiting the fall of the flag, that when war came they meant to make their main advance through Belgium, going wide, and that *pickelhaubes* would be as the sands of the sea for number well beyond Liège within a very few days of the outbreak of hostilities. On getting home I compared notes with the Intelligence Section of the General Staff which was especially interested in these territories, but found little to tell them that they did not know already except with regard to a few very recently completed railway constructions. The General Staff hugged no illusions. They were not so silly as to suppose that the Teuton proposed to respect treaties in the event of the upheaval that was sure to come ere long.

Having a house at Fleet that summer, I cycled over to beyond Camberley one day, just at the stage when coming events were beginning to cast their shadows before after the Serajevo assassinations, to watch the Aldershot Command at work, and talked long with many members of the Command and with some of the Staff College personnel who had turned out to see the show. Some of them—*e.g.* Lieut.-Colonels W. Thwaites and J. T. Burnett-Stuart and Major (or was it Captain ?) W. E. Ironside—were to go far within the next five years. But there were also others whom I met that day for the last time—Brigadier-General Neil Findlay, commanding the artillery, who had been in the same room with me at the " Shop," and Lieut.-Colonel Adrian Grant-Duff of the Black Watch, excusing his presence in the firing-line on the plea that he " really *must* see how his lads worked through the woodlands " ; both had made the supreme sacrifice in France before the leaves were off the trees. How many are alive and unmaimed to-day of those fighting men of all ranks who buzzed about so cheerily amid the heather and the pine trees that afternoon, and who melted away so silently out of Aldershot a very few days later ?

The clouds thereafter gathered thicker from day to day, and on Friday morning, the 31st of July, I received a letter from General Henry Wilson, sent on from my town address, asking me to come and breakfast with him on the following day. I was going down to Winchester to see the Home Counties (Territorial) Division complete a long march from the east on their way to Salisbury Plain, and it happened to be inconvenient to go up to town that night, so I wired to Wilson to say I would call at his house on the Sunday. On getting back, late, to Fleet I however found a peremptory summons from him saying I must come and see him next day, and I went up in the morning. One could not foresee that that breakfast in Draycott Place to which I had been bidden was to take rank as a historic meal. Mr. Maxse has told the story of it in the pages of the *National Review*, and of how the movement was there started by which the Unionist leaders were got together from various quarters to bring pressure on the Government not to leave France in the lurch, a movement which culminated in Mr. Bonar Law's famous letter to Mr. Asquith.

On meeting General Wilson at the War Office about noon he told me that I was to take his place as Director of Military Operations in case of mobilization, and he asked me to join as soon as possible. He further made me acquainted with the political situation, with the very unsatisfactory attitude which a proportion of the Cabinet were disposed to take up, and with the steps which Messrs. George Lloyd, Amery, Maxse, and others were taking to mobilize the Opposition leaders and to compel the Government to play the game. In the last conversation that I ever had with Lord Roberts, two or three days before the great Field-Marshal paid the visit to the Front which was so tragically cut short, he spoke enthusiastically of the services of Lloyd (now Sir George) on this occasion. In consequence of what I had learnt I joined at the War Office for duty on the Monday, although the arrangement was irregular and purely provisional for the moment, seeing that it had not yet been decided whether mobilization was to be ordained or not. But I found Wilson in much more buoyant mood after the week-end of anxiety, for he believed that Mr. Bonar Law's letter had proved the decisive factor. By this time we moreover knew that Germany had already violated the neutrality of Luxemburg and was threatening Belgium openly.

I ought to mention here that this appointment to the post of Director of Military Operations came as a complete surprise—my not having been warned well in advance had been due to an oversight; up to within a few months earlier, when I had ceased to belong to the Reserve of Officers, having passed the age-limit for colonels, my fate in the event of general mobilization was to have been something high up on the staff of the Home Defence Army. One could entertain no illusions. Heavy responsibilities were involved in taking up such an appointment on the eve of war. After five years of civil life it was a large order to find myself suddenly thrust into such a job and to be called upon to take up charge of a War Office Directorate which I knew was overloaded. Ever since 1904, ever since the date when this Directorate had been set up by the Esher Committee as one item in the reconstitution of the office as a whole and when my section of the old Intelligence Division had been absorbed into it, I had insisted that this composite branch was an overburdened and improperly constituted one.

For the Esher triumvirate had amalgamated " operations " and " intelligence," while they had deposited " home defence " in the Military Training Directorate. It was an absurd arrangement in peace-time, and one that was wholly unadapted to the conditions of a great war. Lord Esher and his colleagues would seem, however, to have been actuated by a fear lest the importance of home defence should overshadow that of preparation for oversea warfare if the two sets of duties were in one hand, and, inasmuch as they were making a start with the General Staff at Headquarters and bearing in mind former tendencies, they may have been right. They, moreover, hardly realized perhaps that intelligence must always be the handmaid of operations, and that it is in the interest of both that they should be kept quite distinct. It was natural that the first Chief of the General Staff to be appointed, Sir N. Lyttelton, should have hesitated to overset an organization which had been so recently laid down and which had been accepted by the Government as it stood, even if he recognized its unsuitability ; but I have never been able to understand how his successors, Sir W. Nicholson and Sir J. French, failed to effect the rearrangement of duties which a sound system of administration imperatively called for. That my predecessors, Generals " Jimmy " Grierson, Spencer Ewart, and Henry Wilson, made no move in the matter is rendered the more intelligible to me by the fact that I took no steps in the matter myself, even when the need for a reorganization was driven home by the conditions brought about in the War Office during the early months of the Great War. Somehow one feels no irresistible impulse to abridge one's functions and to depreciate one's importance by one's own act, to lop off one's own members, so to speak. But when Sir W. Robertson turned up ﹒at the end of 1915 to﹒become

C.I.G.S. he straightway split my Directorate in two, and he thus put things at last on a proper footing.

The incongruity of the Esher organization had, it may be mentioned, been well illustrated by an episode that occurred very shortly after the reconstitution of the War Office had been carried into effect in the spring of 1904. Under the distribution of duties then laid down, my section of the Operations Directorate dealt *inter alia* with questions of coast defence in connection with our stations abroad, while a section of the Military Training Directorate dealt *inter alia* with questions of coast defence in connection with our stations at home. It came about that the two sections issued instructions simultaneously about the same thing, and the instructions issued by the two sections were absolutely antagonistic. The consequence was that coast defence people at Malta came to be doing the thing one way, while those at Portsmouth came to be doing it exactly the opposite way, and that the War Office managed to give itself away and to expose itself to troublesome questionings. The blunder no doubt could be put down to lack of co-ordination ; but the primary cause was the existence of a faulty organization under which two different branches at Headquarters were dealing with the one subject.

The earliest experiences in the War Office in August 1914 amounted, it must be confessed, almost to a night mare. There were huge maps working on rollers in my spacious office, and in particular there was one of vast dimensions portraying what even then was coming to be called the Western Front. During the week or so that elapsed before G.H.Q. of the Expeditionary Force proceeded to the theatre of war, its cream thought fit to spend the hours of suspense in creeping on tiptoe in and out of my apartment, clambering on and off a table which fronted this portentous map, discussing strategical problems in blood-curdling whispers, and every now and then expressing an earnest hope that this sort of thing was not a nuisance. It was a most intolerable nuisance, but they were persons of light and leading who could not be addressed in appropriate terms. As hour to hour passed, and H.M. Government could not make up its mind to give the word " go " to the Expeditionary Force, G.H.Q.'s language grew stronger and stronger until the walls resounded with expletives. It was not easy to concentrate one's attention upon questions arising in the performance of novel duties in a time of grave emergency under such conditions, and it was a genuine relief when the party took itself off to France.

One was too busy to keep notes of what went on in those days and I am not sure of exact dates, but I think that it was on the 6th of August that a wire, which seemed on the face of it to be trustworthy, came to hand from a German port, to the effect that transports and troops were being collected there to convey a military force somewhither. This message caused the Government considerable concern and very nearly delayed the despatch of the Expeditionary Force across the Channel. One was too new to the business to take the proper steps to trace the source of that message, which, as far as I remember, purported to emanate from one of our consuls ; but I have a strong suspicion that the message was faked—was really sent off by the Germans. Lord Kitchener had taken up the appointment of Secretary of State that morning, and in the afternoon he walked across Whitehall, accompanied by my immediate chief, Sir C. Douglas the C.I.G.S., General Kiggell, and myself, to discuss the position with Mr. Churchill and the chiefs of the Admiralty in the First Lord's room. Whitehall was rendered almost impassable by a mass of excited citizens, and Lord Kitchener on being recognized was wildly cheered. Nothing could have been clearer and more reassuring than Mr. Churchill's exposition of the naval arrangements to meet any attempt at a landing on our shores, and any one of the War Office quartette who may have been troubled with qualms—I had felt none myself—must have had his anxiety allayed.

It will not be out of place to refer here to one aspect of the virtual emasculation of the General Staff at the War Office on mobilization that has not perhaps quite received the attention that it deserves. That, in spite of his being Director of Military Operations in Whitehall, General Wilson very properly accompanied the Expeditionary Force will hardly be disputed. He had established close and cordial relations with the French higher military authorities, he could talk French like a Parisian, he had worked out the details of the concentration of our troops on the farther side of the Channel months before, and he probably knew more about the theatre where our contingent was expected to operate than any man in the army. But he was not the only member of the Military Operations Directorate staff who disappeared; he took his right-hand man and his left-hand man in respect to actual operations with him. Nevertheless, as I was pretty familiar with the working of the War Office, and as the planting down of the Expeditionary Force beyond Le Cateau was effected, practically automatically, by the Movements branch under the Quartermaster-General, operations question in respect to the war in the West gave no great trouble until my Directorate had had time to settle down after a fashion in its new conditions.

But the Intelligence side of General Wilson's Directorate included a branch which dealt with a number of matters with which no Director brought in from outside was likely to be well acquainted, and about which I knew nothing at all. Very few officers in the regular army are conversant with international law. Nor used they, in the days before 1914, to interest themselves in the status of aliens when the country is engaged in hostilities, nor with problems of censorship of the post and telegraph services, nor with the relations between the military and the Press, nor yet with the organization, the maintenance, and the duties of a secret service. Before mobilization, all this was in the hands of a section under the D.M.O. which was in charge of Colonel (now Lieut.-General Sir G.)

Macdonogh, who had made a special study of these matters, and who had devised a machinery for performing a number of duties in this country which on the outbreak of war necessarily assumed a cardinal importance and called for efficient administration at the hands of a large personnel, only to be got together when the emergency arose. But Colonel Macdonogh on mobilization took up an important appointment with the Expeditionary Force, and went off to France, carrying off his assistants with him. As far as personnel was concerned, this cupboard was left as bare as a fashionable lady's back when *en grande tenue* in " Victory Year." Charge of it was assumed by an extremely capable and energetic substitute brought in from outside (Colonel D. L. MacEwen), who, however, suffered under the disability of knowing practically nothing about the peculiar class of work which he was suddenly called upon to take up.

As an example of the extreme inconvenience which this caused, the following somewhat comical incident may be related. Three or four days after the declaration of war a brace of very distinguished civil servants, one representing the Foreign Office and the other the Home Office, came across Whitehall by appointment and with long faces, and the four of us sat solemnly round a table— they, Colonel MacEwen, and I. It appeared that we had been guilty of terrifying violations of international law. We had seized numbers of German reservists and German males of military age on board ships in British ports, and had consigned some of them to quarters designed for the accommodation of malefactors. This sort of thing would never do. Such steps had not been taken by belligerents in 1870, nor at the time of the American War of Secession, and I am not sure that Messrs. Mason and Slidell were not trotted out. The Foreign and Home Secretaries, the very distinguished civil servants declared, would not unlikely be agitated when they heard of the shocking affair. Soldiers, no doubt, were by nature abrupt and unconventional in their actions, and the Foreign and Home

Offices would make every allowance, realizing that we had acted in good faith. But, hang it all—and they gazed at us in compassionate displeasure.

Will it be believed? My assistant and I knew so little about our business that we did not fall upon that pair of pantaloons and rend them. We took them and their protestation quite seriously. We accepted their courteous, but uncompromising, rebuke like small boys caught stealing apples, whose better feelings have been appealed to. For the space of two or three hours, and until we had pulled ourselves together, we remained content, on the strength of doctrines enunciated by a couple of officials fossilized by having dwelt in a groove for years, to accept it as a principle that this tremendous conflict into which the Empire had been plunged at a moment's notice was to be a kid-glove transaction. Within three weeks the Foreign Office and the Home Office were, however, praying us in the War Office for goodness' sake to take all questions in connection with the internment and so forth of aliens entirely off their hands because they could make nothing of the business.

The above reference to my having been virtually left in the lurch with regard to these, to me, occult matters is not made by way of complaint. It is made because it illustrates with signal force how completely the relative importance of the Expeditionary Force as compared to the task which the War Office had to face had been misunderstood when framing plans in advance for the anticipated emergency. Colonel Macdonogh became head of Sir J. French's Intelligence Department in the field. That was a very important appointment and one for which he was admirably fitted, but it was one which many other experienced officers in the army could have effectually filled. The appointment at the War Office which he gave up was one which no officer in the army was so well qualified—nor nearly so well qualified—to hold as he was, and it was at the outbreak of war incomparably the more important appointment of the two.

The arrangement arrived at in respect to this matter indicated, in fact, a strange lack of sense of proportion. It argued a fundamental misconception of the military problem with which the country was confronted.

In his book, "*1914*," in which he finds so much to say in disparagement of Lord Kitchener, Lord French has very frankly admitted his inability to foresee certain tactical developments in connection with heavy artillery and so forth, which actual experience in the field brought home to him within a few weeks of the opening of hostilities. Most of the superior French and German military authorities who held sway in the early days of the struggle would probably similarly plead guilty, for nobody in high places anticipated these developments. The Field-Marshal, on the other hand, makes no reference to any failure on his part to realize in advance the relatively insignificant part which our original Expeditionary Force would be able to play in the great contest. He makes no admission as to a misconception with regard to the paramount problem which faced the British military authorities as a whole after mobilization was decreed. He would not seem to have been aware, when a conflict of first-rate magnitude came upon us, that the creation of a great national army was of far greater consequence than the operations of the small body of troops which he took with him into the field. The action taken in connection with the personnel of the General Staff in Whitehall is significant evidence of the extent to which the whole situation had been misinterpreted.

It may be urged that Sir J. French (as he then was) was not responsible. He had — under circumstances which will not have been forgotten—ceased to be Chief of the Imperial General Staff some four months before war broke out   But Sir Charles Douglas, who had then taken his place, although a resolute, experienced soldier, equipped with an almost unique knowledge of the army, was a deliberate, cautious Scot ; he was the very last man to shirk responsibility and to shelter himself behind somebody else, but, on the other hand, he was not an impatient thruster who would be panting to be—in gunner's parlance—" re-teaming the battery before the old major was out of the gate." He accepted, and he was indeed bound to accept, the ideas of a predecessor of the highest standing in the Service, who had made a special study of campaigning possibilities under the conditions which actually arose in August 1914, and under whose aegis definite plans and administrative arrangements to meet the case had been elaborated beforehand with meticulous care. Enjoying all the advantages arising from having made a close study of the subject and from having an Intelligence Department brimming over with detailed information at his beck and call, Sir J. French entirely failed to grasp the extent and nature of the war in its early days. Lord Kitchener did. Suddenly summoned to take supreme military charge, a stranger to the War Office and enjoying none of Sir J. French's advantages, the new Secretary of State mastered the realities of the position at once by some sort of instinct, perceived what a stupendous effort would have to be made, took the long view from the start, and foretold that the struggle would last some years.

It must have been about the 11th of August, three days before G.H.Q. crossed the Channel, that I went in with Sir John to see Colonel Dallas, the head of my Intelligence section dealing with Germany. One had been too busy during the previous few days to bother much about the German army, and at the time I knew little more about that formidable fighting machine than what was told in books of reference like the *Statesman's Year-book*, which gave full particulars about First Line Troops, but said uncommonly little about Reserve Formations. Information with regard to these could only be obtained from secret sources. What we were told by Dallas was a revelation to me. There seemed to be no end to the enemy's fighting resources. He kept on producing fresh batches of Reserve Divisions and Extra-

Reserve Divisions, like a conjurer who produces huge glass bowls full of goldfish out of his waistcoat pocket. He seemed to be doing it on purpose—one felt quite angry with the man. But it was made plain to me that we were up against a tougher proposition than I had imagined. The Field-Marshal must have been, or at all events ought to have been, perfectly well aware of all this, seeing that he had been C.I.G.S. up till very recently, and had devoted special attention to the problems involved in a war with Germany.

In a foot-note near the end of "*1914*," Lord French mentions having, on some occasion during the few days when war was still trembling in the balance, suggested to Lord Kitchener that they should repair together to the Prime Minister and propose that Lord Kitchener should be commander-in-chief of the field army, with him (French) as Chief of Staff. That was a self-sacrificing suggestion ; but it surely indicates an absence of what Lord Haldane calls " clear thinking." Sir J. French had been organizing and training the Expeditionary Force for some years previously, knew all about it, was acquainted with its generals and staffs, was up-to-date in connection with progress in tactical details, and had studied the strategical situation in Belgium and France. Lord Kitchener had, on the other hand, been in civil employment and out of touch with most military questions for some considerable time previously. Lord Kitchener would have been thrown away commanding the Expeditionary Force. He was needed for the much more important position which he actually took up.

CHAPTER II

EARLY DAYS AT THE WAR OFFICE

Plan of issuing *communiqués* given up owing to the disposition to conceal reverses that manifested itself—Direct telephonic communication with the battlefield in Belgium—A strange attempt to withhold news as to the fall of Brussels—Anxiety during the retreat from Mons—The work of the Topographical Section at that time—Arrival of refugee officers and other ranks at the War Office—One of the Royal Irish affords valuable information—Candidates for the appointment of " Intelligence Officer "—How one dealt with recommendations in regard to jobs—Linguists—The discoverer of interpreters, fifty produced as if by magic—The Boy Scouts in the War Office—An Admirable Crichton—The scouts' effective method of handling troublesome visitors—Army chaplains in embryo—A famous cricketer doing his bit—A beauty competition outside my door—The Eminent K.C.—An impressive personality—How he benefits the community—The Self-Appointed Spy-Catcher—Gun platforms concealed everywhere—The hidden dangers in disused coal mines in Kent—Procuring officers for the New Armies—" Bill " Elliot's unorthodox methods—The Military Secretary's branch meets with a set-back—Visits from Lord Roberts—His suggestion as to the commander-in-chiefship in China—His last visit—The Antwerp business—The strategical situation with regard to the Belgian field army—The project of our Government—The despatch of the Seventh Division and the Third Cavalry Division to Belgian Flanders—Organization of base and line of communications overlooked—A couple of transports " on their own " come to a halt on the Goodwins—Difficulty of the strategical situation—Death of Sir O. Douglas.

IT will be remembered that although our troops were not engaged during the first fortnight of the war, and were indeed never likely to be engaged so early, events moved quickly on the Western Front, and that the set-back encountered by the Germans when they tried to smother Liège without bringing up heavy artillery aroused a certain enthusiasm in this country. On taking stock of my duties, it had appeared to me that one of these would be the issue of reasoned *communiqués* to the Press from time to time, and I actually drafted one, designed to convey a warning as to excessive jubilation over incidents such as the momentary success of the defending side in the struggle for the stronghold on the Meuse, which appeared in all the newspapers. The following passage occurred in it · " The exaggeration into important triumphs of minor episodes in which the Allies are alleged to have gained the upper hand is misleading." But it speedily became apparent that the powers that be did not mean to be expansive in connection with incidents where our side was getting the worst of it, so the plan of issuing *communiqués* was abandoned almost at once.

One soon learnt that Belgian resistance was being brushed aside by the enemy with comparative ease, and that such delay as the invaders had suffered before Liège did not very appreciably interfere with the plans of the German Great General Staff. Going one afternoon into the room occupied by the head of my Intelligence section which was charged with French and Belgian affairs, I found him on his telephone and holding up his hand to enjoin silence. He was speaking with the late General " Sandy " Du Cane, our representative with King Albert's forces in the field, who was at the moment actually on the battlefield and under fire. While I was in the room, Du Cane wound up the conversation with : " They're giving way all along the line. I'm off." A day or two after this the Boches were in Brussels, and one realized that our Expeditionary Force must very soon be in the thick of it.

For some reason or other those in the highest places at the War Office hesitated to allow the news that Brussels had fallen to leak out to the public—an attitude at which the newspaper editors were not unnaturally incensed— and Mr. F. E. Smith, now Lord Birkenhead, who was head of the Press Bureau, came to see me that evening, and was outspoken as to the absurdity of this sort of thing. The matter did not, however, rest in my hands. The secretiveness in connection with reverses and contretemps which prevailed at that time, and which continued to prevail during the first year and a half of the war—during the very period when I had certain responsibilities in connection with such matters myself— seemed to me then, and seems to me now, to have been a mistake. It did our cause considerable harm, it delayed the putting forth of the full fighting strength of the British nation, it created irritation in the country when it came to be detected, and it even at times caused official reports which were perfectly in accordance with the facts to be regarded with suspicion. The point will be touched upon again in later chapters.

Then came those grey days when we knew that the Entente plan of campaign had broken down, that the forces on our side were not satisfactorily disposed for staying the hostile rush, that the French were unable to hold their ground, and that our little army were sore beset and in full retreat before superior hosts. King's Messengers, the Duke of Marlborough and Major Hankey, came to see me, and told me of the atmosphere of grave anxiety prevalent at G.H.Q. A message from General Henry Wilson, written in pencil late at night on a leaf of a notebook, reached me, of so ominous a character (seeing that he assuredly was not one to quail) that I never showed it to anybody—not even to my chief, Sir C. Douglas. And yet, one felt somehow that we should pull through in spite of all, and even though the demands coming to hand for maps of regions in the very heart of France certainly conveyed no encouragement: One regretted that the country was being kept so much in the dark—the best is never got out of the Anglo-Saxon race until it is in a tight place. A special edition of the *Times*, issued on Sunday morning the 30th of August, which contained a somewhat lurid account of the retreat by some hysterical journalist, and which, it turned out, had been doctored by the head of the Press Bureau, caused great anger in some quarters. But for my part I rather welcomed it. Anything that would help to bring home to the public what they were up against was to the good. Whoever first made use of that pestilent phrase " business as usual," whether it was a Cabinet Minister, or a Fleet Street scribe, or some gag-merchant on the music-hall stage, had much to answer for.

The Topographical Section under Colonel Hedley did fine work during those troubled days before the Battle of the Marne. It was in the highest degree gratifying to find a branch, for which one found oneself suddenly after a fashion responsible, to be capable of so promptly and effectually meeting emergencies. The Expeditionary Force had taken with it generous supplies of maps portraying the regions adjacent to the Franco-Belgian frontier, where it proposed to operate ; a somewhat hasty retreat to a point right away back, south-east of Paris, had formed no part of its programme. A day or two after the first clash of arms near Mons, a wire arrived demanding the instant despatch of maps of the country as far to the rear as the Seine and the Marne. Now, as all units had to be supplied on a liberal scale, this meant hundreds of copies of each of a considerable number of different large-scale sheets, besides hundreds of copies of two or three more general small-scale sheets ; nevertheless, the consignment was on its way before midnight. A day or two later G.H.Q. wired for maps as far back as Orleans, a day or two later, again, for maps as far as the mouth of the Loire, and yet a day or two later, for maps down to Bordeaux—this last request representing thousands of sheets. But on each occasion the demand was met within a few hours and without the slightest hitch. It was a remarkable achievement—an achievement attributable in part to military foresight dating back to the days when Messrs. Asquith, Lloyd George, Churchill and Co., either deliberately or else as a result of sheer ignorance and ineptitude, were deceiving their countrymen as to the gravity of the German menace, an achievement attributable also in part to military administrative efficiency of a high order in a time of crisis. The Topographical Section, it should be added, was able to afford highly appreciated assistance to our French and Belgian allies in the matter of supplying them with maps of their own countries.

During the first two or three weeks after fighting started, waifs and strays who had been run over by the Boches, but who had picked themselves up somehow and had fetched up at the coast, used to turn up at the War Office and to find their way to my department. For some reason or other they always presented themselves after dinner—like the coffee. The first arrival was a young cavalry officer, knocked off his horse in the preliminary encounters by what had evidently been the detonation of a well-pitched-up high-explosive, and who was still suffering from a touch of what we now know as shell-shock. He proved to be the very embodiment of effective military training, because, although he was to the last degree vague as to how he had got back across the Channel and only seemed to know that he had had a bath at the Cavalry Club, he was able to give most useful and detailed information as to what he had noted after recovering consciousness while making his way athwart the German trains and troops in reserve as they poured along behind Von Kluck's troops in front line. One observed the same thing in the case of another cavalry officer who arrived some days later, after a prolonged succession of tramps by night from the Sambre to Ostend. " You'll sleep well to-night," I remarked when thanking him for the valuable information that he had been able to impart—and of a sudden he looked ten years older. " I couldn't sleep a wink last night at Ostend," he muttered in a bewildered sort of way, " and I don't feel as if I'd ever sleep again."

We did not wear uniform in the War Office for the first month or so, and one night about this time, on meeting a disreputable and suspicious-looking character on the stairs, garbed in the vesture affected by the foreign mechanic, I was debating whether to demand of the interloper what he was doing within the sacred precincts, when he abruptly accosted me with : " I say, d'you happen to know where in this infernal rabbit-warren a blighter called the Something of Military Operations hangs out ? " His address indicated him to be a refugee officer looking for my department.

These prodigals had such interesting experiences to recount that, in a weak moment, I gave instructions for them to be brought direct to me, and about 10 P.M. one night, when there happened to be a lot of unfinished stuff to be disposed of before repairing homewards, a tarnished-looking but otherwise smart and well-set-up private soldier was let loose on me. A colloquy somewhat as follows ensued :

" What regiment ? "

" The Rile Irish, sorr." (He said this as if there was no other regiment—they always do.)

"Ah! Well, and how have you got along back here?"

" Sorr, it's the truth I'm tellin' ye, sorra ilse. Sure wasn't I marchin' and fightin' and hidin' and craalin' for wakes and wakes " (the Royal Irish could only have detrained at Le Cateau about ten days before) " before I gits to that place as they calls Boulong—a gran' place, sorr, wid quays and thruck like it was the North Waal— an' a fellah takes me to the Commandant, sorr, where I seen a major-man wid red tabs an' an eye like Polly-famous. ' Sorr,' sez I to him, sez I ; sez I, ' it's gittin' back to the rigimint I'd be afther,' sez I. ' Ye'll not,' sez he, ' divil a stir,' sez he ; ' ye'll go to Lunnon,' sez he. ' Will I ? ' sez I. ' Ye will,' sez he ; ' take him down to the boat at wanst, sergeant,' sez he, and the sergeant right turns me and marches me out. ' Sergeant dear,' sez I, ' sure why can't I be gittin' back to the rigimint?' sez I. ' Agh, t'hell out o' that,' sez he; ' sure didn't ye hear what the major bin and said?' sez he, an' he gin me over to a carpral—one on thim ogly Jocks, sorr—an' down we goes by the quays to the boat—a gran' boat, sorr, wid ladies an' childer an' Frinch an' Bilgians, an' all sorts, as minded me on the ould *Innisfallen*. D'y' iver know the ould *Innisfallen*, sorr, as sails from Carrk to some place as I misremember the name on, sorr ? "

" Crossed over on her once from Cork to Milford."

" Ye did, yer honour—sorr, I mane ? Glory be to God—to think o' that ! Well, sorr, I'd a sup of tay at one on thim shtahls, sorr, an' the Jock gives me me papers an' puts me aboard, sorr. It's mostly onaisy in me inside I am, sorr, on the say, but it was beautiful calm an'——"

" Yes, yes ; but look here—Where was it you left your regiment ? "

" Is it me, sorr ? Me lave me rigimint, sorr ? Me wid three years' sarvis an' sorra intry in my shate at all, only two, wan time I was dthronk wid a cowld in me nose, sorr. Me lave me rigimint ? It was the rigimint lift me, sorr. As I tell ye just now, we'd bin marchin' an' fightin' for wakes and wakes, an' it was tired I was, sorr, bate I was, an' we was havin' a halt, sorr ; an' I sez to Mick Shehan from Mallow, as is in my platoon, ' Mick,' sez I. ' Tim,' sez he, wid his mouth full of shkoff. ' Mick,' sez I, ' it's gwan to have a shlape, I am,' sez I, ' an' ye'll wake me, Mick darlint, when the fall-in goes.' ' Begob an' why wouldn't I, Tim,' sez he, ' so I ain't shlapin' mysilf?' sez he. ' Ye'll no forgit, Mick,' sez I. ' Agh, shut yer mouth, why would I be the wan to forgit?' sez he. But whin I wuk up, the divil a rigimint was there at all, at all, only me, sorr ; an' there was a lot of quare-lookin' chaps as I sinsed by the look on thim was Jarmins. I was concaled by a ditch,[1] an' settin' down by a bit o' whin, I was, sorr, or they seen me for sure. ' Phwat 'll I do at all?' sez I to mysilf, sez I, an'——"

" Just stop a minute ; where was all this ? "

" Where was it ? Why, in Fraance, sorr, where ilse would it be ? Well, sorr, as I was just startin' to tell ye,

----

[1] *Anglice*, bank.

there was a lot of quare-lookin' chaps as I sinsed by the look of thim was Jarmins, an'——"

" Yes, but good Lord, man, what was the name of the place in France where all this happened ? "

" Place is it, sorr ? Sure it wasn't any place at all, but one of thim kind of places as the name on has shlipped me mimry, a bog, sorr—leastways it wasn't a bog as ye'd rightly call a bog in Oireland, sorr—no turf nor there wasn't no wather. I mind now, sorr ! It was what the chaps at the 'Shott calls a ' hathe,' sorr. There was trees contagious, an' whins ; sure wasn't I tellin' ye just now as I was settin' down by a bit of whin, sorr——"

But it had been borne in on me that this had become a young man's job, so I succeeded, not without some difficulty, in consigning the gallant Royal Irishman—still pouring forth priceless intelligence material—into the hands of a messenger to be taken to the officer on duty. Manuals of instruction that deal with the subject of elicit- ing military information in time of war impress upon you that the Oriental always wants to tell you what he thinks you want him to tell you. But the Irishman tells you what he wants to tell you himself, and it isn't the least use trying to stop him.

The Intelligence Department being—directly at home and indirectly abroad—under my control, I was much sought after in the early days, was almost snowed under, indeed, with applications and recommendations for the post of " Intelligence Officer." Bigwigs within the War Office itself, when they were bothered on paper about people, simply passed the note along as it stood with " D.M.O., can you do anything for this creature?" or some- thing of that sort, scribbled in blue pencil at the top. One was treated as if one was a sort of unemployment bureau. Qualifications for this particular class of post turned out to be of the most varied kind. One young gentleman, who was declared to be a veritable jewel, was described as a pianist, fitted out with " technique almost equal to a professional." The leading characteristic of another candidate appeared to be his liability to fits. Algy, " a dear boy and *so* good-looking," had spent a couple of months in Paris after leaving Eton a year or two back. This sounds terribly like petticoat influence ; but resisting petticoat influence is, I can assure you, child's play compared to resisting Parliamentary influence. For good, straightforward, unblushing, shan't-take-no-for-an-answer jobbery, give me the M.P. They are sublime in their hardihood.

My experience in these Whitehall purlieus during the war perhaps provides some explanation of the theory, so sedulously hugged by the community, that interest and influence are all-powerful inside the War Office portals. To be invited to take a hand in obtaining jobs for people about whom one knew nothing and cared less, in services with which one had no connection, was a daily event. The procedure that was followed in such cases was automatic and appropriate. A reply would be dictated intimating that one would do what one could—a mere form of words, needless to say, as one had not the slightest intention of doing anything. And yet, as often as not, there would be a disconcerting sequel. Profuse outpourings of gratitude in letter form would come to hand, two or three weeks later : Jimmy had got his job, entirely owing to one's efforts in his behalf : the memory of one's services in this sacred cause would be carried to the grave : might Jimmy call and express his feeling of obligation in person ? One had not the faintest recollection of what all the bother was about ; but it was easy to dictate another letter expressing one's gratification at the recognition of Jimmy's merits and one's heartfelt regret that owing to stress of work one would be unable to grant him an audience. To hint that the appointment had presumably been made by the responsible official, on the strength of an application received from Jimmy in proper form, that there had been no wheels within wheels, and that backstairs had never got beyond the first landing, would have been disobliging.

Some applicants for " intelligence work " possessed, or gave out that they possessed, the gift of tongues, and the provision of interpreters was one of the many duties which had to be performed by the huge agglomeration of branches over which I exercised—or was supposed to exercise— sway. The subordinate charged with the provision had been retrieved from the Reserve of Officers and business pursuits, but retained the instincts of the soldier—a man with all his wits about him, but who sometimes positively frightened one by his unconventional procedure. One hardly likes to say such a thing of a man behind his back, but I really would not have been surprised to hear that, because he had been unable to concur in the views set out on it by other branches, he had put one of those bloated War Office files, on which one more or less automatically expresses dissent with the last minute without reading the remainder, into the fire. He made up his mind in a moment, which was irregular ; and he generally made it up right, which was unprecedented. Experts in many outlandish vernaculars had to be found from the start, and he always managed to produce the article required at the shortest notice. As a matter of fact, he had laid hands upon a tame professor, whom he kept immured in a fastness somewhere in the attics, and who was always prepared to vouch for the proficiency of anybody in any language when required to do so.

The first Divisions of the " Old Contemptibles " to proceed to the Continent were fitted out with interpreters by the French. But, for some reason or other, a Division going out to the front some few weeks later had not been prepared for, and so we suddenly found that we had to furnish it with its linguists at this end. But the chief of the sub-section responsible for finding them proved fully equal to the occasion. " How many d'yon want, sir ? " he demanded. I intimated that the authorized establishment was about seventy, but that if we could find fifty under the circumstances we should have done very well. " I'll have them ready early to-morrow, sir," he remarked, as if it was the most ordinary thing in the world—and he did. For, next morning the passages in the immediate vicinity of the room which he graced with his presence were congested with swarms of individuals, arrayed in the newest of new uniforms and resplendent in the lightest of light brown belts and gaiters, who were bundled off unceremoniously to regiments and batteries and staffs on the eve of departure for the seat of war. It is quite true that some generals and colonels in this Division wrote from France to complain that their inter- preters did not know French, or if they did know French, did not know English. Still, nobody takes that sort of croaking seriously. In a grumbling match the British officer can keep his end up against the British soldier any day.

An excellent innovation at the War Office synchroniz- ing with mobilization was the introduction of a large number of boy scouts within its gates. They proved most reliable and useful, and did the utmost credit to the fine institution for which we have to thank Sir Robert Baden- Powell. A day or two after joining I wanted to make the acquaintance of a colonel, who I found was under me in charge of a branch—a new hand like myself, but whose apartment nobody in the place could indicate. A War Office messenger despatched to find him came back empty- handed. Another War Office messenger sent on the same errand on the morrow proved no more successful. On the third day I summoned a boy scout into my presence—a very small one—and commanded him to find that colonel and not to come back without him. In about ten minutes' time the door of my room was flung open, and in walked the scout, followed by one of the biggest sort of colonels. " I did not know what I had done or where I was being taken," remarked the colonel, " but the boy made it quite clear that he wasn't going to have any nonsense ; so I thought it best to come quietly."

At a much later stage, one of these youngsters was especially told off to a branch which I then controlled—

an extraordinary boy, who impressed one all the more owing to his looking considerably younger than he really was.   I seldom found anything that he did not know, and never found anything that he could not do.   This Admirable Crichton was spangled all over well-earned badges, indicating his accomplishments.   We really might have gone off, the whole lot of us, masterful staff officer, dainty registration clerks, highly efficient stenographer, etc., and had a good time ; he would have run the show perfectly well without us—a Hirst, a Jimmy Wilde, a " Tetrarch," as he was amongst scouts.

The plan that the lads adopted for making things uncomfortable for troublesome people paid eloquent testimony to that fertility of resource which it is one of the objects of the scout movement to develop in its members. One of the greatest worries to which War Office officials were exposed during these anxious times was a bent on the part of individuals, whom they had not the slightest wish to see, for demanding—and obtaining—interviews. The scouts tumbled to this (if one may use so vulgar an expression) almost from the first day, and they acted with rare judgement and determination.   They chose *lasciate ogni speranza, voi ch' entrate* for their motto, and adopted the method of herding the intruders into an unattractive apartment on the ground floor, as tube attendants herd subterranean travellers into the lifts, and of keeping the intruders there until they verged on a condition of mutiny.   They then enlarged them in big parties, each of which was taken control of by a scout, who led his charges round and round and in and out along the corridors, and up and down between floors, carefully avoiding the elevators, until the victims were in a state of physical and mental collapse.   If one of the party quitted the ranks while on the trek, to read the name marked up on some door that he was passing, the scout called a halt and withered the culprit with· a scowl—it would never have done to permit that sort of thing, because the visitor might conceivably have noticed the name of the very official whom he had come to see. Anybody who came again after undergoing this experience once, probably had just cause for demanding an interview ; but one bout of it satisfied most people. It may be suggested that the scouts were acting under instructions from Sir Reginald Brade, Secretary and Grand Master of the Ceremonies, in this matter. But, if asked, he will own up and admit that in the pressure of his duties he overlooked the point, and that the entire credit belongs to the boys.

Still, perambulation of those furlongs of corridor in the big building in Whitehall might have offered points of interest to a visitor not too exhausted to take notice. By one window was usually to be seen a posse of parsons, of furtive aspect, each nervously twiddling a lissom hat, a love-your-neighbour-as-yourself look frozen on their countenances, and not by any means conveying for the time being an impression of the church militant : they were candidates for the post of army chaplain, and were about to be inspected by the genial prelate who presided over the department responsible for the spiritual welfare of the troops. A day or two later might be seen in the same place some of these very candidates, decked out in khaki raiment, hung about with contrivances into which combatant comrades introduce implements for slaying their fellow-men, erect, martial, terrifying, the very embodiment of the church triumphant, having been accepted for the job and awaiting orders—and no men have done finer service in the Great Adventure.

At another point one encountered a very well-known cricketer, who was doling out commissions. How he did it one had no time to ask. But one strongly suspected that, if one of the young gentlemen whom he took in hand had been in a school eleven or even house eleven (or said he had), crooked ways somehow became straight.

Just outside my own door an attractive-looking civilian had devised a sort of wigwam within which he took cover—one of those arrangements with screens which second lieutenants prepare when there is a regimental dance, and which they designate, until called to order, as " hugging booths." There he was to be seen at any hour of the day in close communion with a fascinating lady, heads close together, murmuring confidences, an idyll in a vestibule—or rather a succession of idylls, because there was a succession of ladies, all of them different except in that all of them were charming. After two or three months he disappeared, and only then did it occur to me to ask what these intimate transactions were on which he had been engaged. It transpired that he was acting vicariously on my behalf, that he was selecting a staff for censorship duties or some such dull occupation, in my place. If good looks were a qualification for such employment, that civilian must have been troubled with an *embarras de richesses.*

Amongst the many privileges and responsibilities which my position in the early months of the war thrust upon me was that of finding myself in more or less official relations with the Eminent K.C. and with the Self-Appointed Spy-Catcher. One may have had the good fortune in pre-war times to meet the former, when disguised as a mere human being—on the links, say, or at the dinner table. The latter, one came into contact with for the first time.

The average soldier seldom finds himself associated with the Eminent K.C. on parade, so to speak, in the piping times of peace. When performing, and on the warpath as you might say, this successful limb of the law is a portentous personage. Persuasive, masterful, clean-shaven, he fixes you with his eye as the boa-constrictor fascinates the rabbit. Pontifically, compassionately, almost affectionately indeed, he makes it plain to you what an ass you in reality are, and he looks so wise the while that you are hardly able to bear it. He handles his arguments with such petrifying precision, he marshals his facts so mercilessly, he becomes so elusive when you approach the real point, and he grows so bewildering if he detects the slightest symptoms of your having dis-

covered what he is driving at, that he will transform an
elementary military question, which you in your folly
have presumed to think that you understand, into a
problem which a very Moltke would ignominiously fail
to elucidate.

Contact with the Eminent K.C. under such conditions
makes you realize to the full what an inestimable boon
lawyers confer upon their fellow-citizens when they sink
all personal ambition and flock into the House of Commons for their country's good. It makes you rejoice in
that time-honoured arrangement under which the Lord
Chancellorship is the reward and recognition, not of
mastery of the principles and practice of jurisprudence,
but of parliamentary services to a political faction. It
convinces you that the importance of judges and
barristers having holidays of a length to make the public-
school-boy's mouth water, immeasurably exceeds the
importance of litigation being conducted with reasonable
despatch. It accounts for the dexterity invariably displayed by Parliament when new enactments are placed on
the Statute-Book, for the simplicity of the language in
which they are couched, and for that minimum of employment to the legal profession to which these specimens of
masterly legislation subsequently give rise.   The Eminent
K.C. is, by the way, reputed to be a somewhat expensive
luxury when you avail yourself of his services in your
civil capacity, but he must be well worth it.   A man who
can be so mystifying when he proposes to be lucid must
prove a priceless asset to his client when he undertakes
the task of bamboozling a dozen unhappy countrymen
penned in a box.   It is hard to picture to yourself this
impressive figure giggling sycophantically at the pleasau-
tries of a humorous judge.   But he must have conformed
to convention in this matter in the past, for how otherwise could he now be an Eminent K.C.?

During many months of acute national emergency,
while the war was settling into its groove, there was no
more zealous, no more persevering, and no more ineffectual

subject of the King than the Self-Appointed Spy-Catcher. You never know what ferocity means until you have been approached by a titled lady who has persuaded herself that she is on the track of a German spy. We Britons are given to boasting of our grit in adversity and of our inability to realize when we are beaten. In no class of the community were these national traits more conspicuous in the early days of the war than in the ranks of the amateur spy-catching fraternity and sisterhood—for the amateur spy-catcher never caught a spy. Only after months of disappointment and failure did these self-appointed protectors of their country begin to abandon a task which they had taken up with enthusiastic fervour, and which they had prosecuted with unfaltering resolution. Although it was at the hands of the despised professional that enemy agents were again and again brought to face the firing party in the Tower ditch, the amateurs entertained, and perhaps still entertain, a profound contempt for the official method. One fair member of the body, indeed, so far forgot herself as to write in a fit of exasperation to say that we must—the whole boiling of us—be in league with the enemy, and that we ought to be " intered."

They were in their element when, after the fall of Maubeuge, it transpired that the Germans had gun-platforms in certain factories situated within range of the forts, that they had established ready prepared for action should they be required. Anybody with an asphalt lawn-tennis court then became suspect. A very bad case was reported from the Chilterns, just the very sort of locality where Boches contemplating invasion of the United Kingdom would naturally propose to set up guns of big calibre. A building with a concrete base— many buildings do have concrete bases nowadays—near Hampstead was the cause of much excitement. When the unemotional official, sent to view the place, suggested that the extremely solid structure overhead would be rather in the way supposing that one proposed to emplace

D

a gun, or guns, on the concrete base, it was urged that there was a flat roof and that ordnance mounted on it would dominate the metropolis. There was a flat roof all right, but it turned out to be of glass.

A number of most worthy people were much concerned over the subject of certain disused coal-mines in Kent, where, they had persuaded themselves, the enemy had stored quantities of war material. What precisely was the nature of the war material they did not know—aircraft as like as not, the aviator finds the bottom of a mine-shaft an ideal place to keep his machine. These catacombs were duly inspected by an expert, but he could find nothing. The worthy people thereupon declared that the penetralia had not been properly examined and desired permission to carry out a searching inspection themselves. They were, if I remember aright, told they might go down the mines or might go to the devil (or words to that effect) for all we cared. Had one not been so busy one could have got a good deal of fun out of the Self-Appointed Spy-Catcher.

The Military Operations Directorate had nothing to do with the formation and organization of the New Armies, but one heard a good deal about their birth and infancy. Apart from the question of their personal equipment, in regard to which the Quartermaster-General's Department (with Lord Kitchener at its back and urging it forward) performed such wonders, the most troublesome question in connection with their creation in the early stages was the provision of officers ; the men were procured almost too fast. This became the business of the Military Secretary's Department. The M.S. Department holds tenaciously to the dogma that maladministration is the child of precipitancy and that deliberation stamps official procedure with the hall-mark of respectability. In later stages of the war one never was gazetted to an appointment until after one had passed on to the next one. But a gunner " dug-out," Colonel " Bill " Elliot, had been roped into the Department on mobilization, having been similarly roped in during the South African War, and by good luck the question of officers for the New Armies was turned over to him.

A believer in the theory that the King's service has to be carried on even in spite of regulations, he worked on lines of his own, and he altered those lines when the occasion called for it.   He was a " mandarin," of course— everybody in a Government office is.   He was to some extent enmeshed in " red tape "—every step taken in a Government office, from sending a note in acknowledge- ment of a written communication, to losing a State paper at a moment when the safety of the country depends upon its being available for reference, comes within the category of " red tape."   But he did get things done somehow, thanks to some extent to his pronounced and never- failing sense of humour.   When one felt worried, weary, worn out, one only had to sit opposite to him at lunch at the club and to listen to some of his tales of manu- facturing New Army officers, to be oneself again; it was like a trip to Margate.   Fortunately he either was given, or gave himself, a free hand, and his quota was not the least considerable of the many quotas from various quarters that contributed towards winning the war.

As, keeper of the Secretary of State's conscience when he has one, the Military Secretary is bound to take himself very seriously indeed.   There is always something dignified and impressive about slow motion, and his branch during the Great War was compelled to take up a firm attitude in exacting the respect that was its due ; " Bill," with his eminently successful, but none the less abnormal and even lawless, methods at times hardly seemed in the picture.   It may be mentioned that in spite of precautions the branch on at least one occasion met with a deplorable affront.   An officer, who had been secured by tumultuary process during the early efforts to expand the land forces, proved to be a disappointment and had to be invited to convert his sword into a ploughshare. His reply is understood to have read somewhat as follows :

SIR—I beg to acknowledge receipt of your letter of —— directing me to resign my commission. I will see you damned first.—Yours,   ——.

New Army officers were so unconventional.

Lord Roberts often came to see me in those anxious early days at the War Office, ever sympathetic, ever encouraging, ever confident. It had not been my privilege while on the active list to be brought into contact with him, except once, many years ago, when a young subaltern at Kabul. But one day, it must have been in 1911, he sent me a message asking me to call and see him at the Athenaeum. On my presenting myself, and on our repairing to the little room by the door where members of that exclusive establishment interviewed outsiders, he made a somewhat unexpected proposal. A gentleman of progressive views hailing from the Far East, called Sun Yat-sen,—one had seen his name in the newspapers and had got the impression that he was a revolutionary, out for trouble—was in England in search of arms, and he required a commander-in-chief for the forces which he proposed to raise for the purpose of bringing the Celestial Empire up to date.[1] The Field-Marshal wanted me to take on the job. But the project somehow did not appeal to me—people do say that the Chinese have old-fashioned ways when they come to deal with persons whose conduct they are unable to approve—and I no doubt cut but a poor figure when manifesting no disposition to jump at the chance. " If I were only forty years younger," exclaimed Lord Roberts, " I would go myself ! Why, you might be Emperor of China before you knew where you were ! " But even the prospect of a seat on the Peacock Throne failed to charm, although I had an interview with Sun Yat-sen (who looked as if butter

[1] He brought his revolution off all right and was for a time President of the Southern China Republic.

would not melt in his mouth) at the Savoy Hotel; bene-factors of the human race coming from foreign parts always put up at that hostelry, comfortable quarters are understood to be procurable.   One could not, however, but be impressed with the amazing vitality of the aged Field-Marshal then, as also a year or two later when he used to come to make enquiries concerning the progress of events in France.

He followed the movements of the contending armies closely, and he always carried the details of the map and of the British order of battle in his head, just as if he were a smart young staff-captain.   At critical junctures he used to call me up, between 9 P.M. and 10 P.M., from his house at Ascot on the telephone, eager for news.   The last time that I saw him was when he came to ask me to tell off some one from my staff to accompany him to the front on the occasion of the visit which in some respects ended so tragically, but which enabled the great soldier to go to his rest within sound of the guns and surrounded by the troops whom he had loved so well.

It was mentioned in the preceding chapter that the Military Operations Directorate found little to do in connection with " operations " question concerning the Western Front just at first, because the concentration of the Expeditionary Force in the war zone was carried out automatically and in accordance with plans worked out in advance.   Indeed almost the first time that such a question arose in at all aggravated form was when the Antwerp affair got going.   That was a queer business altogether, and it seems necessary briefly to deal with what most military men regard as an unfortunate trans-action.

In so far as the Belgian forces as part of the Entente hosts in this theatre of war were concerned, the strategical situation after the great retreat appeared to demand imperatively that these must above all things avoid, firstly, any risk of becoming cut off from their French and British allies, and, secondly, the danger of finding themselves trapped in the entrenched camp of Antwerp or of being hustled up against the Dutch frontier on their way out of the entrenched camp. The Belgian military authorities, as far as one could make out at the time, appreciated the situation quite correctly—they wished to abandon Antwerp, at all events with their field troops. Problems such as those responsible on the Entente side were at this time faced with, undoubtedly admit of difference of opinion ; but most soldiers will surely agree that the Belgian leaders deserve great credit for not allowing themselves to be hypnotized by that huge place of arms which General Brialmont had designed some forty years before, and upon which vast sums of money had been laid out then and since. It has to be remembered in this connection that the famous engineer had always contemplated the retirement of his country's armies into the stronghold, more or less as a matter of course, in case of invasion, and that this had virtually been the military policy of Belgium up till quite recently. Lord French has referred in " *1914* " to the " terrible temptation " which Maubeuge offered to him at the time of the retreat from Mons. If Maubeuge suggested itself as an asylum for the hard-pressed Expeditionary Force, Antwerp would assuredly suggest itself still more strongly as an asylum for King Albert's field army, confronted as it was by an overwhelming hostile array and not in direct contact with the troops under Joffre and Sir J. French.

It was then that those who were directing the British operations as a whole suddenly intervened and induced the Belgians to alter their plan. The very recently improvised Naval Division was set in motion for Antwerp. Mr. Churchill, a bolt from the blue, appeared in the city. And, instead of King Albert's forces getting clear in good time and moving off, practically unmolested, to join the Anglo-French host in Western Flanders, they only escaped by the skin of their teeth after being roughly handled, and the all-important junction was delayed so long that a most critical situation arose. Moreover, the

Seventh Division and a Cavalry Division were packed off in a hurry from this country to help the Belgians out of a mess which they would not have got into had they been left alone, instead of being sent to join the Expeditionary Force where they were badly wanted. That is how I read the proceedings at the time, and how I read them still.

War Office procedure did not at that stage conform to the methods which had held good previous to mobilization, and which had been devised to hold good in time of war ; something further will be said on the subject in a later chapter. The Director of Military Operations did not on this particular occasion hear about the Seventh Division and the cavalry being diverted to the Belgian coast until after instructions for the move had been issued and the troops were preparing to proceed to the port of embarkation. How far my chief, Sir C. Douglas, concurred in this disposition of our limited available fighting forces, how far he was consulted and what part he performed in giving the orders, I do not know. I have no recollection of ever discussing the matter with him. But there was a circumstance in connection with the transaction which does suggest that the C.I.G.S. did not play a very prominent rôle in the business.

Some time after I had learnt what was going forward— it was next day, I think—the idea occurred to me to find out what steps had been, or were being, taken to provide the necessary organization for a base and line of communications for this force which was about to be projected suddenly across the narrow seas. Enquiries elicited the startling information that nothing whatever had been done in the matter ; some of those most concerned in such questions in Whitehall had not even heard that the force was preparing to start. The problem, such as it was, was promptly solved as soon as it was grappled with. The Directors dealing with such subjects met in my room, and in a few minutes the requisite staff had been selected, arrangements had been decided ' upon, and orders had been despatched—it was as easy as falling downstairs once machinery had been set in motion. But how came it that this had not been thought of before? Now, I can quite understand Sir C. Douglas holding that this particular phase of the Antwerp project, sending Generals Capper and Byng with their divisions to sustain the Belgians and the Naval Division by a landing at Zeebrugge, was a sound one from the strategical point of view—such questions are necessarily questions of opinion. But I cannot understand a master of military administration such as he was, a soldier equipped with exceptional knowledge of organization and with wide experience of the requirements of a British army in the field, sending a considerable body of troops off oversea to a theatre of operations, where fighting might be expected almost as soon as they landed, without making provision for their base and communications.

Actually, what turned out to be a tragic episode was not without some little comic relief. There was consternation in Whitehall one evening, just before the dinner-hour, when tidings arrived that a couple of the transports conveying this force to its destination had passed the rendezvous where the convoy was mustering, and were at large, heading without escort or orders for a water-area known to be mined by both sides, and where enemy destroyers and similar pests were apt to make their appearance unexpectedly. Fortunately the panic was of short duration. On returning to the office after dinner one learnt that the straying vessels had both fetched up on the Goodwins—luckily about low water—and were under control again.

In any criticism of H.M. Government's action in connection with the Antwerp affair (as regards the prosecution of the war in the field, H.M. Government for all practical purposes then meant Mr. Asquith, Lord Kitchener, and Mr. Churchill) it must be allowed that the situation at the time was a most complicated and perplexing one. Lord French in his book makes it clear that, while he objected strongly to the Seventh Division and the Third Cavalry Division being sent to the Belgian coast under the independent command of Sir H. Rawlinson instead of their being sent to Boulogne and placed under his own orders, he did not wish Antwerp to be abandoned. Lord Kitchener had, as a matter of fact, seized upon Antwerp as a means of inducing reluctant colleagues to assent to the United Kingdom being denuded of these regular troops and their being hurried to the theatre of war. Knowing what we know now, it seems almost certain that, no matter where the fresh troops from England turned up or whose orders they were under, the Belgian army and the Naval Division would have been lost for good and all had they not cleared out of the fortress when they did. The verdict of history will probably be that both H.M. Government and the commander of the British Expeditionary Force misread the situation, that H.M. Government's misreading was very much the graver of the two, that there was excuse for such misreadings when the inevitable fog of war is taken into consideration, and that the Germans threw away their chances and bungled the business worst of all.

A few days after Antwerp had fallen, and a week or so before that tremendous conflict which has come to be known as the First Battle of Ypres was fairly launched, Sir C. Douglas, who for a long time past had not been in the best of health and upon whom the strain had been telling severely during the previous two and a half months, did not make his appearance at the office one morning. He had struggled on with splendid grit and determination almost to the very end, for he died within a few days, a victim of devotion to duty and of overwork. His place was taken by Sir J. Wolfe-Murray

CHAPTER III

LORD KITCHENER'S START

A first meeting with Lord Kitchener—Sent up to see him in Pretoria
by his brother under unpromising conditions—The interview—
The Chief's pleasant reception—A story of Lord K. from the
Sudan—An unpleasant interview with him in August 1914—
Rare meetings with him during the first two or three months—
His ignorance of War Office organization—His lack of acquaintance with many matters in connection with the existing
organization of the army—His indisposition to listen to advice on
such subjects—Lord K. shy of strangers—His treatment of the
Territorial Forces—Their weak point at the outset of hostilities,
not having the necessary strength to mobilize at war establishment
—Effect of this on the general plans—The way the Territorials
dwindled after taking the field—Lord K. inclined at first to pile
up divisions without providing them with the requisite reservoirs
of reserves—His feat in organizing four regular divisions in addition
to those in the Expeditionary Force—His immediate recognition
of the magnitude of the contest—He makes things hum in the
War Office—His differences of opinion with G.H.Q.—The inability
of G.H.Q. to realize that a vast expansion of the military forces
was the matter of primary importance—Lord K.'s relations with
Sir J. French—The despatch of Sir H. Smith-Dorrien to command
the Second Corps—Sir J. French not well treated at the time of
the Antwerp affair—The relegation of the General Staff at the
War Office to the background in the early days—Question whether
this was entirely due to its having suffered in efficiency by the
withdrawals which took place on mobilization—The General Staff
only eliminated in respect to operations.

MY first meeting with Lord Kitchener had taken place
under conditions that augured no agreeable experience.
It was in March or April 1901.   At that time I had charge
of a heterogeneous collection of guns in a body of troops
operating in the Eastern Transvaal and commanded by
General Walter Kitchener, the Chief's brother, and was
also used by him as a sort of second-in-command to take

charge of portions of the force when detached from time to time. Our commando had trekked out from Belfast and had camped in a likely spot, and on the morrow he took out part of the force in one direction and sent me off with part of the force in another direction, while the remainder stayed in camp guarding the impedimenta. I tumbled across a few snipers, and we enjoyed a harmless scrap; but Walter butted into a whole lot of truculent burghers. These were being reinforced and were full of fight, so he decided to retire, and also to retire the camp; but the message directing me to conform unfortunately went astray. The result was that before long I found myself covering the retirement of the whole gang, and being rather harried to boot—one of those *reculer pour mieux sauter* sort of movements where it is all *reculer* and no *sauter*. The casualties were, however, small, and we lost nothing worth bothering about; but Walter took his big brother very seriously indeed, was much concerned as to how the Chief might regard an operation which we could not possibly represent as a success, and, after much cogitation, packed me off to Pretoria to report in person.

He gave me elaborate directions as to how best to approach the subject when in the presence. " No, don't put it that way, tell it him like this "—" He'll damn me and you, but whatever you do, don't make excuses," and so forth. One had read Steevens' appreciation of the then Sirdar in his *With Kitchener to Khartum,* and had gathered from newspapers (the worst possible source of information about the character and the idiosyncrasies of persons of note) that this commander-in-chief of ours was a cold, exacting, unsympathetic figure, much more given to jumping down your throat than to patting you on the back. The consequence was that when, having fetched up in Pretoria after some adventures, I was wending my way to Lord K.'s headquarters I felt very much as one does when repairing to the dentist. It was worse, indeed, than going to the dentist, because when I got there Colonel Hubert Hamilton, the Military Secretary (who was killed when in command of the Third Division soon after it reached the Lys from the Aisne in October 1914), greeted me with " Very sorry, but the Chief's awfully busy to-day. Roll up about this time to-morrow, will you, like a good chap ? " It was the same story again on the next day—the Chief up to the neck in correspondence. But on presenting myself on the third day, Hamilton promptly ushered me into the great man's study, where he was sitting at his desk.

"What d'you want ? " demanded Lord K. I began explaining about our little affair near Belfast ; but he cut me short with " Oh, I don't want to hear about all that. Had any trouble getting here ? " Yes, the train in front of mine had been blown up, and—— " They'll bag you on the way back," interrupted the Chief cheerily, " so I'd better get what I can out of you now ; my brother writes that you've been about a good deal on the east side, and I'm going to take that in hand very shortly. Come along over here." We went across to where there was a huge great map of the Eastern Transvaal, with the positions of the posts and columns, etc., marked on it, and for twenty minutes or so I found myself enjoying the pleasantest interview with a much senior officer than I had ever had in my life. He listened to my exposition of how it seemed best to round up the enemy commandos, where sedentary forces ought to be dumped down to act as stops, and what lines the mobile columns ought to operate along. Lord K. occasionally inter-jected a question or criticism as to some particular point, but seemed not in the least displeased when I stuck to my own view. When he dismissed me he spoke in a particularly friendly way, and my experience of him on this occasion was nothing short of a revelation.

" Had a satisfactory talk ? " asked Hamilton when I came out, and, on my saying how nice the Chief had been, he remarked, " He's in one of his good moods to-day, but you mightn't always find him quite so tame. He's been down to the Old Colony and back these last two days, and found things moving—that's why he could not see you before. But he always keeps his movements very close, so you mustn't let it go any further."

Walter Kitchener, not unnaturally, entertained unbounded admiration for, and belief in, his brother, and he often told me tales from Egyptian days of things that the Sirdar then did and of the resource he would display in unexpected emergencies. One of these yarns about the great War Minister at a stage of his career when he was still mounting the ladder of success deserves to be repeated here.[1] It happened one day, during the operations for the recovery of the Sudan from the Mahdi-ists, that " K." was riding forward with his staff, there being no troops nor transport actually on the move, he mounted on his camel, the rest on horses and ponies. By the wayside they came upon a heap of rolls of telegraph-wire lying near the track, which some unit had apparently abandoned as lumber or else had been unable to carry. " We can't leave that stuff behind," said the Sirdar to the staff; " bring it along." Two or three of them dismounted to see what could be done, but there was no gear available for lashing and the rolls were heavy. A little party of the small donkeys of the country was, however, being driven along by a native lad and came on the scene just at this juncture. " Hurry up. Put the wire on those donkeys. I don't want to sit here all day," commanded the Sirdar impatiently. The donkeys had no saddles nor equipment of any kind except rope halters of sorts, and the officers sampled various devices, without success, for placing the goods on the donkeys' backs and keeping them there. They experimented with balancing a roll on the back of one, but it promptly fell off again. They tied two rolls together and slung them across the back of another, pannier fashion; but the little beast gave a kick and a

---

[1] While this volume has been in the press Sir G. Arthur's *Life of Lord Kitchener* has appeared, giving a different version of this story and probably the correct one. Walter Kitchener was speaking, I think, from hearsay.

wriggle and deposited the load on the ground. Various dodges were tried, perspiration poured off the faces of the officers, they were covered with dust, their language grew stronger and stronger, and at last, feeling themselves entirely nonplussed, one of them, looking up at their chief as he sat on his camel with a sardonic smile on his face, observed deprecatingly, " I'm afraid we really can't manage it, sir."

" Can't manage it, can't you ! " ejaculated the Sirdar ; " here, let me come " He made his camel kneel, and dismounted, stalked over to one of the donkeys, gripped the animal by the nose, backed it till its hind feet were inside one of the rolls, turned the roll up over the donkey's back from behind, gave the beast a smack on the rump, and after one or two wriggles and kicks, the creature was trotting along, adorned with a loosely fitting girdle of telegraph-wire round its waist which it could not get rid of. The same plan was promptly adopted with the other donkeys. And in a few minutes the party were riding along again, with the donkeys, carrying the whole of the abandoned wire, in close attendance.

That Lord Kitchener would cut up rough at times when things went wrong, as Hubert Hamilton had hinted at Pretoria, was brought home to me convincingly on the occasion of my first interview with him at the War Office after that visit to the Admiralty which is mentioned in Chapter I. General Hanbury Williams had been earmarked in advance for British Military Commissioner at Russian Headquarters, and he dashed off in a great hurry to take up the appointment on mobilization. I believe that he looked in to see me before starting, but I was not in my room at the moment ; I am not sure, indeed, that I knew that he was going until after he had started. A few days later the Chief, when wanting to wire to his representative with the Tsar's armies, discovered that he had gone off without a cipher. It was possible, of course, to communicate through the Foreign Office and our embassy at St. Petersburg (as the capital was still called) ; but Lord K. naturally desired means of direct communication. He was extremely angry about it, and he gave me a most disagreeable five minutes.

Although all this cipher business was under charge of one of my branches, the contretemps was due to no neglect on my own part. Nor was it the fault of the subordinate who actually handled the ciphers, because he did not even know that Hanbury Williams had gone until the row occurred. The mishap had resulted from our Military Commissioner making his exit at the very moment when new hands were taking up their duties and had not yet got the hang of these. But one guessed that explanations would not be received sympathetically by the Secretary of State, and that it would be wisest to take the rebuke " lying down " ; he expected things to be done right, and that was all about it. Still, it was not an altogether encouraging start. Indeed I scarcely ever saw Lord K. during the first two or three months, and when I did, it was generally because some little matter had gone wrong in connection with the Secret Service or the Press, or owing to one of the Amateur Spy-Catchers starting some preposterous hare, or because he needed information as to some point of little importance. The fact is that—to put the matter quite bluntly—when he took up his burden the Chief did not know what the duties of his subordinates were supposed to be, and he took little trouble to find out. One day he sent for me and directed me to carry out a certain measure in connection with a subject that was not my business at all, and I was so ill-advised as to say, " It's a matter for the Adjutant-General's Department, sir, but I'll let them know about it." " I told you to do it yourself," snapped the Chief in a very peremptory tone. Under the circumstances, one could only go to the man concerned in the A.G. Department, explain matters, and beg him for goodness sake to wrestle with the problem and carry out what was wanted.

What, however, was still more unfortunate than Lord K.'s lack of acquaintance with the distribution of work within the Office was that he was by no means familiar with many very essential details of our existing military organization. That is not an unusual state of affairs when a new Secretary of State is let loose in the War Office. But a new Secretary of State as a rule has the time, and is willing, to study questions of organization and policy closely before embarking on fresh projects. Lord Kitchener, however, arrived with certain preconceived ideas and cramped by defective knowledge of the army system. He had scarcely served at home since he had left Chatham as a young subaltern of the Royal Engineers. In Egypt, in India, even to a great extent in South Africa, the troops coming from the United Kingdom with which he had been brought into contact had been regulars. He had never had anything to say to the provision of British military personnel at its source. For the three years previous to the outbreak of the Great War he had been holding a civil appointment afar off, and had necessarily been out of touch with contemporary military thought. There must have been many matters in connection with the organization of His Majesty's land forces, thoroughly known to pretty well every staff-officer in the War Office, of which the incoming Secretary of State was entirely unaware. The British division of all arms of 1914 represented a far larger force than the British divisions of all arms had represented with which he had had to do in the days of Paardeberg and Diamond Hill. The expressions " Special Reserve " and " Territorial Forces " did not, I believe, when he arrived, convey any very clear meaning to him. He was not, in fact, in all respects fully equipped for his task.

With many, indeed with most, men similarly placed this might not have greatly mattered. There were plenty of officers of wide experience in Whitehall who could have posted him up fully in regard to points not within his knowledge. But Lord Kitchener had for many years previously always been absolute master in his own house, with neither the need nor the desire to lean upon others.

Like many men of strong will and commanding ability, he was a centralizer by instinct and in practice. He took over the position of War Minister with very clearly defined conceptions of what must be done to expand the exiguous fighting forces of his country in face of the tremendous emergency with which it stood suddenly confronted. He was little disposed to modify the plans which he had formed for compassing that end, when subordinates pointed out that these clashed with arrangements that were already in full working order, or that they ignored the existence of formations which only stood in need of nursing and of consolidation to render them really valuable assets within a short space of time for the purpose of prosecuting war. The masterful personality and self-confidence to which the phenomenal success that attended his creation of the wonderful New Armies was so largely due, was in some respects a handicap to him in the early days of his stewardship.

My impression of him—an impression unduly influenced perhaps by personal experiences—was that he was shy of strangers or comparative strangers. He did not give his confidence readily to subordinates with whom he found himself associated for the first time. He would not brook remonstrance, still less contradiction, from a man whom he did not know. It was largely due to this, as it seemed to me, that he was rather out of hand, so to speak, during the critical opening months. It was during those opening months that he performed the greatest services to the people of this land, that he introduced the measures which won us the war. But it was also during those opening months, when he was disinclined to listen to advice, that he made his worst mistakes.

I do not believe that there was one single military authority of any standing within the War Office, except himself, who would not have preferred that the cream of the personnel, men who had served in the regulars, who flocked into the ranks in response to his trumpet call to the nation, should have been devoted in the first instance

E

to filling the yawning gaps that existed in the Territorial Forces, and to providing those forces with trained reservists to fill war wastage.   Such a disposition of this very valuable material seemed preferable to absorbing it at the outset in brand-new formations, which in any case would be unable to take the field for many months to come. Parliament would have readily consented to any alteration in the statutes governing the Territorial Forces which might have been necessary.   Lord K.'s actions in this question to some extent antagonized the military side of the War Office just at first : we were thinking of the early future ;   he, as was his wont, was looking far ahead.   My work was nowise concerned with the provision of troops in any form, and in later days, when I was often with the Chief, I never remember discussing the Territorials with him.   But it is conceivable that he became somewhat prejudiced against this category of the land forces at the start on finding that they were unable to perform the very duty for which they were supposed to exist—that of home defence.   Something may, therefore, perhaps be said here on this point.

Mobilization means producing the force concerned, at its full war establishment and composed of officers and men who at least have some pretence to military training.   It is, moreover, supposed to be completed at very short notice.   Owing to their being territorial and to officers and other ranks living in their territorial districts, the Territorial Forces ought to have been mobilized more rapidly by some hours than the Expeditionary Force, and I believe that, in so far as collecting what personnel there was available is concerned, the Territorial Forces beat the Expeditionary Force.   But the ranks of the Territorials had never filled in pre-war days, and there were practically no organized reserves. The war establishment was roughly 315,000 of all ranks ; but at the beginning of August the strength was only about 270,000, and this, be it remembered, included a proportion of totally untrained individuals, as well as sick, absentees, and so forth. To have mobilized these troops properly, the number of officers and men on the books at the start and before the order came ought to have amounted to at least 350,000.

The consequence of this shortage was that, at the very moment when the Government and the country were on the first occasion for a century confronted by a really grave and complex military situation, at the very moment when there was a scare as to German projects of an immediate invasion, that category of our land forces which was especially earmarked for the defence of the British Isles was not in a position to perform its functions. The Sixth Division, properly forming part of the Expeditionary Force, had to be fetched over from Ireland to East Anglia to bolster up the Territorials, and Sir J. French was deprived of its use for six weeks at a very critical time. The ranks of the Territorial Forces filled up very rapidly *after* mobilization, but from the home defence point of view that was too late. We required our home defence army to be ready at once, so that the overseas army could be despatched complete to the Continent without *arrière pensée*. Its failure at the critical moment may have somewhat influenced Lord Kitchener in the estimates that he formed of it thenceforward. Instead of framing his plans with a view to reinforcing the Expeditionary Force as soon as possible with the existing fourteen Territorial divisions which were in some measure going concerns, by affording these special support, he preferred simply to expand the Territorial Forces as a whole. Four divisions were sent out of the country on garrison duty before the end of 1914; but although a number of individual battalions had preceded it, the first division to be sent to the front (the North Midland) did not sail from the United Kingdom till the end of February, more than six months after the outbreak of hostilities, while the two last to take the field did not leave till early in 1916. The policy may in the long run have proved the right one; but at the time it did seem a pity not to have accelerated the preparation of these existing troops for the ordeal of the field. None of us in Whitehall, however, wished the New Armies to be set up under the auspices of the Territorial Associations; that was a different question altogether.

Moreover, whatever was the cause of it, the Territorial divisions after they took the field seemed to be treated as veritable Cinderellas for a long time. They generally set out short of establishment, and they were apt to dwindle away painfully for want of reserves after they had spent a few weeks on the war-path. The Returns show this to have been the case. More than one of the divisional Generals concerned spoke to me, or wrote to me, on the subject in the later months of 1915. This discouraging shrinkage was not manifesting itself to at all the same extent at that stage in such New Army divisions as were at the front.

A good many of us at the War Office also did not, I think, see quite eye to eye with Lord K. in connection with his piling up of New Army divisions without providing them with reserves. The tremendous drain which modern war creates in respect to personnel came as a surprise to all the belligerents; but the surprise came fairly early in the proceedings, and the Adjutant-General's department had fully grasped what this meant, and had realized the scale of the provision necessary to meet it, by the end of 1914. If I remember aright, one whole "New Army" (the Fourth, I think it was) had to be broken up in the summer of 1915, and transformed into a reservoir of reserves, because the First, Second, and Third New Armies practically had none. It had been manifest long before these armies were gradually drawn into the fight that they would suffer heavy wastage, and that they would speedily become mere skeletons unless they had ample backing from home. Had the branches of the War Office which were supposed to deal with these questions been allowed their own way in regard to them, I imagine that greater foresight would have been displayed and that some confusion might have been avoided.

The preceding paragraphs read perhaps rather like a deliberate attempt to belittle the achievements of the greatest of our War Ministers. But they only touch upon one side, the dark side so to speak, of Lord Kitchener's work as an organizer and administrator during the Great War. Little has been said hitherto as to the other and much more important side, the bright side, of that work.

The marvels that he accomplished in respect to multiplying the land forces of the nation by creating improvised armies as it were by magic, have put in the shade a feat for which Lord Kitchener has never been given sufficient credit. Prior to August 1914, no organization existed for placing any portions of our regular army in the field in a Continental theatre of war, other than the Expeditionary Force and one additional division. The additional division was to be constituted if possible on the outbreak of war out of infantry to be withdrawn from certain foreign garrisons, and spare artillery, engineer and departmental units that existed in the United Kingdom. That additional division, the Seventh, was despatched to the Western Front within two months of mobilization. But Lord Kitchener also organized four further regular divisions, the Eighth, Twenty-seventh, Twenty-eighth and Twenty-ninth, of which the first three were in the field within five months of mobilization, joining Sir J. French respectively in November, December and January, and the remaining one was nearly ready to take the field by the end of the six months. The Secretary of State prepared for this immediately on taking up office, by recalling practically the whole of the regulars on foreign service, with the exception of the British troops included in four mixed Indian divisions. Would any War Minister other than Lord Kitchener have had the courage to denude India of British regular troops, artillery as well as infantry, to the extent that he did ? Supposing any other War

Minister to have proposed such a thing, would the Government have backed him up ? It was the handiwork of a very big man.

Still, this was after all a quite minor detail in the constructive labours undertaken by one of the most illustrious public servants of our time. His paramount claim to the gratitude of his countrymen rests upon his nimble perception of the nature of the task which he had been suddenly called upon to perform, and upon the speed with which he set every channel in motion to accomplish his purpose. He realized, as it seemed by instinct, that this contest was going to be a very big business indeed, an incomparably bigger business than these topmost military authorities who had been in the confidence of the Government before the blow fell had any idea of. It is no exaggeration to say that in this matter he was a giant amongst the pigmies. He grasped the truth at once that this world war was to be a protracted struggle, a struggle in which the Entente would not gain the upper hand unless a tremendous effort was to be put forward by the British Empire. He saw almost at a glance that our military system such as it was, and as previously devised with a view to war conditions, provided what represented numerically no more than an insignificant fraction of the host which would ultimately be needed to give us victory. He furthermore—and it is well to insist upon this thus early, in view of fabrications which have been put about on the subject of munitions—clearly discerned the need for a huge expansion in the country's powers of output in respect to war material ; so that under his impulse existing factories and establishments were developed on generous lines, and arrangements were instantly set on foot for creating entirely new factories and establishments. The result was that, after a lean and discouraging period for the troops in the field, the needs of an army which was ten times as strong as the army which soldiers of light and leading had been contemplating before war broke out, were being adequately met within fifteen months of the British ultimatum to Germany.

Within the War Office itself he certainly made things hum. In pre-war, plain-clothes days, those messengers of distinguished presence—dignity personified in their faultlessly-fitting official frock-coats and red waistcoats—had lent a tone of respectability to the precincts, compensating for the unfortunate impression conveyed by Adjutant-Generals and such like who perambulated the corridors in grimy, abandoned-looking " office jackets." (No scarecrow on duty afield in the remotest of rural districts would have been seen in the garment which my predecessor, now F.M., Bart., and G.C.B., left hanging up as a legacy in the apartment which he vacated in my favour.) But—although old hands will hardly credit it and may think I am romancing—I have seen those messengers tearing along the passages with coat-tails flying as though mad monkeys were at their heels, when Lord K. wanted somebody in his sanctum and had invited one of them to take the requisite steps. If the Chief happened to desire the presence of oneself, one did not run. Appearances had to be preserved. But one walked rather fast.

An earlier paragraph has hinted that, owing to military authorities in Whitehall not seeing quite eye to eye with the new Secretary of State when he took up his appointment, he was to some small extent working in an atmosphere of latent hostility to his measures. This state of affairs was, however, of very short duration, and certainly did not hamper his operations in the slightest degree; he would indeed have made uncommonly short work of anybody whom he found to be actively opposing him, or even to be hanging back. But the situation in the case of G.H.Q. of the Expeditionary Force was different. It is a matter of common knowledge—anybody who was unaware of it before the appearance of Lord French's " _1914_ " will have learnt it from that volume—that the relations between Lord Kitchener and some of those up at the top in connection with our troops on the Western Front were, practically from the outset, not quite satisfactory in character.

The attitude taken up by G.H.Q. over a comparatively small matter during the first few days is an example of this.   The Secretary of State had laid his hands upon one officer and one or two non-commissioned officers of each battalion of the Expeditionary Force, and had diverted these to act as drill-instructors, and so forth, for the new formations which he proposed to create.   That his action in this should have been objected to within the bereft units was natural enough ; their officers could hardly be expected to take the long view on the question at such a juncture.   But that the higher authorities of our little army proceeding to the front should have taken the measure so amiss was unfortunate.   And it was, moreover, instructive, indicating as it did in somewhat striking fashion the lack of sense of proportion prevalent amongst some of those included in G.H.Q.   This chapter deals only with early days ; but it may perhaps be mentioned here that there was a disposition to deride and decry the New Army at St. Omer almost up to the date, May 1915, when the first three of its divisions, the Ninth, Twelfth and Fourteenth, made their appearance in the war zone.

Watching the progress of events from behind the scenes, one could not but think that in respect to the occasional *tracasseries* between the War Minister and the Commander-in-Chief of the British troops in France and Flanders, there were faults on both sides.   The wording of some of the telegraphic messages passing between Lord K. and Sir J. French did not strike one as altogether felicitous, and, if messages from G.H.Q. were provocative, the replies were not always calculated to pour oil on troubled waters. The truth is, that when a pair of people both of whom require " handling " become associated under conditions of anxiety and stress that are bound to be trying to the temper and jarring on the nerves, it's a horse to a hen they won't make much of a fist of handling each other.

The Secretary of State's action in sending Sir H. Smith-Dorrien to command the Second Corps at the very outset of the campaign after General Grierson's tragic death, struck me at the time as a mistake. Sir J. French had asked for General Plumer who was available, and his wishes might well have been acceded to. Owing to circumstances of a quite special character the selection was not in any case an altogether happy one, as the relations between the new commander of the Second Corps and the chief of the B.E.F. had not always been too cordial in the past. Having been away from home so much, Lord K. may not have been aware of this; but I imagine that if he had consulted the Military Members of the Army Council they would have mentioned it, as it was almost a matter of common knowledge in the Service.

On that unpleasant controversy with regard to the rights and the wrongs of what occurred when the War Minister paid his sudden visit to Paris during the retreat from Mons, of which so much has been heard, I can throw no light whatever. At a later date " Fitz " (Colonel O. Fitzgerald, Lord K.'s constant companion) and I were in pretty close touch, and he used to keep me informed of what his chief had in his mind; but I hardly knew him to speak to during the early weeks. In respect to the Antwerp business, it certainly did seem to me that our principal commander on the Western Front (for the moment there were two) was not being very well treated. From a perusal of some of the communications that were flying about at a juncture when Sir J. French was confronted by a complex problem, and was virtually embarking on an entirely new set of operations, one gathered that he was hardly being kept so well informed of what was in progress and of what was contemplated as he had a right to expect, and as was indeed demanded by the situation. Still, this was no doubt due to what one might call bad Staff work, and not to any wish to keep Sir John in the dark as to Sir H. Rawlinson's orders, nor as to the position of this new British force that was being planted down in the war zone. It may well have been the direct result of Lord K.'s system of keeping all telegraphic work in connection with operations in his own hands, instead of this being carried out by the General Staff as under the existing regulations it was supposed to be.

Much has been written and has been said in public about the pushing of the General Staff into the background at the War Office during the early months of the war. An idea exists that this subversion was mainly, if not indeed entirely, consequential on the weakening of its personnel as a body owing to a number of its most prominent and experienced members having gone off to the wars. While readily admitting that its efficiency suffered as a result of these withdrawals, I am by no means sure that it would have managed to keep in the foreground even if the whole of its more shining lights had on mobilization remained where they were in Whitehall. Lord Kitchener had never been closely associated with Generals Robertson and Henry Wilson, its two principal members to leave for the front, and it by no means follows that if they had remained they would, during the first few critical weeks, have been much more successful than were Sir C. Douglas and Sir J. Wolfe-Murray in keeping a hand on the helm. The Secretary of State would no doubt have learnt to value their counsel before long, but he would no more have tolerated the slightest attempt at dictation in respect to the general conduct of the war until he knew his men, than he would have put up with dictation as to how the personnel which he was attracting into the ranks at the rate of tens of thousands per week were to be disposed of. The story of how the General Staff gradually recovered much of its lost ground will, however, be touched upon in the next chapter, and on that point no more need be said at present.

It may, however, be remarked here that the comparative elimination of the General Staff was virtually confined to its elimination in respect to what admittedly is its most important function in times of national emergency—advising the Government of the country on the subject of the general conduct of the war—and in respect to the administrative task of actually issuing instructions as to operations to those in supreme command in the theatres of conflict. The duties of the General Staff cover many other matters besides these. They include collection of information, secret service, questions of international law, military education, training of troops, etc. It fulfilled its mission in connection with such subjects just as had always been intended, nor, in so far as they were concerned, was it thrust on one side in any sense. Lord Kitchener's system of centralization only directly affected a small proportion of the very numerous directorates, branches, and sections into which the War Office was divided up.

CHAPTER IV

LORD KITCHENER'S LATER RECORD

The munitions question and the Dardanelles, to be dealt with later—
The Alexandretta project of the winter of 1914–15—Such an
operation presented little difficulty then—H.M.S. *Doris'* doings—
The scheme abandoned—I am sent to Paris about the Italian
conventions just after the Dardanelles landings—Concern at the
situation after the troops had got ashore at Helles and Anzac
—A talk with Lord K. and Sir E. Grey—Its consequences—
Lord K. seemed to have lost some of his confidence in his own
judgement with regard to operations questions—The question of
the withdrawal of the *Queen Elizabeth* from the Aegean—The
discussion about it at the Admiralty—Lord K.'s inability to take
some of his colleagues at their own valuation—Does not know
some of their names—Another officer of distinction gets them
mixed up in his mind—Lord K.'s disappointment at the early
failures of the New Army divisions—His impatience when he
wanted anything in a hurry—My own experiences—Typists'
idiosyncrasies aggravate the trouble—Lord K. in an unreasonable
mood—His knowledge of French—His skilful handling of a
Portuguese mission—His readiness to see foreign officers when
asked to do so—How he handled them—The Serbian Military
Attaché asks for approval of an attack by his country upon
Bulgaria at the time of Bulgarian mobilization—A dramatic interview with Lord K.—Confidence placed in him with regard to
munitions by the Russians—His speeches in the House of Lords—
The heat of his room—His preoccupation about the safety of Egypt
—He disapproves of the General Staff plan with regard to its
defence—His attitude with regard to national service—His
difficulties in this matter—His anxiety to have a reserve in hand
for delivering the decisive blow in the war—My last meeting with
him—His pleasure in going to Russia—His failure to accomplish
his mission, a great disaster to the Entente cause—A final word
about him—He did more than any man on the side of the Allies
to win the war—Fitz.

LORD KITCHENER's actions and attitude in connection
with two particular matters evoked a good deal of criticism
in various quarters at the time, and much has been said
and written about them. One of those matters was the

munitions question, the other was the Dardanelles under-taking ; both of those subjects are, however, discussed in special later chapters, and no reference will therefore be made to them in this one, except incidentally. I have, moreover, no recollection of ever having been brought into contact with the Secretary of State in connection with those projects for combined naval and military operations on the Flanders coast which received considerable attention in the winter of 1914–15, although, as will be mentioned in Chapter VI., aware of what was under review.

That Flanders coast scheme constituted, it may be observed, a question of the general strategical conduct of the war ; it was, in fact, a question of " operations." The first time that I went into any problem coming properly under that heading with the Secretary of State was when a plan of landing troops at or near Alexandretta was on the tapis in December 1914.   There was a good deal to be said for such an enterprise at that particular juncture.   Military opinion invariably favours active in preference to passive defence, so long as active defence can be regarded as reasonably feasible and the troops needed for the purpose are available.   The Turks were mustering for an attack upon Egypt across the Isthmus of Sinai at that time.   It was an axiom in our military policy that the Nile delta must be rendered secure against such efforts.   There was something decidedly attractive about employing the troops—or a portion of them—who must in any case be charged with the protection of Egypt, actively against the enemy's line of communica-tions instead of their hanging about, a stationary force, on the Suez Canal awaiting the onset of the Osmanli. Right through the war, the region about the Gulf of Iskanderun was one of prime strategical importance, seeing that Entente forces planted down in those parts automatically threatened, if they did not actually sever, the Ottoman communications between Anatolia and the theatres of war in Palestine and in Mesopotamia.   But at dates subsequent to the winter of 1914–15 the enemy had fully realized that this was the case, was in a position to provide against the eventuality, and had taken steps accordingly.

At the time I speak of, the Turks were not, however, in strong force at or near Alexandretta. Nor were they in a position to assemble formidable bodies of troops in that neighbourhood at short notice. For railway communications running westward towards Smyrna and the Golden Horn remained interrupted by the great Taurus range of mountains, the tunnels through which were making slow progress; and the tunnels through the Amanus hills which sever Aleppo from the Cilician Plain were likewise incomplete. One of our light cruisers (H.M.S. *Doris*, if my memory is not at fault) was stationed in the Gulf of Iskanderun, and was having a high old time. She dodged up and down the coast, appeared unexpectedly at unwelcome moments, and carried terror into the hearts of the local representatives of the Sublime Porte. She landed boats' crews from time to time just to show that she was top-dog, without their even being fired upon. Somebody ashore having done something that she disapproved of, she ordered the Ottoman officials to blow up certain of the bridges on their own railway, and when these harassed individuals, anxious to oblige, proffered the excuse that they lacked the wherewithal to carry her instructions out, she lent them explosives and saw to it that they were properly used. Her activities made it plain to us that there was absolutely no fight in the enemy at the moment in this quarter.

The whole subject of an expedition to Alexandretta was carefully gone into, in consultation with Sir J. Maxwell who was commanding the forces in Egypt, and we came to the conclusion that a comparatively small force could quite easily effect a landing and gain sufficient ground to make itself comfortable on enemy soil, even if the Turks managed gradually to assemble reinforcements. One realized that securing a considerable sector of ground

at once was essential in an amphibious operation of
this kind, the very thing that was never accomplished
on the Gallipoli Peninsula.   Lord K. was much interested
in the project for a time ; he believed that it would help
the Russians, who were in some straits in Armenia, and he
was satisfied that if it was successfully carried into effect,
hostile designs against the Suez Canal line would automatically be brought to nought.   A job of this sort would
have served as a capital exercise for some of the Australasian troops then in Egypt, who from the training point
of view were still a raw soldiery ; such a task would have
represented a very different class of trial from that which
they were actually to undergo three months later when
getting ashore at Anzac Cove.   But Mr. Churchill's naval
project against the Dardanelles began to take shape early
in January, and it put an end to any thoughts about
Alexandretta.   The matter is, indeed, only mentioned
here because its consideration marked about the first
occasion on which Lord Kitchener made any use of the
General Staff within the War Office in connection with
any operations question outside the United Kingdom.

It was not until another four months had elapsed,
however, that I personally had much say in regard to
those very questions which a Director of Military Operations would, from his title, seem necessarily to be closely
concerned with.   The change that then took place I
attribute very largely to an incident which on that
account deserves recording.   It happened that, on the
very day after welcome tidings came to hand by cable
from Sir I. Hamilton to the effect that he had successfully
landed 29,000 troops on the Gallipoli Peninsula on the
25th of April, I was sent off to Paris to represent the
British Army at a secret conference with French and
Russian commissioners and with representatives of the
Italians (who were coming into the war), at which naval
and military conventions with our fresh ally were to be
drawn up.   Further reference to this conference will be
made in a later chapter.   The consequence was that for

several days I heard no more about Sir Ian's operations beyond what appeared in the newspapers, and it was only when Mr. Churchill turned up somewhat unexpectedly and told me what had occurred, that it was borne in on me that our Dardanelles expeditionary force was completely held up in cramped positions and without elbow-room on an uncomfortable sort of shore. An examination of the telegrams and a discussion with my assistants after getting back from Paris convinced me that the situation was in the highest degree unsatisfactory, and I gathered, furthermore, that H.M. Government did not seem to be aware how unsatisfactory the situation was.

A day or two later, Lord K. summoned me to his room to ask some question, when I found Sir E. Grey closeted with him. Here was an opportunity that was not to be missed. While the Chief was making a note at his desk of the point that he wanted to know, I spoke to Sir Edward, and told him in effect that we had not a dog's chance of getting through the Dardanelles unless he secured the aid of the Bulgars, or of the Greeks, or of both of them — purposely putting the matter more strongly than I actually felt about it, in the hopes of making an impression by a jeremiad. Lord K. stopped writing and looked up. We had a short conversation, and after a few minutes I left the room. The Foreign Minister may not have been impressed, but Lord K. was; for he sent for me again later in the day, and we had a long discussion about Sir I. Hamilton's prospects. The incident, moreover, had a result which I had not anticipated. From that time forward the Chief often talked to me about the position in the Dardanelles and in the Near East generally. He used to take me with him to the Dardanelles Committee which was formed soon afterwards; and when he was away I ordinarily represented him at the deliberations of that body, deliberations which, as a matter of fact, covered a good deal of ground besides the Gallipoli Peninsula.

It struck me at the time that Lord Kitchener's

confidence in himself and his own judgement, in connection with what may be called operations subjects, had been somewhat shaken, and that from this stage onwards he rather welcomed the opinion of others when such points arose. The Antwerp adventure had proved a fiasco. The endeavour to force the Dardanelles by naval power, unaided by troops, had conspicuously failed. Coming on the top of those discouraging experiences, our army thrown ashore on the Gallipoli Peninsula had, after suffering very heavy losses, straightway been brought to a standstill. As regards the Fleet's efforts against the Straits, I gathered at the time (from Fitzgerald, I think) that in taking an optimistic view of the project when it was under discussion by the War Council, Lord K. had been a good deal influenced by recollections of the bombardment of Alexandria, at which he had been present. The Chief always claimed to have been led astray by Mr. Churchill concerning the potentialities of the *Queen Elizabeth*, and had, I should say, come to the conclusion that the judgement of the then First Lord, with whom he had been so closely associated for nine months, was not quite infallible. He cannot but have been aware that his Cabinet colleagues no longer reposed the implicit trust in his own judgement that they had accorded him at the outset. All through the summer of 1915 he grew more and more disposed to listen to the views of the General Staff as regards questions affecting the general conduct of the war, and, after Sir A. Murray became C.I.G.S. in October, that institution was almost occupying its proper position in the consultative sense. It did not recover its proper position in the executive sense, however, until Lord K. arranged that Sir W. Robertson should take up charge at the end of the year.

The question of the *Queen Elizabeth* cropped up in somewhat acute form two or three weeks after my conversation with Sir E. Grey which has been mentioned above. Lord Fisher had, as I knew from himself, been getting decidedly jumpy about the enemy U-boats, which

F

were known to be approaching the Aegean, and about the middle of May he raised the question of fetching away the " *Lizzie*," as Sir I. Hamilton's troops used to call her, lest evil should befall this, the most powerful ship in commission at the time. Lord Fisher has referred to this matter in his book *Memories*. He speaks of great tension between Lord K. and himself over the business, and he mentions an interview at the Admiralty at which, according to him, Lord K. got up from the table and left when he (Lord Fisher) announced that he would resign unless the battleship was ordered out of that forthwith. Now there may have been more than one interview at the Admiralty, but I was present at the conference when the matter was settled, and my recollection of what occurred does not agree with Lord Fisher's account.

Lord Kitchener sent for me early one morning, and on my presenting myself, told me that Lord Fisher was insisting upon recalling the *Queen Elizabeth* owing to enemy submarines, that Mr. Churchill was in two minds but leant towards keeping her where she was, that he (Lord K.) objected to her removal, and that I was to accompany him to a meeting at the Admiralty a little later in connection with the affair. " They've rammed that ship down my throat," said he in effect. " Churchill told me in the first place that she would knock all the Dardanelles batteries into smithereens, firing from goodness knows where. He afterwards told me that she would make everything all right for the troops as they landed, and after they landed. And now, without ' with your leave or by your leave,' old Fisher says he won't let her stop out there." He seemed to be quite as much concerned about the way he had been treated in the matter, as influenced by any great alarm at the prospect of the ship leaving the vicinity of the Dardanelles. Finally, he asked me what I thought myself.

Now, there could be no question as to the *Queen Elizabeth* being a most powerful ship of war ; but the fact was that she had been a regular nuisance. Mr. Churchill had somehow persuaded himself, and what was worse, he had managed to persuade Lord Kitchener as well as Mr. Asquith and others, that she would just about settle the Dardanelles business off her own bat. I had, as it happened (and as will be mentioned in the next chapter), expressed doubts to him six months earlier when the idea of operations in this quarter was first mooted, as to the efficacy of gun-fire from warships in assisting troops on shore or when trying to get ashore. Nothing which had happened since had furnished any reason for altering that view. No battleship depending upon flat trajectory guns could ever play a rôle of paramount importance during fighting ashore, except in quite abnormal circumstances. The whole thing was a delusion. Ships of war, and particularly such a vessel as the *Queen Elizabeth*, did undoubtedly provide moral support to an army operating on land close to the coast, and their aid was by no means to be despised; but their potentialities under such conditions were apt to be greatly overestimated, and had, in fact, been greatly overestimated by the War Council. My reply to the Chief, therefore, was to the effect that it was of secondary importance from the soldier's point of view whether this particular battleship stopped or cleared out, and that, seeing the risks which she obviously was running, it seemed to me a mistake to contest the point. We discussed the matter briefly, and Lord K. gave me to understand that, although he must put up some sort of fight as he had already raised objections, he would make no real stand about it at the coming pow-wow.

When we went across the road we found Mr. Churchill and Lord Fisher waiting in the First Lord's room. After some remarks by Mr. Churchill giving the *pros* and *cons*, Lord Fisher burst out that, unless orders were dispatched to the battleship without delay to " come out of that," he would resign. The First Lord thereupon, somewhat reluctantly as it seemed to me, intimated that in view of the position taken up by his principal expert adviser, he had no option but to recall the vessel.   Lord Kitchener demurred, but he demurred very mildly.   There was no jumping up and going off in a huff.   Some perfectly amicable discussion as to one or two other points of mutual interest ensued, and when we took our departure the Chief was in the very best of humours and asked me if he had made as much fuss as was expedient under the circumstances.

Lord K. seemed quite incapable of taking his Cabinet colleagues so seriously as people of that sort take themselves.   Indeed, but for the more prominent ones, he never could remember what their jobs were, nor even recollect their names.   It put one in a cold perspiration to hear him remark, when recounting what had occurred at a Cabinet séance or at the meeting of some committee bristling with Privy Councillers, " A fellow—I don't know his name but he's got curly hair—said . . ." Other soldiers besides Lord K. have, however, been known on occasion to get these super-men mixed up in their minds.   There were three Ministers, for instance, whom for convenience we will call Messrs. Abraham, Isaac and Jacob.   Mr. Jacob was on one occasion taking part in a conference at the War Office about something or other, a whole lot of the brightest and best sitting round a table trying to look intelligent ; and in the course of the proceedings he felt constrained to give his opinion on a matter that had cropped up.   A soldier of high degree, who was holding a most respectable position in the War Office and was sitting on the opposite side of the table, thereupon lifted up his voice.   " I quite see Mr. Abraham's point," he began argumentatively, " but I——." He was thrown into pitiable confusion, was routed, lost his guns, his baggage, everything, forgot what he was about to say, on being brought up short by a snarl from across the table, " My name is Jacob, not Abraham."

One day in the summer of 1915 when Lord K. had summoned me to ask some question, he appeared to be in particularly low spirits, and presently he showed me a communication (a telegram, I think it was) from Sir J. French, intimating that one of the New Army divisions which had recently proceeded across the water had not borne itself altogether satisfactorily when assailed in the trenches.   The troops had apparently been in a measure caught napping, although they had fought it out gallantly after being taken at a disadvantage owing to keeping careless guard.   That these divisions, in which he naturally enough took such exceptional personal interest, needed a great deal of breaking-in to conditions in presence of the enemy before they could be employed with complete confidence, had been a bitter disappointment to him.   On this subject he was perhaps misled to some extent by the opinions of officers who were particularly well qualified to judge.   The New Army troops had shown magnificent grit and zeal while preparing themselves in this country for the ordeal of the field, under most discouraging conditions, and they had come on very fast in consequence. Their very experienced divisional commanders, many of whom had come conspicuously to the front in the early months of the war and had learnt in the best of schools what fighting meant under existing conditions, were therefore rather disposed to form unduly favourable estimates of what their divisions would be capable of as soon as they entered upon their great task in the war zone.   I remember receiving a letter from that very gallant and popular gunner, General F. Wing (who was afterwards killed at Loos), written very shortly before his division proceeded to France, in which he expressed himself enthusiastically with regard to the potentialities of his troops.   His earnest hope was to find himself pitting them against the Boche as soon as the division took the field.

In one respect we most of us, I think, found Lord K. a little difficult at times.   He was apt to be impatient if, when he was at all in a hurry, he required information from, or wanted something carried out by, a subordinate.

This impatience indeed rather disposed him to rush his fences at times. Your book or your orator always extols the man of lightning decision, and in time of war soldiers do often have to make up their minds for better or for worse on the spur of the moment. But there is a good deal to be said for very carefully examining all the factors bearing upon the question at issue before coming to a conclusion, if there be leisure for consideration. Certain of the Secretary of State's colleagues were perpetually starting some new hare or other overnight, and the result would often be that the Chief would send for me at about 9.30 A.M., would give me some brand-new document or would tell me of some fresh project that was afoot, and would direct me to let him have a note on the subject not later than 11 A.M., so that he should be fully posted up in the matter by 11.30 A.M., when the War Council, or the Cabinet, or the Dardanelles Committee, as the case might be, would be wanting to chat about it.

One would thereupon proceed to investigate the project, or whatever the thing was, would muster one's data, would probably consult some subordinate and get him to lend a hand, and by, say, 10.15 A.M. one had hurriedly drafted out a memorandum, and had handed it to one's typists with injunctions that the draft must be reproduced at all hazards within twenty minutes. About 10.30 A.M. a War Office messenger, wearing a hunted look on his face, would appear at one's door " His Lordship wants to know, sir, if you have that paper ready that he asked you for." " Tell him that he shall have it directly," and one got on to the telephone to the clerks' room and enjoined despatch. In another ten minutes, Lord K.'s Private Secretary, and one of the best, Creedy, would turn up panting but trying not to look heated. " I say, can't you let the S. of S. have that confounded paper he is worrying about ? Do be quick so that we may have some peace." Fresh urgings through the telephone, accompanied by reminders that the twenty minutes had more than elapsed. Five minutes later

Fitzgerald would arrive. " Look here ! K.'s kicking up the devil's own fuss because you won't let him have some paper or other. Typists ? But it's always those typists of yours, General. Why don't you have the lot up against the wall out in the courtyard, and have them shot ? It's the only thing to do in these cases." When one had almost given up hope, the typist would hurry in with a beautifully prepared document, and one would rush off to the Chief. " Oh ! Here you are at last. What a time you've been. Now, let me see what you say. . . Well, that seems all right. But stop. Show me on the map where this place B—— that you mention is. One of them may ask." They were just a little exhausting, those occasions.

What exactly the tomfoolery is that expert typists engage on after they have typed a document, I have never been able to discover. As long as they are at play on their machines these whirr like the propeller of a Handley-Page. They get down millions of words a minute. But when they have got the job apparently done, they simmer away to nothing. They perform mysterious rites with ink-eraser. They scratch feebly with knives. They hold up to the light, they tittivate, they muse and they adorn. It is not the slightest use intimating that you do not care twopence whether there are typographic errors or not—the expert typist treats you with the scorn that the expert always does treat the layman with. At such junctures it is an advantage if the typist happens to be a he, because you can tell him what you think of him. If the typist happens to be a she, and you tell her what you think of her, the odds are she will take cover under a flood of tears, and goodness only knows what one is supposed to do then. Not that my typists were not highly merito-rious—I would not have exchanged them with anybody. They merely played their game according to the rules.

Lord K. could no doubt be really unreasonable on occasion ; but I can only recall one instance of it in my own experience. It all arose over our Military Attaché at our Paris embassy, Colonel H. Yarde-Buller, having taken up his abode from an early date at Chantilly so as to be in close touch with General Joffre's headquarters.   Not being on the spot at the Embassy, his work in the meantime was being done, and very well done, by our Naval Attaché, Captain M. H. Hodges.   I do not know why it was, but one afternoon the Chief sent for me to say that a Military Attaché was required at once in Paris, and that I was to proffer names for him to choose from forthwith.   After consultation with my French experts, I produced a list of desirable candidates for the post, all, to a man, equipped with incontestable qualifications.   But Lord K. would have none of my nominees, although he probably knew uncommonly little about any of them.   I tried one or two more casts, but the Chief was really for the moment in an impossible mood.   Even Fitzgerald was in despair. At last the name of Colonel Le Roy Lewis occurred to me, whom I somehow had not thought of before ; but on repairing to the Chief's anteroom, where Fitz always was, a restful air was noticeable in the apartment, and Fitz acquainted me in a tone of relief that the boss had gone off home.   He moreover counselled me to keep Le Roy Lewis up my sleeve and to lie low, as the whole thing might have blown over by next day, and that is exactly what happened.   One heard no more about it ; but several weeks later I began myself to find that the military work in Paris was getting so heavy that we ought to have an attaché of our own, instead of depending upon the Admiralty's man, Hodges.   So I went to Lord K., proposed the appointment of a second Military Attaché, and suggested Le Roy Lewis for the job.   " Certainly,'.' said Lord K. ; " fix the business up with the Foreign Office, or whatever's necessary."   The fuss there had been a few weeks before had apparently been forgotten.

His intimate acquaintance with the French language stood him in rare stead, and this undoubtedly represented an asset to the country during the period that he was War Minister.   His actual phraseology and his accent might peradventure not have been accounted quite faultless on the boulevards ; but he was wonderfully fluent, he never by any chance paused for a word, and he always appeared to be perfectly familiar with those happy little turns of speech to which the Gallic tongue so particularly lends itself.   The ease with which he took charge of, and dominated, the whole proceedings on the occasion of one or two of the earlier conferences on the farther side of the Channel between our Ministers and the French astonished our representatives, as some of them have told me.   He thoroughly enjoyed discussions with foreign officers who had been sent over officially to consult with the War Office about matters connected with the war, and he always, as far as one could judge, deeply impressed such visitors.   I do not think that the warmth with which some of them spoke about him after such pow-wows when I ushered them out, was a mere manifestation of politeness.   He was gifted with a special bent for diplomacy, and he prided himself with justice on the skill and tact with which he handled such questions.

Quite early in the war—it must have been about November 1914—a small Portuguese military mission turned up, bearers of a proposal that our ancient ally should furnish a division to fight under Sir J. French's orders on the Western Front.   Our Government, as it happened, were not anxious, on political grounds which need not be gone into here, for open and active co-operation on the part of Portugal at this time.   Regarding the question from the purely military point of view, one doubted whether the introduction into the Flanders war zone of Portuguese troops, who would require certain material which we could then ill spare before they took the field, would not be premature at this early juncture. When tactfully interrogating concerning the martial spirit, the training efficiency, and so forth, of the rank and file, one was touched rather than exhilarated by the head of the mission's expression of faith " ils savent mourir." The officers composing the mission were, however, enthusiasts for their project, and they were on that account somewhat difficult to keep, as it were, at arm's length. But Lord K.'s management of the problem was masterly.

In the course of a protracted conference in his room, he contrived to persuade our friends from Lisbon that the despatch of the division at this moment would be a mistake from their, and from everybody else's, point of view, and he extracted promises out of them to let us have many thousands of their excellent Mauser rifles, together with a goodly number of their Schneider-Canet field guns. The small arms (of which we were horribly short at the time) proved invaluable in South Africa and Egypt, while the guns served to re-equip the Belgian army to some extent with field artillery. He managed to convince the mission that this was by far the most effective form of assistance which Portugal could then afford to the Entente —as was indeed the case—and he sent them off, just a little bewildered perhaps, but perfectly satisfied and even gratified. One felt a little bewildered oneself, the whole business had been conducted with such nicety and discretion.

His name counted for much in the armies of the Allies, as I myself found later wherever I went in Russia. Foreign officers coming on official errands to London, attached an enormous importance to obtaining an interview with him, and he was very good about this. " Oh, I can't be bothered with seeing the man," he would say ; " you've told him the thing's out of the question. What's the good of his coming to me, taking up my time ? " " But you see, sir," one would urge ; " he's a little rubbed up the wrong way at not getting what he· wants, and will not put the thing pleasantly to his own people when he fetches up at their end. You can smooth him down as nobody else could, and then he'll go away off out of this like a lamb and be quite good." " Oh well, bring him along. But, look here. You must have him away again sharp out of my room, or he'll keep on giving tongue here all the rest of the day." What actually happened as a rule on such occasions was that Lord K. would not let the missionary get a word in edgeways, smothered him with cordiality, chattered away in French as if he were wound up, and the difficulty was, not to carry the man off but to find an opportunity for jumping up and thereby conveying a hint to our friend that it was time to clear out. " Comme il est charmant, M. le Maréchal," the gratified foreign officer would say after one had grabbed him somehow and conducted him out of the presence ; " je n'oublierai de ma vie que je lui ai serré la main." And he would go off back to where he had come from, as pleased as Punch, having completely failed in his embassy.

But Lord K. could if the occasion called for it, adopt quite a different tone when dealing with an Allied representative, and I have a vivid remembrance of one such interview to which there seems to be no harm in referring now. Some aspects of the tangled political web of 1915, in the Near East, will be dealt with at greater length in Chapter VII. Suffice it to say here that, at the juncture under reference, Serbia, with formidable German and Austro-Hungarian hosts pouring into her territory from the north and aware that her traditional foe, Bulgaria, was mobilizing, desired to attack Tsar Ferdinand's realm before it was ready. That, from the purely military point of view, was unquestionably the sound procedure to adopt. " Thrice is he armed who has his quarrel just, but four times he who gets his blow in fust." We know now that it would have been the sound procedure to adopt, even allowing for arguments against such a course that could be put forward from the political point of view. But our Government's attitude was that, in view of engagements entered into by Greece, the Serbs must not act aggressively against the still neutral Bulgars. Nor do I think that, seeing how contradictory and inconclusive the information was upon which they were relying, they were to blame for maintaining an attitude which in the event had untoward consequences.

One afternoon the Serbian Military Attaché came to see me. He called in to beg us soldiers to do our utmost to induce H.M. Government to acquiesce in an immediate offensive on the part of King Peter's troops against the forces of the neighbouring State, which were mobilizing and were evidently bent on mischief. I presented our Government's case as well as I could, although my sympathies were in fact on military grounds entirely on the side of my visitor. He thereupon besought me to take him to Lord Kitchener, and I did so. The Chief talked the question over in the friendliest and most sympathetic manner, he gave utterance to warm appreciation of the vigorous, heroic stand which the sore-beset little Allied nation had made, and was making, in face of dangers that were gathering ever thicker, he expressed deep regret at our inability to give effective assistance. and he admitted that from the soldier's point of view there was much to be said for the contention that an immediate blow should be struck at Serbia's eastern neighbour. But he stated our Government's attitude in the matter clearly and uncompromisingly, and he would not budge an inch on the subject of our sanctioning or approving an attack upon Bulgaria so long as Bulgaria remained neutral.

The Attaché protested eagerly, volubly, stubbornly, pathetically, but all to no purpose. Then, when at last we rose to our feet, Lord K., finding his visitor wholly unconvinced, drew himself up to his full height. He seemed to tower over the Attaché, who was himself a tall man, and—well, it is hard to set down in words the happenings of a tense situation. The scene was one that I never shall forget, as, by his demeanour rather than by any words of his, Lord K. virtually issued a command that no Serb soldier was to cross the Bulgar border unless the Bulgars embarked on hostilities. The Attaché stood still a moment; then he put his kepi on, saluted gravely, turned round and went out without a word. I followed him out on to the landing. " Mon Dieu ! " he said ;

"mon Dieu!" And then he went slowly down the great marble staircase, looking a broken man. But for that interview the Serbs might perhaps have given their treacherous neighbours an uncommonly nasty jar before these got going, and this might have rendered their own military situation decidedly less tragic than it came to be within a very few days. But I do not see that Lord Kitchener could have done otherwise than support the attitude of the Government of which he was a member.

Striking testimony to the confidence which his name inspired amongst our Allies is afforded by the action of the Russians in the summer of 1915, in entrusting the question of their being furnished with munitions from the United States into his hands. They came to him as a child comes to its mother. This, be it noted, was at a time when our own army fighting in many fields was notoriously none too well fitted out with weapons nor with ammunition for them, at a time when the most powerful group of newspapers in this country had recently been making a pointed attack upon him in connection with this very matter, at a time when an idea undoubtedly existed in many quarters in the United Kingdom that the provision of vital war material had been neglected and botched under his control. That there was no justification whatever for that idea does not alter the fact that the idea prevailed. As I assumed special responsibilities in connection with Russian supplies at a later date, a date subsequent to the *Hampshire* catastrophe, and as the subject of munitions will be dealt with in a later chapter, no more need be said on the subject here. But the point seemed to deserve mention at this stage.

We came rather to dread the occasions when the Chief was going to deliver one of his periodical orations in the House of Lords. Singularly enough, he used to take these speeches of his, in which he took good care never to tell his auditors anything that they did not know before, quite seriously—a good deal more seriously than we did. He prepared them laboriously, absorbing a good deal of his own time, and some of the time of certain of those under him, and then he would read out his rough draft to one, asking for approval and grateful for hints. He was always delighted to have some felicitous turn of expression proffered him, and he would discuss its merits at some length as compared with his own wording, ending by inserting it in the draft or rejecting it, as the case might be. I remember on one occasion, when he was going to fire off one of these addresses, just about the time when the great Boche thrust of 1915 into the heart of Russia came to an end, his making use of the idiom that the German " bolt was about shot." I objected. " Don't you like the phrase ? " demanded Lord K. I admitted that it was an excellent phrase in itself, but urged that it was not altogether applicable, that the enemy seemed to have come to a standstill, not because he could get no farther but because he did not want to go farther, meaning to divert force in some new direction, and that the words somehow represented our principal foe as in worse case than was correct. Lord K. seemed disappointed. He said that he would consider the matter, and he made a note on his draft. But he stuck to his guns as it turned out ; he used the phrase in the Upper House a day or two later, and it was somewhat criticised in the newspapers at the time. He was, I believe, so much captivated by his little figure of speech that he simply could not bear to part with it.

He was a regular salamander. The heat of his room, owing to the huge fire that he always maintained if it was in the least cold outside and to the double windows designed to keep out the noise of Whitehall, was at times almost unbearable. One's head would be in a buzz after being in it for some time. His long sojourn in southern lands no doubt rendered him very susceptible to low temperatures. On one occasion, when General Joffre had sent over a couple of superior staff officers to discuss some questions with him, the four of us sat at his table for an hour and a half, and the two visitors and I were almost in a state of collapse at the end. "Mais, la chaleur! Pouf! C'était assommant!" I heard one say to the other as they left the room, not noticing that I was immediately behind.

Lord Kitchener's judgement in respect to general military policy in the Near East and the Levant, during the time that he was War Minister was, I think, to some small extent warped at times by excessive preoccupation with regard to Egypt and the Sudan. His hesitation to concur in the evacuation of the Gallipoli Peninsula until he had convinced himself of the urgent necessity of the step by personal observation, was, I am sure, prompted by his fears as to the evil moral effect which such a confession of failure would exert in the Nile Delta, and up the valley of the great river. Soon after Sir Archie Murray had become C.I.G.S., and when the War Council had taken to asking for the considered views of the General Staff upon problems of the kind, a paper had to be prepared on the subject of how best to secure Egypt. This document I drafted in the rough in the first instance. Sir Archie and we Directors of the General Staff then went carefully through it and modified it in some respects. Its purport when presented was that the proper course to pursue with regard to Egypt would be to depend upon holding the line of the Suez Canal, and some minor areas in front of it, as a comparatively small force would suffice for the purpose.

Lord K. was much disappointed. He sent for me, expressed himself as strongly opposed to our view, and he seemed rather hurt at the attitude we had taken up. He favoured the despatch of a body of troops to the Gulf of Alexandretta with the idea of carrying on a very active defence ; he wished to keep the enemy as far away from Egypt as possible for fear of internal disturbances, and this opinion was, I know, concurred in by Sir R. Wingate and Sir J. Maxwell. We should, no doubt, have concurred in that view likewise, had there been unlimited numbers of divisions to dispose of, and had there been no U-boats about. But an army merely sufficient to hold the

Egyptian frontier would have been entirely inadequate to start a campaign based on the sea in northern Syria, and experiences in the Dardanelles theatre of war hardly offered encouragement for embarking on ventures on the shores of the Levant.   Lord K. called Sir D. Haig, who happened to be over on short leave at the time, into counsel ; Sir Douglas supported the contention that a comparatively small force distributed about the Canal would render things secure.   The Chief then despatched General Horne (who in those days was known rather as an expert gunner than as commander of aggregates of army corps) to Egypt to report ; I had ceased to be D.M.O. before the report came to hand, but I believe that it favoured our plan, the plan which actually was adopted and which served its purpose for many months.

A good many of us in the War Office were a little inclined to cavil at our Chief's deliberation in the matter of demanding a system of national service, when the country had arrived at the stage where expansion of the fighting forces was no longer hopelessly retarded by lack of war material.   But, looking back upon the events of the first year of the war, one realizes now that if he made a mistake over this subject it was in not establishing the principle by statute at the very beginning, in the days when he was occupying a position in the eyes of his countrymen such as no British citizen had enjoyed for generations.   He could have done what he liked at the start.   The nation was solid behind him.   Not Great Britain alone, but also Ireland, would have swallowed conscription with gusto in September 1914, after the retreat from Mons.   Our man-power could in that case have been tapped gradually, by methods that were at once scientific and equitable, so as to cause the least possible disturbance to the country's productive capacity.

Twelve months later, he had ceased to present quite so commanding a figure to the proletariat as he had presented when first he was called in to save the situation. Of this he was probably quite aware himself, and it is a great mistake to suppose that he was indifferent to public opinion or even to the opinion of the Press. By that time, moreover, he was probably a good deal hampered by some of his colleagues and their pestilent pre-war pledges. A good many politicians nowadays find it convenient to forget that during those very days when the secret information reaching them must surely have made them aware of Germany's determination to make war on a suitable opportunity presenting itself, they were making the question of compulsory service virtually a party matter, and were binding themselves to oppose it tooth and nail. The statemonger always assumes that the public take his pledges (which he never boggles over breaking for some purely factious object) seriously. The public may be silly, but they are not quite so silly as that.

Having missed the tide when it was at the flood, Lord K. was wise in acting with circumspection, and in rather shrinking from insisting upon compulsion so long as it had not become manifestly and imperatively necessary. When, in the early autumn of 1915, he told me off as a kind of bear-leader to a Cabinet Committee presided over by Lord Crewe, which was to go into the general question of man-power and of the future development of the forces—a Committee which was intended, as far as I could make out, to advise as to whether compulsory service was to be adopted or not—I found him a little unapproachable and disinclined to commit himself. I was, of course, only supposed to assist in respect to information and as regards technical military points; but it would have been a help to know exactly what one's Chief desired and thought. Fitzgerald was a great stand-by on such occasions. I gathered from him that the Secretary of State was not anxious to precipitate bringing the question to a head, with the conception ever at the back of his mind of conserving sufficient fighting resources under his hand to deal the decisive blow in the war when the psychological moment should come, months ahead. He was not, in 1915, looking to 1916; he was looking to

G

1917, having made up his mind from the outset that this was to be a prolonged war of attrition. He, no more than all others, could foresee that the Russian revolution was to occur and was to delay the final triumph of the Entente for full twelve months.

The last time that I saw the greatest of our War Ministers was a day or two before he started on his fatal expedition to Russia. I had recently come back from that country, and had been able to give him and Fitzgerald some useful hints as to minor points—kit, having all available decorations handy to put on for special occasions, taking large-sized photographs to dole out as presents, and so forth. He was very anxious to get back speedily, and had been somewhat disturbed to hear that things moved slowly in the Tsar's dominions, and that the trip would inevitably take considerably longer than he had counted on. I had urged him not to be in too great haste— to visit several groups of armies, and to show himself in Moscow and Kieff, feeling absolutely convinced that if the most was made of his progress through Russian territory it would do an immense amount of good. But he was in just as great a hurry to get journeys over in 1916 as he had been in South African days, when he used to risk a smash by requiring the trains in which he roamed the theatre of war to travel at a speed beyond that which was safe on such tortuous tracks ; and it is easy to understand how hard-set, with so impetuous a passenger, the Admiralissimo of the Grand Fleet would have been to delay the departure of the *Hampshire* merely on the grounds of rough weather on the day on which she put to sea.

On that last occasion when I saw him the Field-Marshal was in rare spirits, looking forward eagerly to his time in Russia, merry as a schoolboy starting for his holidays, only anxious to be off. With that incomparable gift of his for interpreting the essentials of a situation, he fully realized how far-reaching might be the consequences of the undertaking to which he stood committed. The public of this country perhaps hardly realize that the most unfortunate feature of his death at that time, from the national point of view, was that it prevented his Russian trip. Had it not been for the disaster of the 5th of June 1916 off the Orkneys, that convulsion of March 1917 in the territories of our great eastern Ally might never have occurred, or it might at least have been deferred until after the war had been brought to a happy termination. Apart from this, Lord Kitchener's work was almost done. Thanks to him, the United Kingdom had, alike in respect to men and to material, been transformed into a great military Power, and yet further developments had been assured. The employing of the instrument which he had created could be left to other hands.

Many appreciations of him appeared at the time of his lamented passing, and have appeared since. His character and his qualifications as man of action and elaborator had not always been appraised quite correctly during his lifetime, and they are a subject of differences of opinion still. Often was he spoken of as a great organizer and administrator. But his claim to possess such qualifications rested rather upon the results that he obtained than upon the methods by which he obtained them. Of detail he possessed no special mastery, and yet he would concern himself with questions of detail which might well have been left to subordinates to deal with. He won the confidence of those under him not so much through trusting them in the sense of leaving them responsibility, as through compelling them to trust him by the force of his personality and by the wide compass of his outlook upon the numberless questions that were ever at issue. He had been described as harsh, taciturn, and unbending. He was on the contrary a delightful chief to serve once one understood his ways, although he would stand no nonsense and, like most people, was occasionally out of humour and exacting.

A more cunning hand than mine is needed to depict adequately the great soldier-statesman. But this I would say. There has been much foolish talk as to this individual and to that having won the war. That any one person could have won the war is on the face of it an absurdity. The greatest factor in achieving the result was the British Navy; but who would claim that any one of the chieftains in our fleets or pulling the naval strings ashore decided the issue of the struggle? Next, however, to what our sailors achieved afloat, the most important influence in giving victory to the side of the Entente was the development, to an extent previously undreamt of, of the British fighting resources ashore. That was primarily the handiwork of Lord Kitchener. His country can fairly claim that he accomplished more than did any other individual — French, American, Italian, Russian, British—to bring German militarism to the ground.

No reference to the famous Field-Marshal's career during the Great War would be complete without one word as to " Fitz." Fitzgerald was, after a fashion, the complement of his Chief. We in Whitehall would have been lost without him. A comparatively junior officer, he was looked upon with some suspicion by those high up in the War Office just at first, in consequence of the exceptional influence that he enjoyed with the War Minister, and of his always knowing more about what was going on than anybody else but the War Minister himself. But all hands speedily came to appreciate the rare qualities of this seeming interloper, to realize what useful services he was able and ever ready to perform, and to turn his presence at his Chief's elbow to the best account. Sometimes he would be acting as a buffer; at other times he assumed the rôle of coupling-chain. Lord Kitchener frequently employed him to convey instructions verbally, and on such occasions the emissary always knew exactly what was in the War Minister's mind. If after an interview with the Chief one felt any doubts as to what was required of one, a hint to Fitz would be sure to secure the information of which one stood in need. Lord K. reposed implicit confidence in the judgement of this Personal Military Secretary of his, and with good reason. Often when the solution of some problem under discussion appeared to be open to question, he would say, " Let's have in Fitz and see what he thinks."

The relations between them were like father and son. Each swore by the other, and Lord K. indeed never seemed better pleased than when one showed a liking for the Bengal Lancer whom he had chosen when in India and attached to himself. " I'll go and talk it over with Fitz, sir," was sure to be rewarded with a pleasant smile and a " Yes, do." Possessing a charming personality, a keen intellect, a fund of humour and a considerable knowledge of the world, Fitz was an extremely attractive figure quite apart from the exceptional qualifications which he possessed for a post which he filled with so much credit to himself, and with such advantage to others. Of the thousands who went down in the great struggle, few were probably more sincerely mourned by hosts of friends than the gallant soldier whose body, washed ashore on the iron-bound coast of the Orkneys, we laid to rest one showery June afternoon in the hillside cemetery overlooking Eastbourne.

CHAPTER V

THE DARDANELLES

The Tabah incident—The Dardanelles memorandum of 1906—Special steps taken with regard to it by Sir H. Campbell-Bannerman—Mr. Churchill first raises the question—My conference with him in October 1914—The naval project against the Straits—Its fundamental errors—Would never have been carried into effect had there been a conference between the Naval War Staff and the General Staff—The bad start—The causes of the final failure on the 18th of March—Lord K.'s instructions to Sir I. Hamilton—The question of the packing of the transports—Sir l. Hamilton's complaint as to there being no plan prepared—The 1906 memorandum—Sir Ian's complaint about insufficient information—How the 1906 memorandum affected this question—Misunderstanding as to the difficulty of obtaining information—The information not in reality so defective—My anxiety at the time of the first landing—The plan, a failure by early in May—Impossibility of sending out reinforcements then—Question whether the delay in sending out reinforcements greatly affected the result in August 1915—The Dardanelles Committee—Its anxiety—Sir E. Carson and Mr. Churchill, allies—The question of clearing out—My disinclination to accept the principle before September—Sir C. Monro sent out—The delay of the Government in deciding—Lord K. proceeds to the Aegean—My own experiences—A trip to Paris with a special message to the French Government—Sent on a fool's errand, thanks to the Cabinet—A notable state paper on the subject—Mr. Lloyd George and the " sanhedrin "—Decision to evacuate only Anzac and Suvla—Sir W. Robertson arrives and orders are sent to evacuate Helles—I give up the appointment of D.M.O.

No sooner did disquieting intelligence come to hand to the effect that the Ottoman authorities had given the *Goeben* and the *Breslau* a suspicious welcome in Turkish waters during the opening weeks of the great struggle, than it became apparent that war with a fresh antagonist was at least on the cards. It was, moreover, obvious that if there were to be a rupture between the Entente and the Sublime Porte, the Bosphorus was certain to be closed as a line of communication between the Western Powers and Russia. Such an eventuality was bound to exercise a far-reaching influence over the course of the war as a whole. One therefore naturally gave some attention to the possibilities involved in an undertaking against Constantinople and the Straits—a subject with which by chance I happened to be probably as familiar as anybody in the army.

Some eight years before, in the early part of 1906, H.M. Government had found itself at variance with the Sublime Porte in connection with a spot called Tabah at the head of the Gulf of Akaba, which we regarded as within the dominions of the Khedive but which Osmanli troops had truculently taken possession of. The Sultan's advisers had been rather troublesome about the business, and Downing Street and the Foreign Office had been obliged to take up a firm attitude before the Ottoman Government unwillingly climbed down. I had been in charge of the strategical section of the Military Operations Directorate at that time, and, in considering what we might be able to do in the military line supposing that things came to a head, had investigated the problems involved in gaining possession of the Dardanelles. Some years earlier, moreover, I had passed through the Straits and had spent a night at Chanak in the Narrows, taking careful note of the lie of the land, of the batteries as then existing, and so forth.

After an accommodation had been arrived at with Johnny Turk in 1906, the Committee of Imperial Defence had followed up this question of operations against the Hellespont, more or less as an academic question; and I had drafted a paper on the subject, which was gone through line by line by General Spencer Ewart who was then D.M.O., in consultation with myself, was modified in some minor respects by him, was initialed by General Lyttelton, the Chief of the General Staff, and was accepted in principle by the C.I.D., Sir J. Fisher (as he then was) having as First Sea Lord expressed his full concurrence with the views therein expressed. These in effect " turned " the project " down." When about the end of August I searched for the 1906 memorandum in the files of the Committee of Imperial Defence papers which were in my safe, I found a note in the file concerned to say that by order of the Prime Minister the memorandum had been withdrawn. The reason for this I discovered at a later date. Sir H. Campbell-Bannerman had fully realized the importance of this Dardanelles transaction of 1906. He had perceived that it was a matter of quite exceptional secrecy. He had dreaded the disastrous results which might well arise were news by any mischance to leak out and to reach the Sublime Porte that the naval and military authorities in this country had expressed the opinion that successful attack upon the Dardanelles was virtually impracticable, and that H.M. Government had endorsed this view. Tell the Turk that, and our trump card was gone. We could then no longer bluff the Ottoman Government in the event of war with feints of operations against the Straits—the very course which I believe would have been adopted in 1914–1915, had the Admiralty War Staff and the General Staff considered the question together without Cabinet interference and submitted a joint report for the information of the War Council. That 1906 memorandum and the Committee of Imperial Defence transactions in connection with it were treated differently from any C.I.D. documents of analogous kind then or, as far as I know, subsequently. I never saw the memorandum from 1906 till one day in May 1915, when Mr. Asquith pushed a copy across the table to me at a meeting of the War Council in Downing Street, and I recognized it at once as in great measure my own production. It would not seem to have been brought to the notice of the Dardanelles Commission that the memorandum (to which several references are made in their Reports) was practically accepted by the Committee of Imperial Defence as governing the military policy of the country with respect to attack on the Straits in the event of war.

The consequence of my having made myself familiar with the question in the past was that, when at the beginning of September 1914 Mr. Churchill raised the question of a conjunct Greek and British enterprise against the Straits, it was a simple matter for me to prepare a short memorandum on the subject, a memorandum of a decidedly discouraging nature. As a matter of fact, what was perhaps the strongest argument against the undertaking at that time was by oversight omitted from the document—the Greeks had no howitzers or mobile heavy artillery worth mentioning, and any ordnance of that class that we disposed of in the Mediterranean was of the prehistoric kind. The slip was of no great importance, however, because there never was the remotest chance of King Constantine, who was no mean judge of warlike problems, letting his country in for so dubious an enterprise.

We were not actually at war with the Ottoman Empire for another two months. But hostilities had virtually become certain during the month of October, and one morning in the latter part of that month the First Lord sent a message across asking me to come over to his room and discuss possibilities in connection with the Dardanelles. I found the First Sea Lord (Prince Louis of Battenberg) and the Fourth Sea Lord (Commodore C. F. Lambert) waiting, as well as Mr. Churchill, and we sat round a table with all the maps and charts that were necessary for our purpose spread out on it. The problem of mastering the Straits was examined entirely from the point of view of a military operation based upon, and supported by, naval power. If the question of a fleet attack upon the defences within the defile was mentioned at all, it was only referred to quite incidentally.

From my own observation on the spot, and as a result of later examination of maps, charts, confidential reports, and so forth, I had come to the conclusion that the key to the Dardanelles lay in the Kilid Bahr plateau, which dominates the channel at its very narrowest point from the European (Gallipoli Peninsula) side. By far the best plan of gaining possession of this high ground would, I considered, be to land, by surprise if possible, the biggest military force that could be very rapidly put ashore on that long stretch of coast-line practicable for troops to disembark from boats in fine weather, which was situated about the locality that has since become immortalized as Anzac Cove. A project on these lines is what we actually discussed that morning in the First Lord's room. I pointed out the difficulties and the dangers involved, *i.e.* the virtual impossibility of effecting a real surprise, the perils inseparable from a disembarkation in face of opposition, the certainty that the enemy was even now improving the land defences of the Gallipoli Peninsula, and the fact that, at the moment, we had no troops to carry such a scheme out and that we were most unlikely to have any to spare for such an object for months to come. One somewhat controversial tactical point I gave particular attention to—the efficacy of the fire of warships when covering a military landing and when endeavouring to silence field-guns on shore ; my own view was that the potentialities of a fleet under such conditions were apt to be greatly overestimated. My exposition was intended to be dissuasive, and I think that Mr. Churchill was disappointed.

We had a most pleasant discussion, the First Lord having a good working knowledge of military questions owing to his early career and training, and being therefore able to appreciate professional points which might puzzle the majority of civilians. At the end of it he seemed to clearly realize what a very serious operation of war a military undertaking against the Straits was likely to be, but he dwelt forcibly, and indeed enthusiastically, upon the results that would be gained by the Entente in the event of such an undertaking being successfully carried out—on that subject we were all quite at one. The story of this informal pow-wow has been recorded thus at length, because it was really the only occasion on which the General Staff were afforded anything like a proper opportunity of expressing an opinion as to operations against the Dardanelles, until after the country had been engulfed up to the neck in the morass and was irretrievably committed to an amphibious campaign on a great scale in the Gallipoli Peninsula. Prince Louis resigned his position as First Sea Lord a few days later; Commodore Lambert often mentioned the pow-wow in conversation with me in later days, after the mischief (for which the professional side of the Admiralty was only very partially to blame) had been done.

As one gradually became acquainted in the following January with the nature of the naval scheme for dealing with the Straits, it was difficult not to feel apprehension. While, as Brigade-Major R.A. in the Western Command and later as commanding a company of R.G.A. at Malta, concerned with coast defence principles, the tactical rather than the technical scientific side of such problems had always interested me. When musing, during those interminable waits which take place in the course of a day's gun practice from a coast-defence battery, as to what would be likely to happen in the event of the work actually engaging a hostile armament, one could picture oneself driven from the guns under the hail of flying fragments of rock, concrete, and metal thrown up by the ships' huge projectiles. But one did not picture the battery as destroyed and rendered of no effect. Anybody who has tried both is aware how infinitely easier gun practice is at even a moving target on the water than it is at a target on land. One foresaw that the enemy's warships would plaster the vicinity of the work with projectiles, and would create conditions disastrous to human life if the gun-detachments did not go to ground, but that they would not often, if ever, actually hit the mark and demolish guns and mountings.

The Admiralty's creeping form of attack, chosen on

Admiral Carden's initiative, ignored this aspect of the question altogether. The whole scheme hinged upon *destroying* the Ottoman coast batteries, the very thing that ships find it hardest to do. They can silence batteries; but what is the good of that if they then clear out and allow the defenders to come back and clean up? The creeping plan, moreover, obviously played into the hands of Turkish mobile guns, which would turn up in new positions on successive days, and which, as I had told Mr. Churchill three months before, our ships would find most difficult to deal with; these guns would probably give the mine-sweepers much more trouble than the heavy ordnance in the enemy's fixed defences. Then, again, one could not but be aware that the Sister Service was none too well equipped for dealing with the enigma of mines in any form—that had become obvious to those behind the scenes during the first six months of the war—and one's information pointed to the Turkish mine-defence of the Dardanelles being more up to date than was their gun-defence. Finally, and much the most important of all, this deliberate procedure was the worst possible method to adopt from the army's point of view, supposing the plan to fail and the army then to be called in to pull the chestnuts out of the fire. The enemy would have been given full warning, and would deliberately have been allowed what the Turk always stands in need of when on the war-path—time to prepare.

The "First Report" of the Dardanelles Commission, as well as sidelights thrown upon the affair from other quarters, have established that of the three eminent naval experts who dealt with the project and who were more or less responsible for its being put into execution, two, Sir Arthur Wilson and Sir Henry Jackson, were by no means enthusiastic about it, while the third, Lord Fisher, was opposed to it but allowed himself to be overruled by the War Council. Had those three admirals met three representatives of the General Staff, Sir J. Wolfe-Murray, General Kiggell and myself, let us say, sitting round a table with no Cabinet Ministers present, I am certain that the report that we should have drawn up would have been dead against the whole thing. The objections raised from the military side would have been quite sufficient to dispel any doubts that the sailors had left on the subject. As for that naïve theory that we might draw back in the middle of the naval operations supposing that the business went awry, of which I do not remember hearing at the time—— Pooh! We could hardly, left to ourselves, have been such flats as to take that seriously.

The cable message from Tenedos which announced the result of the first effort against the conspicuous and comparatively feeble works that defended the mouth of the Straits, was the reverse of heartening. The bombarding squadron enjoyed an overwhelming superiority in armament from every point of view—range, weight of metal, and accuracy. The conditions were almost ideal for the attacking side, as there was plenty of sea-room and no worry about mines. If the warships could not finally dispose of Turkish works such as this, and with everything favourable, by long-range fire, then long-range fire was " off." Once inside the Straits, the fleet, manœuvring without elbow-room, would have to get pretty near its work, mines or no mines, if it was going to do any good. The idea of the *Queen Elizabeth* pitching her stuff over the top of the Gallipoli Peninsula left one cold. Several days before Admiral de Robeck delivered his determined attack upon the defences of the Narrows of the 18th of March, one had pretty well made up one's mind that the thing was going to be a failure, and that the army was going to be let in for an extremely uncomfortable business.

Accounts emanating from the Turkish side have suggested that the naval operations were within an ace of succeeding, and that they only had to be pressed a little further to achieve their object. An examination of the books by Mr. Morgenthau and others does not bear this out. The Turks imagined that our fleet had been ·beaten off by gun-fire on the 18th, and they appear to have got nervous because the ammunition for certain of their heaviest guns was running short. Their heavy-guns, and the ammunition for them, was a matter of quite secondary importance. The fleet was beaten off owing to the effect of the drifting mines. The Turks thought that the damage done to the ships was due to their batteries, when it was in reality caused by their mines. They did not appreciate the situation correctly, for they do not appear to have been short of mines. The Russian plan of letting these engines of destruction loose at the Black Sea end of the Bosphorus to drift down with the current indeed provided the Osmanlis with a constant supply of excellent ones ; they were picked up, shipped down to the Dardanelles, and used against the Allies' fleet. These weapons, drifting and fixed, together with the mobile artillery which so seriously interfered with mine-sweeping, proved to be the trump cards in the hands of Johnny Turk and his Boche assistants.

I was present when Lord Kitchener met Sir I. Hamilton and his chief staff-officer, General Braithwaite, and gave Sir Ian his instructions. At that time Lord K. still hoped that, in so far as forcing the Dardanelles was concerned, the fleet would effect its purpose, practically if not wholly unaided by the troops. These were designed rather for operations subsequent to the fall of what was after all but the first line of Ottoman defence. It was only after Sir Ian arrived on the spot that the naval attack actually failed and that military operations on an ambitious scale against the Gallipoli Peninsula took the stage. The fact that when the transports arrived at Mudros they were found not to be packed suitably for effecting an immediate disembarkation on hostile soil, has been a good deal criticized. Although it was not a matter within my responsibility, I was sharply heckled over the point by Captain Stephen Gwynne when before the Dardanelles Commission. But the troops left before there was any question of attempting a landing in force in face of the enemy in the immediate vicinity of the Straits. At the date when they sailed it remained quite an open question as to what exactly their task was to be. The transports could not have been appropriately packed even after military operations in the Gallipoli Peninsula had been decided upon, without knowing exactly what was Sir Ian's plan.

Sir Ian complained to the Dardanelles Commission that no preliminary scheme of operations had been drawn up by the War Office ; and he certainly got little assistance in that direction, although it might not have been of much use to him if he had.[1] He also complained that there was a great want of staff preparation, no arrangements for water, for instance, having been made. This was in effect the consequence of the General Staff at this time not exercising its proper functions or being invested with the powers to which it was entitled. There never was a meeting of the various directors in the War Office concerned, under the aegis of the General Staff, to go into these matters in detail. The troops would certainly be called upon to land somewhere, sooner or later, whether the fleet forced the Dardanelles or not, and all the arrangements as regards supplies, transport, water, hospitals, material for piers, etc., required to be worked out by those responsible after getting a lead from the General Staff. If the commodities of all kinds involved could not be procured locally or in Egypt, then it was up to the War

---

[1] A single "preliminary scheme of operations" would have been of little service to the C.-in-C. of "Medforce"—it must have been based on the mistaken assumption (which held good when he started) that the fleet would force the Straits, and it would consequently have concerned itself with undertakings totally different from those which, in the event, Sir Ian had to carry out. If the army was to derive any benefit from projects elaborated in the War Office, there must have been a second "preliminary scheme of operations" based on the assumption that the fleet was going to fail. What profit is there in a plan of campaign that dictates procedure to be followed after the first great clash of arms ? In the case under consideration, the first great clash of arms befell on the 18th of March, five days after Sir Ian left London with his instructions, and it turned the whole business upside down.

Office to see that they should be sent out from home, and be sent out, moreover, practically at the same time as the troops left so that they should be on the spot when needed.

Sir Ian also mentioned that he had not been shown the 1906 memorandum before going to the Near East. As it turned out, the mystery made about this document (although there was excellent reason for the special steps that were taken in connection with it at the time of its coming before the Committee of Imperial Defence) proved inconvenient in 1914–15. One wonders, indeed, whether it was ever seen by the Admiralty experts at the time when they had Admiral Carden's plan of a creeping naval attack upon the Dardanelles under consideration, because the memorandum expressed considerable doubts as to the efficacy of gun-fire from on board ship against the land, and the event proved that these doubts were fully justified. Had I had a copy in my possession I should certainly have shown it to Sir Ian, or else to Braithwaite, with whom, as he had been a brother-Director on the General Staff at the War Office for some months previously, I was in close touch.

Sir Ian, the Report says, " dwelt strongly on the total absence of information furnished him by the War Office staff," and he complained very justly that the map, or maps, given him had proved inaccurate and inadequate. Now, that reflected upon Generals Ewart and H. Wilson, who had been holding the appointment of D.M.O. between 1906 and 1914, and it reflected upon Sir N. Lyttelton, the late Lord Nicholson (actually a member of the Commission) and Sir J. French, who had successively been Chiefs of the General Staff during the same period: Topographical information cannot be procured after hostilities have broken out ; it has to be obtained in advance. On noting what was said about this in the " First Report " of the Dardanelles Commission, I asked to be allowed to give evidence again, and the Commission were good enough to recall me in due course. The object was, not to contest Sir I. Hamilton's assertions but to point out that under the circumstances of the case no blame was fairly attributable to those who were responsible for information of some sort being available.

To have obtained full information as to the Gallipoli Peninsula and the region around the Dardanelles, but especially as to the peninsula, was a matter of money— and plenty of it. In no country in the world in pre-war days was spying on fortified areas of strategical importance without money a more unprofitable game than in the Ottoman dominions. There were, on the other hand, few countries where money, if you had enough of it, was more sure to procure you the information that you required. Ever since the late General Brackenbury was at the head of the Intelligence Department of the War Office in the eighties secret funds have been at its disposal, but they have not been large, and there have always been plenty of desirable objects to devote those funds to. Had the Committee of Imperial Defence in 1906 taken the line that, even admitting an attack upon the Straits to be a difficult business, its effect if successful was nevertheless likely to be so great that the matter was one to be followed up, a pretty substantial share of the secret funds coming to hand in the Intelligence Department between 1906 and 1914 would surely have been devoted to this region. All kinds of topographical details concerning the immediate neighbourhood of the Dardanelles would thereby have been got together, ready for use ; it would somehow have been discovered in the environs of Stambul that the Gallipoli Peninsula had been surveyed and that good large-scale maps of that region actually existed, and copies of those large-scale maps would have found their way into the War Office, where they would speedily have been reproduced.

It was made plain to me when giving evidence before the Commission that the Rt. Hon. A. Fisher and Sir T. Mackenzie, its members representing the Antipodes, considered that there had been great neglect on the part of the War Office in obtaining information with regard

H

to the environs of the Dardanelles in advance. But, quite apart from the peculiar situation created by the decision of the Committee of Imperial Defence, there must have been serious difficulties in obtaining such information about the Gallipoli Peninsula—only those who have had experience in such matters know how great the difficulties are. Intelligence service in peace time is a subject of which the average civilian does not understand the meaning nor realize the dangers. The Commission, which included experts in such matters in the shape of Admiral Sir W. May and Lord Nicholson, made no comment on this point in its final Report, evidently taking the broad view that the lack of information was, under all the circumstances of the case, excusable. In his special Report, Sir T. Mackenzie on the other hand blames the Imperial General Staff for being " unprepared for operations against the Dardanelles and Bosphorus," obviously having the question of information in his mind, as he must be perfectly well aware that the planning of actual operations was just as much a matter for the Admiralty as for the General Staff, the whole problem being manifestly an amphibious one.

As a matter of fact, considering the kind of place that the Gallipoli Peninsula was, and taking into consideration the extreme jealousy with which the Turks, quite properly from their point of view, had always regarded the appearance of strangers in that well-watched region, the information contained in the secret official publications which the Mediterranean Expeditionary Force took out with it was by no means to be despised. All but one of the landing places actually utilized on the famous 25th of April were, I think, designated in these booklets, and that one was unsuitable for landing anything but infantry. A great deal of the information proved to be perfectly correct, and a good deal more of it might have proved to be correct had the Expeditionary Force ever penetrated far enough into the interior of the Peninsula to test it.

There had been many occasions giving grounds for disquietude since the days of Mons, but I never felt greater anxiety at any time during the war than when awaiting tidings as to the landing on the Aegean shore. We knew that this was about to take place, but I was not aware of the details of Sir I. Hamilton's plan. Soldiers who had examined carefully into the factors likely to govern a disembarkation in force in face of an enemy who was fully prepared, were unanimous in viewing such an operation as a somewhat desperate enterprise. There was no modern precedent for an undertaking of the kind. One dreaded some grave disaster, feared that the troops might entirely fail to gain a footing on shore, and pictured them as driven off after suffering overwhelming losses. The message announcing that a large part of the army was safely disembarked came as an immense relief. Although disappointed at learning that only a portion of the troops had been put ashore at Anzac on the outside of the Peninsula, which, I had presumed, would be the point selected for the main attack, I felt decidedly optimistic for the moment. What had appeared to be the greatest obstacle to success had been overcome, for a landing had been effected in spite of all that the enemy could do to hinder it. As mentioned in the previous chapter, I left London immediately afterwards, and it was a bitter disappointment to hear the truth a few days later, to realize that my first appreciation had been incorrect, and to learn that gaining a footing on shore did not connote an immediate advance into the interior. It provides a good example of how difficult it is to forecast results in war.

By fairly early in May, there already seemed to be little prospect of the Expeditionary Force achieving its object unless very strong reinforcements in men and munitions were sent out to the Aegean. But there was shortage of both men and munitions, and men and munitions alike were needed elsewhere. The second Battle of Ypres, coupled with the miscarriage of the Franco-British offensive about La Bassée, indicated that the enemy was formidable on the Western Front. Although there was every prospect of an improvement before long in respect to munitions output, the shell shortage was at the moment almost at its worst. We knew at the War Office that the Russians were in grave straits in respect to weapons and ammunition, and one could not tell whether the German Great General Staff, probably quite as well aware of this as we were, would assume the offensive in the Eastern theatre of war, or would transfer great bodies of troops from East to West to make some determined effort against the French and ourselves. The change of Government which introduced Mr. Asquith's Coalition Cabinet, moreover, came about at this time, and political palaver seriously delayed decisions.

It was, no doubt, unfortunate, from the point of view of the Dardanelles campaign, that there was so much hesitation about sending out the very substantial reinforcements which only actually reached Sir I. Hamilton at the end of July and during the early days of August. But it by no means necessarily follows that if they had reached their destination, say, six weeks sooner, the Straits would have been won. Much stress has always been laid upon the torpor that descended upon Suvla during the very critical hours which followed the successful disembarkation of the new force in that region ; but those inexperienced troops and their leaders must have acted with extraordinary resolution and energy to have appreciably changed the fortunes of General Birdwood's great offensive against Sari Bair. Information from the Turkish side does not suggest that Liman von Sanders gained any great accessions of strength during July and early August. It was the ample warning which the enemy received of what was impending before ever a soldier was landed on the Gallipoli Peninsula that, far more than anything which occurred subsequently, rendered the Dardanelles operations abortive.

The Dardanelles Committee came into being in June. This body included most of the more prominent figures in the Coalition Cabinet. Attending its deliberations from time to time one acquired the impression that an undue amount of attention was being given in Government circles to the Aegean theatre of war, an attention out of all proportion either to its importance or to our prospects of success ; for the talk ranged over the whole wide world at times and the Committee dealt with a good deal besides the Dardanelles. Its members always took the utmost interest in the events in the Gallipoli Peninsula, and, up to the date when the August offensive in that region definitely failed, they were mostly in sanguine mood. One or two optimistic statements made in public at that time were indeed quite inappropriate and had much better been left unspoken. The amateur strategist, that inexhaustible source of original and unprofitable proposals, was by no means inarticulate at these confabulations in 10 Downing Street. He would pick up Sir I. Hamilton's Army and would deposit it in some new locality, just as one might pick up one's penwiper and shift it from one side of the blotting-pad to the other. That is how some people who are simply bursting with intelligence, people who will produce whole newspaper columns of what to the uninformed reads like sensible matter, love to make war. In a way, the U-boats in the Aegean served as a blessing in disguise ; they helped to squash many hare-brained schemes inchoated around Whitehall, and to consign them to oblivion before they became really dangerous.

After the failure of the August offensive in the Gallipoli Peninsula, the members of the Dardanelles Committee became extremely anxious, and with good reason. They would come round to my room and discuss the situation individually, and I am afraid they seldom found me in optimistic vein. I had run over to Ulster in April 1914 on the occasion of certain stirring events taking place, which brought General Hubert Gough and his cavalry brigade into some public prominence, and which robbed the War Office of the services of Colonel Seely, Sir J. French and

Sir Spencer Ewart. I had been allowed behind the scenes in the north of Ireland as a sympathiser, had visited Omagh, Enniskillen, historic Derry and other places, had noted the grim determination of the loyalists, and had been deeply impressed by the efficiency and the foresight of the inner organization. Necessity makes strange bed-fellows. It was almost startling to find within fifteen months of that experience Sir E. Carson arriving in my apartment together with Mr. Churchill, their relations verging on the mutually affectionate, eager to discuss as colleagues the very unpromising position of affairs on the shores of the Thracian Chersonese.

From a very early stage in the Dardanelles venture there had been a feeling in some quarters within the War Office that we ought to cut our losses and clear out of the Gallipoli Peninsula, and that sending out reinforcements to the Aegean which could ill be spared from other scenes of warlike activity looked uncommonly like throwing good money after bad. My friends at G.H.Q., from whom I used to hear frequently, and who would look in when over on duty or on short leave, were strongly of this opinion; but they naturally were somewhat biassed. One took a long time to reconcile oneself to this idea, even when no hope of real success remained. It was not until September indeed, and after the decision had been come to to send out no more fresh troops to Sir I. Hamilton, that I personally came to the conclusion that no other course was open than to have done with the business and to come away out of that with the least possible delay. Sir Ian had sent home a trusted staff-officer, Major (now Major-General) the Hon. Guy Dawnay, to report and to try to secure help. Dawnay fought his corner resolutely and was loyalty itself to his chief, but the information that he had to give and his appreciation of the situation as it stood were the reverse of encouraging. By the middle of October, when the Salonika affair had begun to create fresh demands on our limited resources and when Sir C. Monro was sent out to take up command of the Mediterranean Expeditionary Force, any doubts which remained on the subject had been dispelled, and I was glad to gather from the new chief's attitude when he left that, in so far as he understood the situation before satisfying himself of the various factors on the spot, he leant towards complete and prompt evacuation.

If a withdrawal was to be effected, it was manifest that this ought to be carried out as soon as possible in view of the virtual certainty of bad weather during the winter months. But the War Council, which had superseded the Dardanelles Committee, unfortunately appeared to halt helplessly between two opinions. Even Sir C. Monro's uncompromising recommendation failed to decide its members. Lord Kitchener was loth to agree to the step, as he feared the effect which a British retreat might exert in Egypt and elsewhere in the East. As will be remembered he proceeded to the Aegean himself at the beginning of November to take stock, but he soon decided for evacuation after examining the conditions on the spot. The whole question remained in abeyance for some three weeks.

My own experiences of what followed were so singular that a careful note of dates and details was made at the time, because one realized even then that incidents of the kind require to be made known. They may serve as a warning. On the 23rd of November my chief, Sir A. Murray, summoned me, after a meeting of the War Council, to say that that body wished me to repair straightway to Paris and to make General Gallieni, the War Minister, acquainted with a decision which they had just arrived at—viz., that the Gallipoli Peninsula was to be abandoned without further ado. The full Cabinet would meet on the morrow (the 24th) to endorse the decision. That afternoon Mr. Asquith, who was acting as Secretary of State for War in the absence of Lord Kitchener, sent for me and repeated these instructions.

I left by the morning boat-train next day, having wired to our Military Attaché to arrange, if possible, an interview with General Gallieni that evening ; and he met me at the Gare du Nord, bearer of an invitation to dinner from the War Minister, and of a telegram from General Murray intimating that the Cabinet, having met as arranged, had been unable to come to a decision but were going to have another try on the morrow. Here was a contingency that was not covered by instructions and for which one was not prepared, but I decided to tell General Gallieni exactly how matters stood. (Adroitly drawn out for my benefit by his personal staff during dinner, the great soldier told us that stirring tale of how, as Governor of Paris, he despatched its garrison in buses and taxis and any vehicles that he could lay hands upon, to buttress the army which, under Maunoury's stalwart leadership, was to fall upon Von Kluck's flank, and was to usher in the victory of the Marne.)

A fresh wire came to hand from the War Office on the following afternoon, announcing that the Cabinet had again been unable to clinch the business, but contemplated a further séance two days later, the 27th. On the afternoon of the 27th, however, a message arrived from General Murray, to say that our rulers had yet again failed to make up their minds, and that the best thing I could do under the circumstances was to return to the War Office. General Gallieni, when the position of affairs was explained to him, was most sympathetic, quoted somebody's dictum that " la politique n'a pas d'entrailles," and hinted that he did not always find it quite plain sailing with his own gang. Still, there it was. The Twenty-Three had thrown the War Council over (it was then composed of Messrs. Asquith, Bonar Law, Lloyd George, and Balfour, and Sir E. Grey, assisted by the First Sea Lord and the C.I.G.S.) and they were leaving our army marooned on the Gallipoli Peninsula, with the winter approaching apace, in a position growing more and more precarious owing to Serbia's collapse and to Bulgaria's accession to the enemy ranks having freed the great artery of communications connecting Germany with the Golden Horn.

Life in the War Office during the Great War, even during those early anxious days of 1914 and 1915, had its lighter side. The astonishing cheeriness of the British soldier under the most trying circumstances has become proverbial; but his officer shares this priceless characteristic with him and displays it even amid the deadening surroundings of the big building in Whitehall. The best laugh that we enjoyed during that strenuous period was on the morning when news came that Anzac and Suvla had been evacuated at the cost of only some half-dozen casualties and of the abandonment of a very few worn-out guns. Then it was that an official, who was very much behind the scenes, extracted a document on the familiar grey-green paper from his safe and read it out with appropriate " business " to a joyous party.

This State paper, a model of incisive diction and of moving prose, conceived in the best Oxford manner, drew a terrible picture of what might occur in withdrawing troops from a foreshore in presence of a ferocious foe. Its polished periods portrayed a scene of horror and despair, of a bullet-swept beach, of drowning soldiers and of shattered boats. It quoted the case of some similar military operation, where warriors who had gained a footing on a hostile coast-line had been obliged to remove themselves in haste and had had the very father and mother of a time during the process—it was Marathon or Syracuse or some such contemporary martial event, if I remember aright. This masterly production, there is reason to believe, had not been without its influence when the question of abandoning the Gallipoli Peninsula was under consideration of those responsible. Well did Mr. Lloyd George say in the House of Commons many months later in the course of his first speech after becoming Prime Minister : " You cannot run a war with a Sanhedrin."

When the War Council, or the Cabinet, or whatever set of men in authority it was who at last got something settled, made up their minds that a withdrawal of sorts was really to take place, they in a measure reversed the decision which I had been charged to convey to the French Government a fortnight before. The orders sent out to Sir C. Monro only directed an evacuation of Anzac and Suvla to take place. This, it may be observed, seems to some extent to have been the fault of the sailor-men. They butted in, wanting to hang on to Helles on watching-the-Straits grounds ; they were apparently ready to impose upon our naval forces in the Aegean the very grave responsibility of mothering a small army, which was blockaded and dominated on the land side, as it clung to the inhospitable, storm-driven toe of the Gallipoli Penin-sula in mid-winter.

Sir W. Robertson arrived a few days later to take up the appointment of C.I.G.S., which, I knew, meant the splitting up of my Directorate. Being aware of his views beforehand as we had often talked it over, I had a paper ready drafted for his approval urging an immediate total evacuation of Turkish soil in this region. This he at once submitted to the War Council, and within two or three days orders were telegraphed out to the Aegean to the effect that Helles was to be abandoned. After remaining a few days longer at the War Office as Director of Military Intelligence, I was sent by the C.I.G.S. on a special mission to Russia, and my direct connection with the General Staff came to an end but for a short period in the summer of 1917. It is a satisfaction to remember that the last question of importance in which I was concerned before leaving Whitehall for the East was in lending a hand towards getting our troops out of the impossible position they were in at the mouth of the Dardanelles.

CHAPTER VI

SOME EXPERIENCES IN THE WAR OFFICE

A reversion to earlier dates—The statisticians in the winter of 1914–15
—The efforts to prove that German man-power would shortly give
out—Lack of the necessary premises upon which to found such
calculations—Views on the maritime blockade—The projects for
operations against the Belgian coast district in the winter of
1914–15—Nature of my staff—The " dug-outs "—The services
of one of them, " Z "—His care of me in foreign parts—His
activities in other Departments of State—An alarming discovery
—How " Z " grappled with a threatening situation—He hears
about the Admiralty working on the Tanks—The cold-shouldering
of Colonel Swinton when he raised this question at the War Office
in January 1915—Lord Fisher proposes to construct large numbers
of motor-lighters, and I am told off to go into the matter with
him—The Baltic project—The way it was approached—Meetings
with Lord Fisher—The " beetles "—Visits from the First Sea
Lord—The question of secrecy in connection with war operations—A parable—The land service behind the sea service in
this matter—Interviews with Mr. Asquith—His ways on such
occasions.

THESE random jottings scarcely lend themselves to the
scrupulous preservation of a chronological continuity.
Many other matters meriting some mention as affecting
the War Office had claimed one's attention before the
Dardanelles campaign finally fizzled out early in January
1916. The General Staff had to some extent been concerned in the solutions arrived at by the Entente during
the year 1915 of those acutely complex problems which
kept arising in the Balkans. Then, again, quite a number
of " side-shows " had been embarked on at various dates
since the outbreak of the conflict, of which some had been
carried through to a successful conclusion to the advantage
of the cause, while the course of others had been of a

decidedly chequered character. The munitions question, furthermore, which had for a time caused most serious difficulty but which had been disposed of in great measure by the end of 1915 owing to the foresight and the labours of Lord Kitchener and of the Master-General of the Ordnance's Department, was necessarily one in which the Military Operations Directorate was deeply interested. These and a number of other matters will be dealt with in special chapters, but some more or less personal experiences in and around Whitehall may appropriately be placed on record here.

Already, early in the winter of 1914–15, the statisticians were busily at work. They had found a bone and they were gnawing at it to their heart's content. Individuals of indisputable capacity and of infinite application set themselves to work to calculate how soon Boche man-power would be exhausted. Lord Haldane hurled himself into the breach with a zest that could hardly have been exceeded had he been contriving a totally new Territorial Army organization. Professor Oman abandoned Wellington somewhere amidst the declivities of the sierras without one qualm, and immersed himself in computations warranted to make the plain man's hair stand on end. The enthusiasts who voluntarily undertook this onerous task arrived at results of the most encouraging kind, for one learnt that the Hun as a warrior would within quite a short space of time be a phantom of the past, that adult males within the Kaiser's dominions would speedily comprise only the very aged, the mentally afflicted or the maimed wreckage from the battlefields of France and Poland, and that if this attractive Sovereign proposed to continue hostilities he must ere long, as Lincoln said of Jefferson Davis, " rob the cradle and the grave." Even Lord Kitchener displayed some interest in these mathematical exercises, and was not wholly unimpressed when figures established the gratifying fact that the German legions were a vanishing proposition. I was always in this matter graded in the " doubting Thomas " class.

The question seemed to base itself upon what premises you thought fit to start from. You could no doubt calculate with some certainty upon the total number of Teuton males of fighting age being somewhere about fifteen millions in August 1914, upon 700,000, or so, youths annually reaching the age of eighteen, and upon Germany being obliged to have under arms continually some five million soldiers. After that you were handling rather indeterminate factors. You might put down indispensables in civil life at half a million or at four millions just as you liked; but it made the difference of three and a half millions in your pool to start with, according to which estimate you preferred. After that you had to cut out the unfit—another problematical figure. Finally came the question of casualties based on suspicious enemy statistics, and the perplexities involved in the number of wounded who would, and who would not, be able to return to the ranks. The only conclusion that one seemed to be justified in arriving at was that the wastage was in excess of the intake of youngsters, that the outflow was greater than the inflow, and that if the war went on long enough German man-power would give out. When that happy consummation would be arrived at, it was in the winter of 1914–15 impossible to say and fruitless to take a shot at.

The Director of Military Operations received copies of most Foreign Office telegrams as a matter of course, and during the early months of the war many of these documents as they came to hand were found to be concerned with that very ticklish question, the maritime blockade. The attitude taken up by those responsible in this country regarding this matter has been severely criticized in many quarters, certain organs of the Press were loud in their condemnation of our kid-glove methods in those days, and the Sister Service seemed to be in discontented mood. But there was a good deal to be said on the other side. Lack of familiarity with international law, with precedents, and with the tenour and result of the discussions which had at various times taken place with foreign countries over the, manners and customs of naval blockade, made any conclusions which I might arrive at over so complex a problem of little profit. But it always did seem to me that the policy actually adopted was in the main the right one, and that to have bowed before advocates of more drastic measures might well have landed us in a most horrible mess. You can play tricks with neutrals whose fighting potentialities are restricted, which you had better not try on with non-belligerents who may be able to make things hot for you. The progress of the war in the early months was not so wholly reassuring as to justify hazarding fresh complications.

In his book, "*1914*," Lord French has dealt at some length with an operations question which was much in debate during the winter of 1914–15. He and Mr. Churchill were at this time bent on joint naval and military undertakings designed to recover possession of part, or of the whole, of the Belgian coast-line—in itself a most desirable objective. Although I did not see most of the communications which passed between the French Government and ours on the subject, nor those which passed between Lord Kitchener and the Commander-in-Chief of the B.E.F., I gathered the nature of what was afoot from Sir J. Wolfe Murray and Fitzgerald, as also from G.H.Q. in France, and examined the problem which was involved with the aid of large-scale maps and charts and such other information as was available. The experts of St. Omer did not appear to accept the scheme with absolutely whole-hearted concurrence. By some of them —it may have been a mistaken impression on my part— the visits of the First Lord of the Admiralty to their Chief hardly seemed to be welcomed with the enthusiasm that might have been expected. Whisperings from across the Channel perhaps made one more critical than one ought to have been, but, be that as it may, the project hardly struck one as an especially inviting method of employing force at that particular juncture. We were deplorably short of heavy howitzers, and we were already feeling the lack of artillery ammunition of all sorts. Although some reinforcements—the Twenty-Seventh and Twenty-Eighth Divisions—were pretty well ready to take the field, no really substantial augmentation of our fighting forces on the Western Front was to be anticipated for some months. The end was attractive enough, but the means appeared to be lacking.

In long-range—or, for the matter of that, short-range—bombardments of the Flanders littoral by warships I placed no trust. Mr. Churchill's " we could give you 100 or 200 guns from the sea in absolutely devastating support " of the 22nd of November to Sir J. French would not have excited me in the very least. In his book, the Field-Marshal ascribes the final decision of our Government to refuse sanction to a plan of operations which they had approved of at the first blush, partly to French objections and partly to the sudden fancy taken by the War Council for offensive endeavour in far-distant fields. That may be the correct explanation ; but it is also possible that after careful consideration of the subject Lord Kitchener perceived the tactical and strategical weakness of the plan in itself.

My staff was from the outset a fairly substantial one— much the largest of that in any War Office Directorate— and, although I am no great believer in a multitudinous personnel swarming in a public office, it somehow grew. It was composed partly of officers and others whom I found on arrival, partly of new hands brought in automatically on mobilization like myself to fill the places of picked men who had been spirited away with the Expeditionary Force, and partly of individuals acquired later on as other regular occupants were received up into the framework of the growing fighting forces of the country. A proportion of the new-comers were dug-outs, and it may not be out of place to say a word concerning this particular class of officer as introduced into the War Office, of whom I formed one myself. Instigated thereunto by that gushing fountain of unimpeachable information, the Press, the public were during the early part of the war disposed to attribute all high crimes and misdemeanours, of which the central administration of the nation's military forces was pronounced to have been guilty, to the "dug-out." That the personnel of the War Office was always set out in detail at the beginning of the *Monthly Army List*, the omniscient Fourth Estate was naturally aware ; but the management of a newspaper could hardly be expected to purchase a copy (it was not made confidential for a year). Nor could a journalistic staff condescend to study this work of reference at some library or club. Under the circumstances, and having heard that such people as " dug-outs " actually existed, the Press as a matter of course assumed that within the portals in Whitehall Lord Kitchener was struggling in vain against the ineptitude and reactionary tendencies of a set of prehistoric creatures who constituted the whole of his staff. The fact, however, was that all the higher appointments (with scarcely an exception other than that of myself) were occupied by soldiers who had been on the active list at the time of mobilization, and the great majority of whom simply remained at their posts after war was declared.

Nor were " dug-outs," whether inside or outside of the War Office, by necessity and in obedience to some inviolable rule individuals languishing in the last stage of mental and bodily decay. Some of them were held to be not too effete to bear their burden even amid the stress and turmoil of the battlefield. One, after serving with conspicuous distinction in several theatres of war, finished up as Chief of the General Staff and right-hand man to Sir Douglas Haig in 1918. Those members of the band who were at my beck and call within the War Office generally contrived to grapple effectually with whatever they undertook, and amongst them certainly not the least competent and interesting was a Rip Van Winkle, whom we will call " Z "—for short.

A subaltern at the start, " Z " was fitted out with all the virtues of the typical subaltern, but was furnished in addition with certain virtues that the typical subaltern does not necessarily possess. It could not be said of him that

> deep on his brow engraven
> Deliberation sat and sovereign care,

but he treated Cabinet Ministers with an engaging blend of firmness and familiarity, and he could, when occasion called for it, keep Royalty in its place. Once when he thought fit to pay a visit on duty to Paris and the front, he took me with him, explaining that unless he had a general officer in his train there might be difficulties as to his being accompanied by his soldier servant. Generals and colonels and people of that kind doing duty at the War Office did not then have soldier servants—but " Z " did. It is, however, bare justice to him to acknowledge that, after I had served his purpose and when he came to send me back to England from Boulogne before he resumed his inspection of troops and trenches, he was grandmotherly in his solicitude that I should meet with no misadventure. " Have you got your yellow form all right, sir ? You'd better look. No, no ; that's not it, that's another thing altogether. Surely you haven't lost it already ! Ah, that's it. Now, do put it in your right-hand breast pocket, where you won't get it messed up with your pocket-handkerchief, sir, and remember where it is." It reminded one of being sent off as a small boy to school.

It was his practice to make a round of the different Public Departments of a forenoon, and to draw the attention of those concerned in each of them to any matters that appeared to him to call for comment. The Admiralty and the Foreign Office naturally engaged his attention more than others, but he was a familiar figure in them all. His activities were so varied indeed that they almost might have been summed up as universal, which being the case, it is not perhaps altogether to be

I

wondered at that he did occasionally make a mistake. For instance :

He burst tumultuously into my room one morning flourishing a paper. " Have you seen this, sir ? " As a matter of fact I had seen it ; but as the document had conveyed no meaning to my mind, dissembled. Its purport was that 580 tons of a substance of which I had never heard before, and of which I have forgotten the name, had been landed somewhere or other in Scandinavia. " But do you know what it is, sir ? It's the most appalling poison ! It's the concoction that the South Sea Islanders smear their bows and arrows with—cyanide and prussic acid are soothing-syrup compared to it. Of course it's for those filthy Boches. Five hundred and eighty tons of it ! There won't be a bullet or a zeppelin or a shell or a bayonet or a dart or a strand of barbed-wire that won't be reeking with the stuff." I was aghast. " Shall I go and see the Director-General, A.M.S., about it, sir ? "

" Yes, do, by all means. The very thing."

He came back presently. " I've seen the D.-G., sir, and he's frightfully excited. He's got hold of all his deputies and hangers-on, and the whole gang of them are talking as if they were wound up. One of them says he thinks he has heard of an antidote, but of course he knows nothing whatever about it really, and is only talking through his hat. I tell you what, sir, we ought to lend them a hand in this business. I know Professor Stingo ; he's miles and away the biggest man on smells and that sort of thing in London, if not in Europe. So, if you'll let me, I'll charter a taxi and be off and hunt him up, and get him to work. If the thing can be done, sir, he's the lad for the job. May I go, sir ? "

" Very well, do as you propose, and let me know the result."

He turned up again in the afternoon. " I've seen old man Stingo, sir, and he's for it all right. He's going to collect a lot more sportsmen of the same kidney, and they're going to have the time of their lives, and to make a regular night of it. You see, sir, I pointed out to him that this was a matter of the utmost urgency—not merely a question of finding an antidote, but also of distributing it methodically and broadcast. After it's been invented or made or procured, or whatever's got to be done, some comedian in the Quartermaster-General's show will insist on the result being packed up in receptacles warranted rot-proof against everything that the mind of man can conceive till the Day of Judgment—you know the absurd way those sort of people go on, sir—and all that will take ages, æons." He really thought of everything. " And there'll have to be books of instructions and classes, and the Lord knows what besides ! After that the stuff'll have to be carted off to France and the Dardanelles, and maybe to Archangel and Mesopotamia ; so Stingo and Co. are going to be up all night, and mean to arrive at some result or to perish in the attempt. And now, sir, what have you done about it at the Foreign Office ? "

This was disconcerting, seeing that I had done nothing.

" Oh, but, sir," sounding that note of submissive expostulation which the tactful staff-officer contrives to introduce when he feels himself obliged reluctantly to express disapproval of superior military authority, " oughtn't we to do something ? How would it be if I were to go down and see Grey, or one of them, and to talk to him like a father ? "

" Well, perhaps it might be advisable to make a guarded suggestion to them on the subject. Give my compliments to —— " But he was gone.

He returned in about half an hour. " I've been down to the Foreign Office, sir, and as you might have expected, they haven't done a blooming thing. What those ' dips ' think they're paid for always beats me ! However, I've got them to promise to cable out to their ambassadors and consuls and bottle-washers in Scandinavia to keep their wits about them. I offered to draft the wires for them ; but they seemed to think that they could do it themselves, and I daresay they'll manage all right now that I've told them exactly what they are to say. I really do not know that we can do anything more about it this evening," he added doubtfully, and with a worried, far-away look on his face. Good heavens, he was never going to think of something else! He took himself off, however, still evidently dissatisfied and communing with himself.

Next forenoon " Z " came into my room in a hurry. " I've been hearing about the caterpillars, sir," he exclaimed joyously.

" The caterpillars ? "

" Oh, not crawly things like one finds in one's salad, sir. The ones the Admiralty are making [1]—armoured motor contrivances, with great big feet that will go across country and jump canals, and go bang through Boche trenches and barbed wire as if they weren't there. They'll be perfectly splendid—full of platoons and bombs and machine guns, and all the rest of it. I *will* say this for Winston and those mariners across Whitehall, when they get an idea they carry it out and do not bother whether the thing'll be any use or can be made at all— care no more for the Treasury than if it was so much dirt, and quite right too! Just what it is. But when they've got their caterpillars made, they won't know what to do with them any more than the Babes in the Wood. Then we'll collar them; but in the meantime I might be able to give them some hints, so, if you'll let me, I'll go across and—— "

" Yes, yes; but just one moment. How about the poison ? "

" The poison, sir ? What poi—oh, that stuff. ·Didn't I tell you, sir ? It isn't poison at all. You see, sir, it's this way. There are two forms of it. There's the white form, and that *is* poison, shocking poison ; it's what the Fijians use when they want to pacify a busybody like Captain Cook who comes butting in where he isn't wanted.

---

[1] The first I heard of the Tanks, which made so dramatic a debut near the Somme a year and a half later.

As a matter of fact there's uncommon little of it—they don't get a hundredweight in a generation. Then there's the red form, and that's what Johnnies have been dumping down 580 tons of at What's-its-name. It's quite innocuous, and is used for commercial purposes—tanning leather, or making spills, or something of that kind. Now may I go to the Ad——"

"But have you told all this to the Director-General ? "

"Oh yes, sir. I told him first thing this morning."

"Did he pass no remarks as to your having started him off after this absurd hare of yours ? "

"Well, you see, sir, he's an uncommonly busy man, and I didn't feel justified in wasting his time. So, after relieving his mind, I cleared out at once."

"And your professors ? "

"Oh, those professor-men—it would never do to tell them, sir. They'd be perfectly miserable if they were deprived of the excitement of muddling about with their crucibles and blow-pipes and retorts and things. It would be cruelty to animals to enlighten them—it would indeed, sir ; and I know that you would not wish me to do anything to discourage scientific investigation. Now, sir, may I go over to the Admiralty ? " And off he went, with instructions to find out all that he could about these contrivances that he had heard about, and to do what he could to promote their production. A treasure : unconventional, resourceful, exceptionally well informed, determined ; the man to get a thing done that one wanted done—even if he did at times get a thing done that one didn't particularly want done—and in some respects quite the best intelligence officer I have come across in a fairly wide experience. To-day " Z " commands the applause of listening senates in the purlieus of St. Stephen's and has given up to party what was meant for mankind ; but although he is not Prime Minister yet, nor even a Secretary of State, that will come in due course.

It was in May 1915 that " Z " told me that the Admiralty were at work on some sort of land-ship, and set about finding out what was being done ; he had previously been in communication with Colonel E. D. Swinton over at the front. Only in the latter part of 1919, when the question of claims in connection with the invention and the development of Tanks had been investigated by a Royal Commission, did I learn to my astonishment that this matter had been brought by Swinton before the War Office so early as the beginning of January 1915, and that his projects had then been " turned down " by a technical branch to which he had, unfortunately, referred them. It does not seem possible that the technical branch can have brought the question to the notice of the General Staff, or I must have heard of it. The value of some contrivance such as he was confident could be constructed was from the tactical point of view incontestable, and had been incontestable ever since trench warfare became the order of the day on the Western Front in the late autumn of 1914. But the idea of the land-ship appeared to be an idle dream, and there was perhaps some excuse for the General Staff in its not of its own accord pressing upon the technical people that something of the sort must be produced somehow. Knowledge that a thoroughly practical man possessed of engineering knowledge and distinguished for his prescience like Swinton was convinced that the thing was feasible, was just what was required to set the General Staff in motion.

Thanks to Swinton, and also to " Z," the General Staff did get into touch with the Admiralty in May, and then found that a good deal had already been done, owing to Mr. Churchill's imagination and foresight and to the energy and ingenuity with which the land-ship idea had been taken up at his instigation. But the War Office came badly out of the business, and the severe criticisms to which it has been exposed in connection with the subject are better deserved than a good many of the criticisms of which it has been the victim. The blunder was not perhaps so much the fault of individuals as of the system. The technical branches had not been put in their place before the war, they did not understand their position and did not realize that on broad questions of policy they were subject to the General Staff.   It is worthy of note, incidentally, that Swinton never seems to have got much satisfaction with G.H.Q. in France until he brought his ideas direct before the General Staff out there on the 1st of June by submitting a memorandum to the Commander-in-Chief. It is to be hoped that the subserviency of all other branches to the General Staff in connection with matters of principle has been established once for all by this time; it was, I think, pretty well established by Sir W. Robertson when he became C.I.G.S. Should there ever be any doubt about the matter—well, remember the start of the Tanks!

One morning in January or February 1915, Lord K. sent for me to his room. It appeared that Lord Fisher had in mind a project of constructing a flotilla of lighters of special type, to be driven by motor power and designed for the express purpose of landing large bodies of troops rapidly on an enemy's coast. The First Sea Lord was anxious to discuss details with somebody from our side of Whitehall, and the Chief wished me to take the thing up, the whole business being of a most secret character. Lord Fisher, I gathered, contemplated descents upon German shores; Lord K. did not appear to take these very seriously, but he did foresee that a flotilla of the nature proposed might prove extremely useful in connection with possible future operations on the Flanders littoral. In any case, seeing that the Admiralty were prepared to undertake a construction job of this kind more or less in the interests of us soldiers, we ought to give the plan every encouragement.

Vague suggestions had reached me from across the road shortly before—I do not recollect exactly how they came to hand—to the effect that one ought to examine into the possibilities offered by military operations based on the German Baltic coast and against the Frisian

Islands. Attacks upon these islands presented concrete problems ; the question in their case had been already gone into carefully by other hands before the war, and schemes of this particular kind had not been found to offer much attraction when their details came to be considered. As for the Baltic coast, one was given nothing whatever to go upon—was groping in the dark. You wondered how it was proposed to obtain command of these protected waters, bearing in mind the nature of the approaches through defiles which happened to be in the main in neutral hands, but you realized that this was a naval question and therefore somebody else's job. Still, even given this command, what then ? Investigations of the subject, based upon uncertain premises, did not lead to the conclusion that, beyond " containing " hostile forces which otherwise might be available for warfare in some other quarter, a landing in large force on these shores was likely to prove an effective operation of war ; and it was bound to be an extremely hazardous one.

It has since transpired from Lord Fisher's volcanic *Memories* that the First Sea Lord had, with his " own hands alone to preserve secret all arrangements," prepared plans for depositing three " great armies " at different places in the Baltic, " two of them being feints that could be turned into reality." How the First Sea Lord could draw up plans of this kind that were capable of being put into effective execution without some military assistance I do not pretend to understand. A venture such as this does not begin and end with dumping down any sort of army you like at a spot on the enemy's shores where it happens to be practicable to disembark troops rapidly. Once landed, the army still has to go ahead and do its business, whatever this is, as a military undertaking, and it stands in need of some definite and practicable objective. The numbers of which it is to consist and its detailed organization have to be worked out in advance, with a clear idea of what service it is intended to perform and of the strength of the enemy forces which it is likely to encounter while carrying out its purpose. It has to be fed and has to be supplied with war material after it has been deposited on *terra firma*. Is it to take its transport with it, or will it pick this up on arrival? Even the constitution of the armada which is to convey it to its point of disembarkation by no means represents a purely naval problem. Until the sailors know what the composition of the military force in respect to men, animals, vehicles, etc., is to be, they cannot calculate what tonnage will be required, or decide how that tonnage is to be allotted for transporting the troops over-sea. For a project of this kind to be worked out solely by naval experts would be no less ridiculous than for it to be worked out solely by military experts. Secrecy in a situation of this kind is no doubt imperative, but you must trust somebody or you will head straight for catastrophe.

When I went over by appointment to see Lord Fisher, he got to work at once in that inimitable way of his. He explained that what he had in view was to place sufficient motor-lighters at Lord Kitchener's disposal, each carrying about 500 men, to land 50,000 troops on a beach at one time. He insisted upon the most absolute secrecy. What he wanted me to do was to discuss the construction of the lighters in detail with the admiral who had the job in charge, so as to ensure that their design would fall in with purely military requirements. I had, some sixteen years before when Lord Fisher had been Commander-in-Chief on the Mediterranean station, enjoyed a confidential discussion with him in Malta concerning certain strategical questions in that part of the world, and had been·amazed at the alertness of his brain, his originality of thought, his intoxicating enthusiasm, and his relentless driving power. Now, in 1915, he seemed to be even younger than he had seemed then. He covered the ground at such a pace that I was speedily toiling breathless and dishevelled far in rear. It is all very well to carry off *Memories* into a quiet corner and to try to assimilate limited portions of that work at a time, deliberately and in solitude. But to have a hotch-potch of Shakespeare, internal combustion engines, chemical devices for smoke screens, principles of the utilization of sea power in war, Holy Writ, and details of ship construction dolloped out on one's plate, and to have to bolt it then and there, imposes a strain on the interior economy that is greater than this will stand. After an interview with the First Sea Lord you suffered from that giddy, bewildered, exhausted sort of feeling that no doubt has you in thrall when you have been run over by a motor bus without suffering actual physical injury.

The main point that I insisted upon when in due course discussing the construction details of the motor-lighters with the admiral who was supervising the work, was that they should be so designed as to let the troops aboard of them rush out quickly as soon as the prow should touch the shore. The vessels were put together rapidly, and one or two of those first completed were experimented with in the Solent towards the end of April, when they were found quite satisfactory. Although they were never turned to account for the purpose which Lord Fisher had had in mind when the decision was taken to build them, a number of these mobile barges proved extremely useful to our troops in the later stages of the Dardanelles campaign, notably on the occasion of the landing at Suvla and while the final evacuations were being carried out. Indeed, but for the " beetles " (as the soldiers christened these new-fangled craft), our army would never have got away from the Gallipoli Peninsula with such small loss of stores and impedimenta as it did, and the last troops told off to leave Helles on the stormy night of the 8th-9th of January 1916 might have been unable to embark and might have met with a deplorable disaster.

After that first meeting with him at the Admiralty, I frequently saw Lord Fisher, and he kept me acquainted with his views on many points, notably on what was involved in the threat of the U-boats after Sir I. Hamilton had landed his troops in the Gallipoli Peninsula. On more than one occasion he honoured me with a surprise visit in my office. These interviews in my sanctum were of quite a dramatic, Harrison-Ainsworth, Gunpowder-Treason, Man-in-the-Iron-Mask character. He gave me no warning, scorning the normal procedure of induction by a messenger. He would appear of a sudden peeping in at the door to see if I was at home, would then thrust the door to and lock it on the inside with a deft turn of the wrist, would screw up the lean-to ventilator above the door in frantic haste, and would have darted over and be sitting down beside me, talking earnestly and *ventre-à-terre* of matters of grave moment, almost before I could rise to my feet and conform to those deferential observances that are customary when a junior officer has to deal with one of much higher standing. Some subjects treated of on these occasions were of an extremely confidential nature, and in view of the laxity of many eminent officials and—if the truth be told—of military officers as a body, the precautions taken by the First Sea Lord within my apartment were perhaps not without justification.

War is too serious a business to warrant the proclamation of prospective naval and military operations from the housetops. Reasonable precautions must be taken. One thing one did learn during those early months of the war, and that was that the fewer the individuals are—no matter who they may be—who are made acquainted with secrets the better. But this is not of such vital importance when the secret concerns some matter of limited interest to the ordinary person as it is when the secret happens to relate to what is calculated to attract public attention.

Of course it was most reprehensible on the part of that expansive youth, Geoffrey, to have acquainted Gladys— strictly between themselves of course—that his company had been " dished out with a brand-new, slap-up, experimental automatic rifle, that'll make Mr. Boche sit up when we get across." Still it did no harm, because Gladys doesn't care twopence about rifles of any kind, and had forgotten all about it before she had swallowed the chocolate that was in her mouth. But when Geoffrey informed Gladys a fortnight later—again strictly between themselves—that the regiment was booked for a stunt at Cuxhaven, it did a great deal of harm. Because, although Gladys did not know where Cuxhaven was, she looked it up in the atlas when she got home, and she thereupon realized, with a wriggle of gratification, that she was " in the know," and under the circumstances she could hardly have been expected not to tell Agatha—under pledge, needless to say, of inviolable secrecy. Nor would you have been well advised to have bet that Agatha would not —in confidence—mention the matter to Genevieve, because you would have lost your money if you had. Then, it was only to be expected that Genevieve should let the cat out of the bag that afternoon at the meeting of Lady Blabit's Committee for the Development of Discretion in Damsels, observing that in *such* company a secret was bound to be absolutely safe. However, that was how the whole story came to be known, and Geoffrey might just as well have done the thing handsomely, and have placarded what was contemplated in Trafalgar Square alongside Mr. Bonar Law's frenzied incitements to buy war bonds.

Speaking seriously, there is rather too much of the sieve about the soldier officer when information comes to his knowledge which it is his duty to keep to himself. He has much to learn in this respect from his sailor brother. You won't get much to windward of the naval cadet or the midshipman if you try to extract out of him details concerning the vessel which has him on her books in time of war—what she is, where she is, or how she occupies her time. These youngsters cannot have absorbed this reticence simply automatically and as one of the traditions of that great Silent Service, to which, more than to any other factor, we and our Allies owe our common triumph in the Great War. It must have been dinned into them at Osborne and Dartmouth, and it must have been impressed upon them—forcibly as is the way amongst those whose dwelling is in the Great Waters—day by day by their superiors afloat. The subject used not to be mentioned at the Woolwich Academy in the seventies. Nor was secretiveness inculcated amongst battery subalterns a few years subsequently. One does not recollect hearing anything about it during the Staff College course, nor call to mind having preached the virtues of discretion in this matter to one's juniors oneself at a later date. Here is a matter which has been grossly neglected and which the General Staff must see to.

When Lord Kitchener was going to be away from town for two or three days in the summer of 1915, he sometimes instructed me to be at Mr. Asquith's beck and call during his absence in case some important question should suddenly arise, and once or twice I was summoned to 10 Downing Street of a morning in consequence, and was ushered into the precincts. On these occasions the Prime Minister was to be found in a big room upstairs; and he was always walking up and down, like Aristotle only that he had his hands in his pockets. His demeanour would be a blend of boredom with the benign. " Whatch-think of this ? " he would demand, snatching up some paper from his desk, cramming it into my hand, and continuing his promenade. Such observations on my part in response to the invitation as seemed to meet the case would be acknowledged with a grunt—dissent, concurrence, incredulity, or a desire for further information being communicated by modulations in the grunt. Once, when the document under survey elaborated one of Mr. Churchill's virgin plans of revolutionizing the conduct of the war as a whole, the Right Honourable Gentleman in an access of exuberance became garrulous to the extent of muttering, " 'Tslike a hen laying eggs."

But, all the same, when instructions came to be given at the end of such an interview, they invariably were lucid, concise, and very much to the point. You knew exactly where you were. For condensing what was needed in a case like this into a convincing form of words, for epitomizing in a single sentence the conclusions arrived at (supposing conclusions by any chance to have been arrived at) after prolonged discussions by a War Council, or at a gathering of the Dardanelles Committee, I have never come across anybody in the same street with Mr. Asquith.

CHAPTER VII

FURTHER EXPERIENCES IN THE WAR OFFICE

Varied nature ot my responsibilities—Inconvenience caused by a
Heath-Caldwell being a brother-Director on the General Staff—
An interview with Lord Methuen—The Man of Business—His
methods when in charge of a Government Department—War
Office branches under Men of Business—The art of advertisement
—This not understood by War Office officials—The paltry staff
and accommodation at the disposal of the Director of Supplies
and Transport, and what was accomplished—Good work of the
Committee of Imperial Defence in providing certain organizations
for special purposes before the war—The contre-espionage branch
—The Government's singular conduct on the occasion of the first
enemy spy being executed at the Tower—The cable censorship—
The post office censorship—A visit from Admiral Bacon—His
plan of landing troops by night at Ostend—Some observations on
the subject—Sir J. Wolfe Murray leaves the War Office—An
appreciation of his work—The Dardanelles papers to be presented
to Parliament referred to me—My action in the matter and the
appointment of the Dardanelles Committee in consequence—Mr.
Lloyd George, Secretary of State for War—His activities—I act
as D.C.I.G.S. for a month—Sound organization introduced by Sir
W. Robertson—Normal trench-warfare casualties and battle
casualties—I learn the facts about the strengths of the different
armies in the field—Troubles with the Cabinet over man-power—
Question of resignation of the Army Council—The Tank Corps and
Tanks—The War Office helps in the reorganization of the Ad-
miralty—Some of the War Cabinet want to divert troops to the
Isonzo—The folly of such a plan—Objections to it indicated—
Arrival of General Pershing in London—I form one of the party
that proceeds to Devonport to meet Colonel House and the
United States Commissioners—Its adventures—Admirals adrift—
Mr. Balfour meets the Commissioners at Paddington.

DURING those months as Director of Military Operations
my responsibilities were in reality of a most varied nature.
They covered pretty well the whole field of endeavour,
from drafting documents bearing upon operations—subjects
for the edification of the very elect—down to returning

to him by King's Messenger the teeth which a well-known staff-officer had inadvertently left behind him at his club when returning to the front from short leave. One was for various reasons brought into contact with numbers of public men who were quite outside of Government circles and official institutions, and whose acquaintance it was agreeable to make. Moreover, officers of high standing, over from the front or holding commands at home, would look in to pass the time of day and keep one posted with what was going on afield. Soldiers appointed to some new billet overseas had constantly to be fitted out with instructions, or to be provided with books, maps, and cipher. The last that I was to see of that brilliant leader, General Maude, was when I went down to Victoria to see him and my old contemporary of " Shop " days, General E. A. Fanshawe, off on their hurried journey to the Dardanelles in August 1915.

A certain amount of minor inconvenience in connection with telephones, correspondence, visits, and so on, arose owing to General Heath-Caldwell taking up the appointment of Director of Military Training about six months after mobilization. That two out of the four Directors on the General Staff within the War Office should have practically the same name, was something of a coincidence. Lord Methuen, who was then holding a very important appointment in connection with the home army (with which I had nothing to do), was ushered into my room one day. He had scarcely sat down when he began, " Now I know how tremendously busy all you people are, and I won't keep you one moment, but . . .," and he embarked on some question in connection with the training of the troops in the United Kingdom. I tried to interrupt ; but he checked me with a gesture, and took complete command of the situation. " No, no. Just let me finish what I want to say . . ." and off he was again in full cry, entirely out of control. After one or two other attempts to stop him, I had to give it up. You can't coerce a Field-Marshal : it isn't done. At last, after about five minutes of rapid and eager exposition of what he had come to the War Office to discuss, he wound up with " Well, what d'you think of that. I haven't kept you long, have I ? " It was then up to me to explain that he had attacked the wrong man, that the question he was interested in did not concern me, and that the best thing I could do was to conduct him forthwith to Heath-Caldwell's lair.

One saw something of the Man of Business in those days, as also later. Next to the " Skilled Workman," the " Man of Business " is the greatest impostor amongst the many impostors at present preying on the community. Just as there are plenty of genuine Skilled Workmen, so also are there numbers of Men of Business who, thanks to their capacity and to the advantage that they have taken of experience, constitute real assets to the nation. Latter-day events have, however, taught us that the majority of the individuals who pose as Skilled Workmen are in reality engaged on operations which anybody in full power of his faculties and of the most ordinary capacity can learn to carry on within a very few hours, if not within a very few minutes. What occurred in Government departments during the war proved that a very large percentage of the Men of Business, who somehow found their way into public employ, were no great catch even if they did manage to spend a good deal of the taxpayer's money. To draw a sharp dividing-line between the nation's good bargains and the nation's bad bargains in this respect would be out of the question. To try to separate the sheep from the goats would be as invidious as it would be vain—there were a lot of hybrids. But it was not military men within the War Office alone who suffered considerable disillusionment on being brought into contact with the Man of Business in the aggregate ; that was also the experience of the Civil Service in general.

The successful Man of Business has owed his triumphs to aptitude in capturing the business of other people. Therefore when he blossoms out as a Government official

K

in charge of a department, he devotes his principal energies to trying to absorb rival departments. It was a case of fat kine endeavouring to swallow lean kine, but finding at times that the lean kine were not so badly nourished after all—and took a deal of swallowing. And yet successful Men of Business, when introduced into Government departments, do have their points. One wonders how much the income-tax payer would be saved during the next decade or two had some really great knight of industry, content to do his own work and not covetous of that of other people (assuming such a combination of the paragon and the freak to exist), been placed in charge of the Ministry of Munitions as soon as Mr. Lloyd George had, with his defiance of Treasury convention, with his wealth of imagination, and with his irrepressible and buoyant courage, set the thing up on the vast foundations already laid by the War Office. Unsuccessful Men of Business, when introduced into Government departments, have their points too, but they are mostly bad points.

The Man of Business' procedure, when he is placed at the head of a Government department, or of some branch of a Government department, in time of war is well known. He makes himself master of some gigantic building or some set of buildings. He then sets to work to people the premises with creatures of his own. He then, with the assistance of the superior grades amongst the creatures, becomes wrapped up in devising employment for the multitudinous personnel that has been got together. He then finds that he has not got sufficient accommodation to house his legions—and so it goes on. He talks in moments of relaxation of " introducing business methods into Whitehall." But that is absurd. You could not introduce business methods into Whitehall, because there is not room enough ; you would have to commandeer the whole of the West End, and then you would be cramped. While the big men at the top are wrestling with housing problems, the staff are engaged in writing minutes to each other—a process which, when indulged in in out-of-date institutions of the War Office, Admiralty, Colonial Office type, is called " red tape," but which, when put in force in a department watched over by Men of Business, is called " push and go."   Engulfed in one of the mushroom branches that were introduced into the War Office in the later stages of the war, I could not but be impressed by what I saw.   The women were splendid: the way in which they kept the lifts in exercise, each lady spending her time going up and down, burdened with a tea-cup or a towel and sometimes with both, was beyond all praise.

One is prejudiced perhaps, and may not on that account do full justice to the achievements of some of those civilian branches which were evolved within the War Office and which elbowed out military branches altogether or else absorbed them.   But they enjoyed great advantages, and on that account much could fairly be expected of them.   Your civilian, introduced into the place with full powers, a blank cheque and the uniform of a general officer, stood on a very different footing from the soldier ever hampered by a control that was not always beneficently administered — financial experts on the War Office staff are apt to deliver their onsets upon the Treasury to the battle-cry of *Kamerad*.   Still, should the civilian elect to maintain on its military lines the branch that he had taken over, he sometimes turned out to be an asset. When the new broom adopted the plan of picking out the best men on the existing staff, of giving those preferred a couple of steps in rank, of providing them with large numbers of assistants, and of housing the result in some spacious edifice or group of edifices especially devised for the purpose, he sometimes contrived to develop what had been an efficient organization before into a still more efficient one.   In that case the spirit of the branch remained, it carried on as a military institution but with a free hand and with extended liberty of action—and the public service benefited although the cost was considerably greater.   But that was not always the procedure decided upon.

Whatever procedure was decided upon, every care was taken to advertise. Advertisement is an art that the Man of Business thoroughly understands, and as to which he has little to learn even from the politician with a Press syndicate at his back. Soldiers are deplorably apathetic in this respect. It will hardly be believed that during the war the military department charged with works and construction often left the immediate supervision of the creation of some set of buildings in the hands of a single foreman of works, acting under an officer of Royal Engineers who only paid a visit daily as he would have several other duties of the same nature to perform. But if that set of buildings under construction came to be transferred to a civilian department or branch—the Ministry of Munitions, let us say—a large staff of supervisors of all kinds was at once introduced. Offices for them to carry on their supervisory duties in were erected. The thing was done in style, employment was given to a number of worthy people at the public expense, and it is quite possible that the supervisory duties were carried on no less efficiently than they had previously been by the foreman of works, visited daily by the officer of Royal Engineers.

From the outbreak of war and for nearly two years afterwards, the headquarters administration of the supply branch of our armies in all theatres except Mesopotamia and East Africa was carried out at the War Office by one director, five military assistants and some thirty clerks, together with one " permanent official " civilian aided by half-a-dozen assistants and about thirty clerks. It administered and controlled and supervised the obtaining and distribution of all requirements in food and forage, as also of fuel, petrol, disinfectants, and special hospital comforts, not only for the armies in the field but also for the troops in the United Kingdom. This meant an expenditure which by the end of the two years had increased to about half a million sterling per diem. Affiliated to this branch, as being under the same director, was the headquarters administration of the military transport service, consisting of some fifteen military assistants and fifty or sixty clerks.   The military transport service included a personnel of fully 300,000 officers and men, and the branch was charged with the obtaining of tens of thousands of motor vehicles of all kinds and of the masses of spare parts needed to keep them in working order, together with many other forms of transport material.   The whole of these two affiliated military branches of the War Office could have been accommodated comfortably on one single floor of the Hotel Metropole !   Well has it been said that soldiers have no imagination.

There were four especial branches under me to which some reference ought to be made.   Of two of them little was, in the nature of things, heard during the war ; these two were secret service branches, the one obtaining information with regard to the enemy, the other preventing the enemy from receiving information with regard to us.   Of the other two, one dealt with the cable censorship and the other with the postal censorship.   The Committee of Imperial Defence has been taken to task in some ill-informed quarters because of that crying lack of sufficient land forces and of munitions of certain kinds which made itself apparent when the crisis came upon us.   It was, however, merely a consultative and not an executive body.   It had no hold over the purse-strings. Shortcomings in these respects were the fault not of the Committee of Imperial Defence but of the Government of the day.   On the other hand, the Committee did splendid work in getting expert sub-committees to compile regulations that were to be brought into force in each Government department on the outbreak of war— compiling regulations cost practically nothing.   Moreover, thanks to its representations and to its action, organizations were created in peace-time for prosecuting espionage in time of war and for ensuring an effective system of contre-espionage ; these were under the control of the Director of Military Operations, and were the two secret branches referred to above.

About the former nothing can appropriately be disclosed. So much interesting information about the latter has appeared in *German Spies at Bay* that little need be said about it, except to repeat what has already appeared in that volume—the branch had already achieved a notable triumph more than a fortnight before our Expeditionary Force fired a shot and some hours before the Royal Navy brought off their first success. For the whole enemy spy system within the United Kingdom was virtually laid by the heels within twenty-four hours of the declaration of war. Every effort to set it up afresh subsequently was nipped in the bud before it could do mischief.

One point, however, deserves to be placed on record. The disinclination of H.M. Government to announce the execution of the first enemy agent to meet his fate, Lodi, was one of the most extraordinary incidents that came to my knowledge in connection with enemy spies. Lodi was an officer, or ex-officer, and a brave man who in the service of his country had gambled with his life as the stake—and had lost. He had fully acknowledged the justice of his conviction. All who were acquainted with the facts felt sympathy for him, although there could, of course, be no question of not carrying out the inevitable sentence of the court-martial. And yet our Government wanted to hush the whole thing up. They did not seem to realize that the shooting of a spy does not, when the spy is an enemy, mean punishment for a crime, that it represents a penalty which has to be inflicted as a deterrent, and which if it is to fulfil its purpose must be made known. Those of us who knew the facts were greatly incensed at the most improper, and indeed fatuous, attitude which the Executive for a time took up. What made them change their minds I do not know.

Then there was the cable censorship, an organization

which did admirable work and got little thanks for it. The personnel consisted largely of retired officers, and many of them broke down under the prolonged strain. The potentialities of the cable censorship had not been fully foreseen when it was automatically established on mobilization, and of what it accomplished the general public know practically nothing at all.   The conception of this institution had at the outset merely been that of setting up a barrier intended to prevent naval and military information that was calculated to be of service to the enemy from passing over the wires, whether in cipher or in clear.   But an enterprising, prescient, and masterful staff perceived ere long that their powers could be developed and turned to account in other directions with advantage to the State, notably in that of stifling the commercial activities of the Central Powers in the Western Hemisphere.   The consequence was that within a very few months the cable censorship had transformed itself to a great extent out of an effective shield for defence into a potent weapon of attack.   The measure of its services to the country will never be known, as some of its procedure cannot perhaps advantageously be disclosed.   Its labours were unadvertised, and its praises remained unsung.   But those who were behind the scenes are well aware of what it accomplished, creeping along unseen tracks, to bring about the downfall of the Hun.

The postal censorship started as a branch of comparatively modest dimensions; but it gradually developed into a huge department, employing a personnel which necessarily included large numbers of efficient linguists. The remarkable success achieved by the contre-espionage service in preventing the re-establishment of the enemy spy system after it had been smashed at the start was in no small degree due to the work of the censorship. That the requisite number of individuals well acquainted with some of the outlandish lingoes which had to be grappled with proved to be forthcoming, is a matter of surprise and a subject for congratulation.   This was not a case merely of French, German, Italian, and languages more or less familiar to our educated and travelled classes. Much of the work was in Scandinavian and in occult Slav tongues, a good deal of it not even written in the Roman character. The staff was largely composed, it should be mentioned, of ladies, some of them quite young ; but young or old—no, that won't do, for ladies are never old—quite young or only moderately young, they took to the work like ducks to the water and did yeoman service. As in the case of the cable censorship, employment in the postal censorship was a thankless job ; but the labourers of both sexes in the branch had at least the satisfaction of knowing that they had done their bit— some of them a good deal more than their bit—for their country in its hour of trial.

Reference was made in the last chapter to certain discussions which took place in the winter of 1914–15 on the subject of suggested conjunct naval and military operations on the Flanders coast. The possibility of such undertakings was never entirely lost sight of during 1915, although the diversion of considerable British forces to far-off theatres of war necessarily enhanced the difficulties that stood in the way of a form of project which had much to recommend it from the strategical point of view. Our hosts on the Western Front were absolutely dependent upon the security of the Narrow Seas, and that security was being menaced owing to the enemy having laid his grip upon Ostend and Zeebrugge. One afternoon in the autumn of 1915 Admiral Bacon of the Dover Patrol, who believed in an extremely active defence, came to see me and we had a long and interesting conversation. He was full of a scheme for running some ship-loads of troops right into Ostend harbour at night and landing the men by surprise about the mole and the docks. His plans were not, however, at this time worked out so elaborately, nor had such effective preparations been taken in hand with regard to them, as was the case at a later date after Sir D. Haig had taken up command of the B.E.F.   The

Admiral describes these preparations and his developed plans in *The Dover Patrol.*

On the occasion of this talk in the War Office, Admiral Bacon was, if I recollect aright, contemplating landing the troops straight off the ordinary type of vessel, not off craft especially designed and constructed for the particular purpose, as was intended in his improved project. Nor was it, I think, proposed to use " beetles " (these may perhaps all have gone to the Mediterranean). My impression at the time was that the scheme had very much to recommend it in principle, but that its execution as it stood must represent an extremely hazardous operation of war. Nor was this a moment when one felt much leaning towards new - fangled tactical and strategical devices, for we had a large force locked up under most depressing conditions in the Gallipoli Peninsula, we were apparently going to be let in for trouble in Macedonia, and, although the United Kingdom and the Dominions had by this time very large forces under arms, a considerable proportion of the troops could hardly be looked upon as efficient owing to lack of training.

Looking at this question of the Flanders littoral from what, in a naval and military sense, may be called the academical point of view, it is certainly a great pity that neither the project worked out by Admiral Bacon in the winter of 1915–16 in agreement with G.H.Q., nor yet the later plan for conjunct operations to take place in this coast region had the Passchendael offensive of 1917 not been so disastrously delayed, was put into execution. Had either of them actually been carried out this must, whatever the result was, have provided one of the most dramatic and remarkable incidents in the course of the Great War.

Passing reference has already been made to Sir Archie Murray's assumption of the position of C.I.G.S. in October 1915, when he replaced the late Sir James Wolfe-Murray. Shrewd, indefatigable, of very varied experience, an excellent administrator and a man of such charming personality that he could always get the very best out of his subordinates, Sir James would have admirably filled any high, non-technical appointment within the War Office during the early part of the contest, other than that which he was suddenly called upon to take up on the death of Sir C. Douglas. Absolutely disinterested, his energies wholly devoted to the service of the State, compelling the respect, indeed the affection, of all of us who were under him in those troublous times, a more considerate chief, nor one whose opinion when you put a point to him you could accept with more implicit confidence, it would have been impossible to find. But for occupying the headship of the General Staff under the existing circumstances he lacked certain desirable qualifications. Although well acquainted with the principles that should govern the general conduct of war and no mean judge of such questions, he was not disposed by instinct to interest himself in the broader aspects of strategy and of military policy. His bent was rather to concern himself with the details. Somewhat cautious, nay diffident, by nature, he moreover shrank from pressing his views, worthy of all respect as they were, on others, and he was always guarded in expressing them even when invited to do so.

Dealing with a Secretary of State of Lord Kitchener's temperament, reticence of this kind did not work. Lord K. liked you to say what you thought without hesitation, and, once he knew you, he never resented your giving an opinion even uninvited if you did so tactfully. As for the personnel who constitute War Councils and their like, it is not the habit of the politician to hide his light under a bushel, nor to recoil from laying down the law about any matter with which he has a bowing acquaintance. That an expert should sit mute when his own subject is in debate, surprises your statesman profoundly. That the expert should not be brimming over with a didactic and confident flow of words when he has been invited to promulgate his views, confounds your statesman altogether. General Wolfe-Murray never seemed to succeed in getting on quite the proper terms either with his immediate superior, the War Minister, or yet with the members of the Government included in the War Council and the Dardanelles Committee ; and it was cruel luck that, with so fine a record in almost all parts of the world to look back upon, this most meritorious public servant should towards the close of his career have found himself unwillingly thrust into a position for which, as he foresaw himself when he assumed it, he was not altogether well suited.

Subsequent to returning from Russia, and very shortly after the loss of the *Hampshire* with Lord Kitchener and his party, I came to be for some weeks unemployed, afterwards taking up a fresh appointment—one in connection with Russian supplies, which later developed into one covering supplies for all the Allies and to which reference will be made in a special chapter. But the result was that, as a retired officer, I ceased for the time being to be on the active list and became a gentleman at large. Thereby hangs a tale ; because it was just at this juncture that I was asked by the Army Council to go into the question of papers which were to be presented to the House of Commons in connection with the Dardanelles Campaign. Badgered by inquisitive members of that assembly, Mr. Asquith had committed himself to the production of papers ; and Mr. Churchill had got together a dossier dealing with his share in the affair, which was sent to me to consider, together with all the telegrams, and so forth, that bore on the operations and their prologue.

On examining all this stuff, it soon became manifest that the publication of any papers at all during the war, in connection with this controversial subject, was to be deprecated. Still, one recognized that the Prime Minister's promise had to be fulfilled somehow ; so the great object to be kept in view seemed to be to keep publication within the narrowest possible limits compatible with satisfying the curiosity of the people in Parliament. As a matter of fact, there were passages in some of the documents which Mr. Churchill proposed for production that must obviously be expunged, in view of Allies' susceptibilities and of their conveying information which might still be of value to the enemy. There could be no question that, no matter how drastic might be the cutting-down process, the Admiralty, the War Office and the Government would come badly out of the business. Furthermore, any publication of papers must make known to the world that Lord Kitchener's judgement in connection with this particular phase of the war had been somewhat at fault.

When asking me to take the matter up, the Army Council had probably overlooked my civilian status or forgotten what a strong position this placed me in. An ex-soldier does not often get an opportunity of enjoying an official heart-to-heart talk, on paper, with the powers-that-be in the War Office. My report was to the effect that it was undesirable to produce any papers at all during the war, but that, as some had to be produced, they ought to be cut down to a minimum, that everybody official concerned in the business at home would be more or less shown up, that this was particularly unfortunate just at this time in view of Lord Kitchener's lamented death, that the papers must be limited to those bearing upon the period antecedent to the actual landing of the army in the Gallipoli Peninsula, that if this last proviso was accepted I would go fully into the question and report in detail, and that if the proviso was not accepted I declined to act and they might all go to the —— well, one did not quite put it in those words, but they would take it that way. The result was not quite what one had either expected or desired. The production-of-papers project was dropped, and the Dardanelles Commission was appointed instead.

Mr. Lloyd George had become Secretary of State for War by this time. He was full of zeal and of original

ideas, nor had he any intention of being merely a
" passenger." He had, after the manner of new War
Ministers, introduced a fresh personal entourage into the
place, and a momentary panic, caused by the news that
telephonic communications into and out of the place were
passing in an unknown guttural language not wholly
unlike German, was only allayed on its being ascertained
that certain of his hangers-on conversed over the wires
in Welsh. Besides being full of original ideas, the new
Secretary of State was in a somewhat restless mood. He
took so keen an interest in some wonderful scheme in
connection with Russian railways (about which I was
freely consulted) that he evidently was hankering after
going on a mission to that part, of the world himself. He
no doubt believed that a visit from him would be an
equivalent for the visit by Lord Kitchener which had
been interrupted so tragically. To anybody who had
recently been to Russia, such an idea was preposterous.
Few who counted in the Tsar's dominions had ever heard
of the Right Honourable Gentleman at this time ; Lord
Kitchener's name, on the other hand, had been known,
and his personality had counted as an asset (as I knew
from my own experience), from Tornea on the Lappland
borders to the highlands of Erzerum. The project did
not strike one as deserving encouragement, and I did
what I could to damp it down unobtrusively.

It was nearly a year later than this, in the summer of
1917, that, owing to the horse of General Whigham, the
Deputy C.I.G.S., slipping up with him near the Marble
Arch and giving him a nasty fall, he became incapacitated
for a month. Sir W. Robertson thereupon called me in
to act as *locum tenens*. From many points of view this
proved to be a particularly edifying and instructive
experience. One could not fail to be impressed with
the smoothness with which the military side of the
War Office was working under the system which Sir
William had introduced, and one furthermore found
oneself behind the scenes in respect to the progress of

the war and to numbers of matters only known to the very few.

The plan under which nearly all routine work in connection with the General Staff, work that the C.I.G.S. would otherwise be obliged to concern himself with personally to a large extent, was delegated to a Deputy who was a Member of the Army Council was an admirable arrangement. It worked almost to perfection as far as I could see. It allowed Sir W. Robertson, in consultation with his Directors of Military Operations and of Intelligence, Generals Maurice and Macdonogh, to devote his attention to major questions embracing the conduct of the war on land as a whole. The Deputy in the meantime wrestled with the details, with the correspondence about points of secondary importance, in fact with the red tape if you like to call it that, while keeping in close and constant touch with the administrative departments and branches. Everybody advocates de - centralization in theory ; Sir William actually carried it out in practice, reminding me of that Prince of military administrators, the late Sir H. Brackenbury. The Deputy's room opened off that of the C.I.G.S. ; but on many days I never even saw him except when he looked in for a minute to ask if I had anything for him, or when I happened to walk home some part of the way to York House with him after the trouble was over for the day.

It was intensely interesting to have the daily reports of casualties at the Western Front passing through one's hands, and to note the extent to which these mounted up on what might be called non-fighting days as compared to days of attack. As this was during the opening stages of the Flanders offensive subsequent to General Plumer's victory at Messines, these statistics were extremely instructive. I do not know whether the details have ever been worked out for the years 1915–17, but it looked to me at that time as if the losses in three weeks of ordinary trench-warfare came on the average to about the same total as did the losses in a regular formal assault of some section of the enemy's lines. Or, putting the thing in another form and supposing the above calculation to be correct, you would in three weeks of continuous attack in a given zone only lose the same number of men as you would lose in that same zone in a year of stagnant, unprofitable trench-warfare. Some of our offensives on the Western Front have been condemned on the grounds of their costliness in human life ; but it has not been sufficiently realized in the country how heavy the losses were during periods of quiescence.

As acting D.C.I.G.S. one, moreover, enjoyed opportunities of examining the various compiled statements showing the numbers of our forces in the various theatres, with full information as to the strength of our Allies' armies in all quarters, as well as the carefully prepared estimates of the enemy's fighting resources as these were arrived at by our Intelligence organizations in consultation with those of the French, Italians, Belgians, and others. One learnt the full details of our " order of battle " for the time being, exactly where the different divisions, army corps, etc., were located, and who commanded them. It transpired that the Entente host on the Salonika Front at this time comprised no fewer than 655,000 of all ranks, without counting in the Serbs who would have brought the total up to about 800,000, while the enemy forces opposed to them were calculated to muster only about 450,000 ; the situation was, in fact, much worse than one had imagined. One discovered that, while slightly over 17 per cent of the male population of Great Britain had been enrolled as soldiers, only 5 per cent of the Irish male population had come forward, and that but for north-east Ulster the figure would not have reached 3 per cent. One became aware, moreover, that the Army Council, or at least its Military Members, were at loggerheads with the War Cabinet over the problem of man-power, and that this question was from the military point of view giving grounds for grave anxiety.

In one of my drawers there was the first draft of a

secret paper on this subject, which expressed the views of the Military Members of the Council in blunt terms, and which amounted in reality to a crushing indictment of the Prime Minister and his Cabinet. I have a copy of the draft in my possession, but as it was a secret document it would be improper to give details of its contents ; it, moreover, was somewhat modified and mellowed in certain particulars before the paper was actually sent to Downing Street. The final discussion took place at a full meeting of the Army Council while I was acting as D.C.I.G.S., but which I did not attend as not being a statutory member of that body. Parliament ought to call for this paper ; it was presented in July 1917 ; it practically foreshadowed what actually occurred in March 1918. The Military Members of the Council nearly resigned in a body over this business; but they were not unanimous on the question of resignation, although perfectly unanimous as regards the seriousness of the position. It may be mentioned that at a considerably later date the Army Council did, including its civilian members, threaten resignation as a body when Sir N. Macready gave up the position of Adjutant-General to become Commissioner of the Metropolitan Police, owing to an attempt made from Downing Street to civilianize the Adjutant-General's department. The Army Council beat Downing Street, hands down.

The disquieting conditions in respect to man-power were, incidentally, hampering the development of two important combatant branches at this time, the Machine-Gun Corps and the Tank Corps. The heavy demands of these two branches, coupled with the fact that infantry wastage was practically exceeding the intake of recruits, threatened a gradual disappearance of the principal arm of the Service. We had by this time got long past the stage with which, when D.M.O., I had been familiar, where lack of material and munitions was checking the growth of our armies in the field. We had arrived at the stage where material and munitions were ample, but where it was becoming very difficult to maintain our armies in the field from lack of personnel—a state of things directly attributable to the Government's opportunist, hand-to-mouth policy in the matter, and to their disinclination to insist upon practically the whole of the younger categories of male adults joining the colours. The organization of the Tank Corps was finally decided actually while I was acting as D.C.I.G.S. In so far as the general control of Tank design and the numbers of these engines of war to be turned out was concerned, it seemed to me to be a case of " pull devil, pull baker " between the military and the civilians as to how far these matters were to be left entirely to the technicalist ; but the technicalist was not perhaps getting quite so much to say in the matter as was reasonable. The personal factor maybe entered into the question.

When the War Office had been reconstituted by the Esher Committee in 1904, the Admiralty organization had been to a great extent taken as a model for the Army Council arrangement which the triumvirate then introduced. Thirteen years later the Admiralty was reorganized, and on this occasion the War Office system of 1904, as modified and developed in the light of experience in peace and in war, was taken as the model for the rival institution. Whigham had played a part in the carrying out of this important reform, lending his advice to the sailors and explaining the distribution of duties amongst the higher professional authorities on our side of Whitehall, especially in connection with the General Staff. The most urgently needed alteration to be sought after was the relieving of the First Sea Lord of a multitude of duties which were quite incompatible with his giving full attention to really vital questions in connection with employing the Royal Navy. For years past he had been a sort of Pooh Bah, holding a position in some respects analogous to that occupied by Lord Wolseley and Lord Roberts when they had been nominally " Commander-in-chief " of the army. Under the arrangements made

with the assistance of the War Office in 1917, a post somewhat analogous to that of D.C.I.G.S. was set up at the
Admiralty, and the First Sea Lord was thenceforward
enabled to see to the things that really mattered as he
never had been before.   Although the amount of current
work to be got through daily when acting as Deputy
C.I.G.S. proved heavy enough during the month when I
was *locum tenens*, it was not so heavy as to preclude my
looking through the instructive documents dealing with
this matter amongst Whigham's papers.

The glorious uncertainty of cricket is acknowledged
to be one of the main attractions of our national game.
But the glorious uncertainty of cricket is as nothing
compared to the glorious uncertainty which obtains in
time of war as to what silly thing H.M. Government—
or some of its shining lights—will be wanting to do next.
At this time the War Cabinet, or perhaps one ought
rather to say certain members of that body, had got it
into their heads that to send round a lot of Sir Douglas
Haig's troops (who were pretty well occupied as it was)
to the Isonzo Front would be a capital plan, the idea being
to catch the Central Powers no end of a " biff " in this
particular quarter.   That fairly banged Banagher.   For
sheer fatuity it was the absolute limit.

Ever since the era of Hannibal, if not indeed since
even earlier epochs, trampling, hope-bestirred armies
have from generation to generation been bursting forth
like a pent-up torrent from that broad zone of tumbled
Alpine peaks which overshadows Piedmont, Lombardy
and Venetia, to flood their smiling plains with hosts of
fighting men.   Who ever heard of an army bursting in
the opposite direction ?   Napoleon tried it, and rugged,
thrusting Suvorof ; but they did not get much change out
of it.   The mountain region has invariably either been in
possession of the conquerors at the start, or else it has been
acquired by deliberate, protracted process during the course
of a lengthy struggle, before the dramatic coup has been
delivered by which the levels have been won.   The wide

belt of highlands extending from Switzerland to Croatia remained in the enemy's hands up to the time of the final collapse of the Dual Monarchy subsequent to the rout of the Emperor Francis' legions on the Piave. The Italians had in the summer of 1917 for two years been striving to force their way into these mountain fastnesses, and they had progressed but a very few miles. They had not only been fighting the soldiery of the Central Powers, but had also been fighting Nature. Nature often proves a yet more formidable foe than do swarms of warriors, even supposing these to be furnished with all modern requirements for prosecuting operations in the field.

Roads are inevitably few and far between in a mountainous region. In such terrain, roads and railways can be destroyed particularly easily and particularly effectively by a retiring host. In this kind of theatre, troops can only quit the main lines of communications with difficulty, and localities abound where a very inferior force will for a long time stay the advance of much more imposing columns. You can no more cram above a given number of men on to a certain stretch of road when on the move, than you can get a quart into a pint pot. Even if your enemy simply falls back without fighting, destroying all viaducts, tunnels, embankments, culverts, and so forth, your army will take a long time to traverse the highlands—unless it be an uncommonly small one. Armies in these days are inevitably of somewhat bloated dimensions if they are to do any good. Theatrical strategy of the flags-on-the-map order is consequently rather at a discount in an arena such as the War Cabinet, or some members of that body, proposed to exploit. Even had there been no other obvious objections to a diversion of force such as they contemplated, the project ignored certain elementary aspects of the conduct of warlike operations which might be summed up in the simple expression " common-sense."

But there were other obvious objections. To switch any force worth bothering about from northern France to the Friuli flats was bound to be a protracted process, because only two railways led over the Alps from Dauphiné and Provence into the basin of the Po; and those lines were distinguished for their severe gradients. It was, as a matter of fact, incomparably easier for the enemy to mass reinforcements in the Julian Alps than it was for the two Western Powers to mass reinforcements in the low ground facing that great area of rugged hills. The question of a transfer of six divisions from the Western Front to Venetia had, however, been gone into very thoroughly by the General Staff in view of conceivable eventualities. An elaborate scheme had been drawn up by experienced officers, who had examined the question in consultation with the Italian military authorities, and had traversed the communications that would have to be brought into play were such a move to be carried out. What time the transfer would take was a matter of calculation based on close examination of the details. The final report came to hand while I was acting as Deputy C.I.G.S., although its general purport had already been communicated several weeks before. Two or three months later, when it suddenly became necessary to rush British and French troops round from northern France to the eastern portions of the Po basin after the singular *débâcle* of Caporetto, actual experience proved the forecasts made in this report to have been quite correct. There was not much " rushing " about the move. It took weeks to complete.

General Pershing and his staff arrived in England just at this time, and I enjoyed the pleasure of meeting them and discussing many matters. The attitude of these distinguished soldiers, one and all, impressed us most agreeably. One had heard something about " Yankee bounce " in the past, which exists no doubt amongst some of the citizens of the great Republic across the water. But here we found a body of officers who, while manifestly knowing uncommonly well what they were about, were bent on learning from us everything that they possibly could, and who from the outset proved themselves singularly ready to fall in with our methods of doing business even where those methods differed widely from what they had been accustomed to.

Some weeks later (in the capacity of War Office representative) I accompanied Lord Jellicoe and Admiral Sims, together with Sir I. Malcolm and Sir W. Wiseman of the Foreign Office, to Devonport to meet a large party of high officials from the United States who were coming over to Europe to take general charge of things in connection with the American share in the war. It was headed by Colonel House, and included the Chiefs of the Naval and Military Staffs with their assistants, as well as financial and other delegates. We arrived some time before the two cruisers conveying the party were due, so we proceeded to Admiralty House. While waiting there, one was afforded a most welcome opportunity of learning something about how the strings were being pulled over the great water-area which was under special charge of the local commander-in-chief. The whole thing was set out on a huge fixed map covering, I think, the billiard-table. On it were shown where the various convoys were at the moment, the minefields, the positions where German U-boats had recently been located, and numberless other important details. To a landsman it was absorbingly interesting to have all this explained, just as it had been interesting, a few days before, to visit General Ashmore's office at the Horse Guards and to learn on the map how the London anti-aircraft defences were controlled during an attack.

Just about dusk the two cruisers were descried coming in past the breakwater, so it became a question of getting to the Keyham dockyard where they were to fetch up. Ever keen for exercise in any form, Lord Jellicoe decided to walk, and the commander-in-chief went with him. Knowing the distance and the somewhat unattractive approaches leading to the Keyham naval establishments, and as it, moreover, looked and felt uncommonly like rain, I preferred to wait and to proceed in due course by car, as did all the rest of our party. The flag-lieutenant and the naval officer who had come down with Lord Jellicoe from the Admiralty likewise thought that a motor was good enough for them. By the time that the automobile party reached the dockyard it was pitch dark and pouring rain, and the cruisers were already reported as practically alongside ; but to our consternation there was no sign of the two flag-officers. Now, a dog who has lost his master is an unperturbed, torpid, contented creature compared with a flag-lieutenant who has lost his admiral, and there was a terrible to-do. All the telephones were buzzing and ringing, the dockyard police were eagerly interrogated, and there was already talk of despatching search-parties, when the two distinguished truants suddenly turned up, exceedingly hot, decidedly wet, and, if the truth must be told, looking a little muddy and bedraggled. However, there was no time to be lost, and we all rushed off into the night heading for where the vessels were to berth. How we did not break our necks tumbling into a dry-dock or find a watery grave tumbling into a wet one, I do not know. We certainly most of us barked our shins against anchors, chains, bollards, and every sort of pernicious litter such as the sister service loves to fondle, and the language would have been atrocious had we not been out of breath —the Foreign Office indeed contrived to be explosive even as it was. However, we managed to reach the jetty after all just as the two big warships had been warped alongside, winning by a nose. So all was well.

Colonel House and his party had not been fortunate in their weather during the crossing, and they had come to the conclusion that a fighting ship represented an over-rated form of ocean liner. More than one of the soldiers and civilians confided to me that if there was no other way of getting across the herring-pond on the way back than by cruiser, they would stop this side. They were all quite pleased to find themselves on dry land, and during the journey up to town by special there was plenty of time to make acquaintance and to discuss general questions. One point was made plain. Mr. Balfour's recently concluded mission to the United States had been a tremendous success. Junior officers who had not met him spoke of him almost with bated breath, and a hint that he might be at the terminus to greet the party caused unbounded satisfaction. When we steamed into Paddington about 1 o'clock A.M. and his tall figure was descried on the platform, the whole crowd burst out of the train in a disorderly swarm, jostling each other in trying to get near him and have a chance of shaking his hand; it was quite a business getting them sorted and under control again so as to start them off in the waiting cars to Claridge's. We do not always send the right man as envoy to foreign parts, but we had managed it that time.

CHAPTER VIII

THE NEAR EAST

"IF you've 'eard the East a-callin', you won't never 'eed nought else," Rudyard Kipling's old soldier sings, mindful of spacious days along the road to Mandalay. The worst of the East, however, is that people hear it calling who have never been there in their lives. That there were individuals in high places who were subject to this mysterious influence, became apparent at a comparatively early stage of the World War.

The first occasion on which, apart from a few outpost affairs over the Dardanelles with Mr. Churchill to which reference has already been made, " easternism " (as it came to be called later) raised its head to my knowledge to any alarming extent, was when Colonel Hankey asked me, one day early in December 1914, to go across to

Treasury Buildings to meet Sir E. Grey and Mr. Lloyd George. There is not a more depressing structure in existence than Treasury Buildings. The arrangement of the interior is a miracle of inconvenience, on the most cloudless of days its apartments are wrapped in gloom, and no decorator has been permitted to pass its portals since it was declared fit for occupation in some forgotten age. But Mr. Lloyd George, who was Chancellor of the Exchequer at this time, is ever like a ray of sunshine illumining otherwise dark places, and on this occasion he was at his very brightest. He had made a discovery. He had found on a map that there was quite a big place— it was shown in block capitals—called Salonika, tucked away in a corner of the Balkans right down by the sea. The map furthermore indicated by means of an interminable centipede that a railway led from this place Salonika right away up into Serbia, and on from thence towards the very heart of the Dual Monarchy. Here was a chance of starting an absolutely new hare. The Chancellor, *allegro con fuoco*, was in a buoyant mood, as was indeed only to be expected under such circumstances, and he was geniality itself when I appeared in the apartment where Sir E. Grey and Hankey were awaiting me together with himself. We should be able to deal the enemy a blow from an entirely unexpected direction, the days of stalemate in the half-frozen morasses of Flanders would be at an end, we would carry the Balkans with us, it would be absolutely top-hole. Although obviously interested— it could hardly be otherwise when the words " Near East " were mentioned—the Foreign Secretary was careful not to give himself away. You have to make a practice of that when you are Foreign Secretary.

Now, it so happened that I had been at Salonika more than once, and also that I had travelled along this very railway more than once and had carefully noted matters in connection with it so long as daylight served. Much more important than that, there were in the archives of my branch at the War Office very elaborate reports on the railway, and there was moreover full information as to the capabilities and the incapabilities of the port of Salonika' for the discharge of what was animate and what was inanimate.   It was a case of an extensive haven that provided shelter in all weathers for ocean-going ships, but possessing most indifferent facilities for landing merchandise, or animals, or persons, considering the importance of the site.   And it was, moreover, a case of one single line of railway meandering up a trough-like valley which at some points narrowed into a defile, a railway of severe gradients with few passing stations, a railway which assuredly would be very short of rolling stock—although this latter disability could no doubt be overcome easily enough.   One somehow did not quite picture to oneself an army of many divisions comfortably advancing from Belgrade on Vienna based on Salonika, and depending upon the Salonika-Belgrade railway for its food, for its munitions, and for its own means of transit from the Mediterranean to its launching place.   Besides, there were no reserves of troops ready to hand for projecting into the Balkans at this juncture.   Only a very few weeks had passed since those days of peril when Sir J. French and the " Old Contemptibles " had, thanks to resolute leadership and to a splendid heroism on the part of regimental officers and rank-and-file, just managed to bring the German multitudes up short as these were surging towards the Channel Ports.   Fancy stunts seemed to be at a discount at the moment, and I found it hard to be encouraging.

Some statesmen are ever, unconsciously perhaps but none the less instinctively, gravitating towards the line of least resistance, or towards what they imagine to be the line of least resistance.   This, peradventure, accounts to some extent for the singular attraction which operations in the Near East, or Palestine, or anywhere other than on the Western Front, always seemed to present to certain highly placed men of affairs.   The idea that the actual strategical position in those somewhat remote regions was such as to constitute any one of them the line of least resistance from the Entente point of view, was based on a complete misreading of the military situation. That theory was founded on the fallacy that the Western Front represented the enemy's strongest point. It was, on the contrary, the enemy's weakest point, because this front was from its geographical position the one where British and French troops could most easily be assembled, and it was the one on which a serious defeat to the enemy necessarily threatened that enemy with a grave, if not an irretrievable, disaster. It is true that for the comparatively short period during which Russia really counted, that is to say during the early months before Russian munitions gave out, the Eastern Front—the Poland Front—was a weak point for the Germans. But the Russian bubble had been pricked in the eyes of those behind the scenes long before the great advance of the German and Austro-Hungarian armies over the Vistula and into the heart of the Tsar's dominions began in the early summer of 1915.

Scarcely had the Salonika venture been mooted than the Dardanelles venture cropped up and was actually embarked on ; so that for the nonce the advocates of an advance through Serbia—I am not sure that there was more than one at the time—abandoned that project. But although the Serbs had succeeded early in the winter of 1914–15 in driving the Austro-Hungarian invading columns ignominiously back over the Save and the Danube, the position of this isolated Ally of ours was giving grounds for anxiety from an early period in 1915, and it always presented a serious problem for the Entente. Colonel Basil Buckley, my right-hand man with regard to the Near East, had it constantly in mind.

It is always easy to be wise after the event ; what in the world would become of the noble army of critics if it were not so ? Still, looking back in the light of the sequel upon the political and strategical situation that existed in the Near East early in 1915, it does look as if the right course for the Western Powers to have adopted then (so soon as there were troops available for another theatre without hopelessly queering the Entente pitch on the Western Front) would have been to use those troops for lending Serbia a hand instead of despatching them to the Dardanelles. Even a weaker force than that with which Sir I. Hamilton embarked on the Gallipoli venture (nominally five Anglo-Australasian and two French divisions) would have proved an invaluable moral, and an effective actual, support to the Serbs; and its arrival on the Morava and the Save could hardly have failed to influence to some extent the attitude of Bulgaria and Roumania, and assuredly would have caused the Austro-Hungarian monarchy some heart-burnings. It has been said that M. Briand (who did not assume the premiership in France until a somewhat later date) advocated the despatch of Entente troops to Serbia in the spring of 1915, and that the question was discussed between the British and French Governments ; but I know nothing of this, only having come to be behind the scenes of the Near Eastern drama at a somewhat later date.

Objections to such a course undoubtedly existed, even leaving out of account the fact that our Government was, with the approval of that of Paris, committing itself at the time more and more definitely to the Hellespont-Bosphorus - Black Sea project. In the first place, Salonika happened to be in the hands of neutral Greece, although that difficulty would probably have been got over readily enough then. In the second place, the despatch of a Franco-British force to Serbia in the spring would have been playing the enemy's game to the extent of virtually tying up that force and of condemning it to inactivity for the time being, so as to provide against a danger—hostile attack on Serbia—which might never materialize, and which actually did not materialize until the autumn. In the third place, there was always, with amateur strategists about, the grave risk that a measure taken with the object of safeguarding Serbia as far as possible, might translate itself into a great offensive operation against the Central Powers from the south, absorbing huge Anglo-French forces, conducted under great difficulties in respect to communications with the sea, and playing into the hands of the German Great General Staff by enabling that wide-awake body to make the very fullest use of its strategical assets in respect to " interior lines." Finally, we could not depend upon Bulgaria siding with the Entente, nor even Roumania ; and although Italy would certainly not take up arms against us she had not yet declared herself an Ally.

The above reference to Bulgaria introduces a question which added greatly to the perplexities of the Near Eastern problem then and afterwards, perplexities that were aggravated by the well-founded suspicion with which Bulgaria's monarch was on all hands regarded. The Bulgars coveted Macedonia. But the greater part of Macedonia happened as a result of the Balkan upheavals of 1912 and 1913 to belong to Serbia, and the rest of it belonged to Greece. Into the ethnographical aspect of the Macedonian problem it is not necessary to enter here. The cardinal fact remained that Bulgaria wanted, and practically demanded, this region. While we might have been ready enough to give away Greek territory which did not belong to us, we really could not give away Serbian territory which did not belong to us seeing that Serbia was an Ally actually embattled on our side and with a victorious campaign already to her credit. Macedonia at a later date upset the apple-cart.

Things were already from our point of view in something of a tangle in the Balkans by the vernal equinox of 1915 ; but they had got into much more of a tangle by the time that spring was merging into summer. At that stage, the failure of our naval effort against the Dardanelles had been followed by our military effort coming to a disconcerting standstill, and the Bulgarian and Greek Governments in common with their military authorities made up their minds that the operation against the Straits was doomed. That was bad enough in all conscience, but worse was to follow. Because then the Russian bubble was suddenly, dramatically, and publicly pricked, the Tsar's stubborn soldiery, without ammunition and almost without weapons, could not even maintain themselves against the Austro-Hungarian forces, much less against the formidable German hosts that were suddenly turned loose upon them, and within the space of a very few weeks the situation on the Eastern Front, which at least in appearance had been favourable enough during the winter and the early spring, suddenly became transformed into one of profoundest gloom from the Entente point of view. Even a much less unpromising diplomatic situation than that which had existed in the Balkans between December and May was bound to become an untoward one under such conditions. Our side had come to be looked upon as the losing side. No amount of skill on the part of our Foreign Office nor of the Quai d'Orsay could compensate for the logic of disastrous facts. The performances of H.M. Government in connection with Bulgaria and Greece at this time have been the subject of much acid criticism. But in time of war it is the victorious battalions that count, not the wiles of a Talleyrand nor of a Great Elchi. The failure in the Dardanelles and the Russian collapse settled our hash in the Near East for the time being, and no amount of diplomatic juggling could have effectually repaired the mischief.

Exactly what line the General Staff would have taken up had they been called upon, say at the beginning of July, to give a considered opinion in the form of a carefully prepared memorandum as to the course that ought to be followed in connection with the Dardanelles and Serbia, it is hard to say. That there was considerable risk of Serbia being assailed in force by the Central Powers before long was manifest. On the other hand, there we were, up to the neck in the Dardanelles venture, and strong reinforcements were at this time belatedly on their way out to Sir I. Hamilton from home. The position was a decidedly awkward one. To despatch further contingents to this part of the world, over and above those already on the way or under orders, was virtually out of the question, unless the Near East was to be accepted as the Entente's main theatre of war—which way madness lay. To divert the Dardanelles reinforcements to Salonika destroyed such hopes as remained of the Gallipoli campaign proving a success after all. Human nature being what it is, there would have been a sore temptation to adopt the attitude of " wait and see " which might perhaps have commended itself to Mr. Asquith, to let things take their course, to be governed by how Sir I. Hamilton's contemplated offensive panned out, and to trust to a decision in that quarter taking place before isolated Serbia should actually be imperilled. But in those days the General Staff never was asked to give a considered opinion. At the Dardanelles Committee which had all these matters in hand, one seldom, if ever, was given an opportunity of expressing views on the broader aspects of any question. The methods in vogue on the part of that body are indeed well illustrated by the following incident.

One evening in August, about 7 P.M., just when I was getting to the end of my work for the day, Colonel Swinton, who for many months past had been acting as " Eye-Witness " with Sir J. French's forces, turned up unexpectedly in my room. My pleasure at meeting an old friend, recently from the hub of things in France and whom I had not seen for a long time, gave place to resentment when he explained what he had come for. It appeared that he had a short time previously arrived in the United Kingdom to act temporarily as Secretary of the Committee of Imperial Defence (which practically meant the Dardanelles Committee at the moment), and he had been called upon, right off the reel, to prepare a memorandum on the Dardanelles situation, which was to be ready next morning. Knowing comparatively little about the

Dardanelles, he had come to consult me. In the first instance I absolutely declined to oblige. I had no authority from Lord K. or the C.I.G.S. to express views on this subject on paper for the benefit of the Committee. Furthermore—and perhaps this weighed more heavily in the scale than did official considerations—I was "fed up." One generally was by 7 P.M. at the War Office. The very idea of starting at this hour upon a memorandum about anything, let alone the Dardanelles, was infuriating.

Swinton, however, eventually prevailed upon me to lend a hand on the distinct understanding, pressed for by me, that it remained a hidden hand. After all, this intrusion of his did provide some sort of opportunity for putting the situation plainly before the Committee, and for expressing a vertebrate opinion. We proceeded to the club and dined together, and thereafter, refreshed and my equanimity restored by a rest and hearing the news from across the water, we grappled with the subject in the C.I.D. office. "Ole Luke Oie" could be trusted to put a thing tersely and with vigour once he knew what to say, and the document did not take long to draft. We took the line that in the Gallipoli Peninsula it was a case of getting on or of getting out. The core of this memorandum is quoted in the "Final Report" of the Dardanelles Commission, where it is pointed out that no mention is made of a middle course. That was intentional. A middle course was regarded by us as wholly unjustifiable, although it was the one which the Dardanelles Committee adopted; for that body did not take our advice—it neither got on nor got out.

The situation in the Near East as a whole became a more anxious one than ever after the failure of Sir I. Hamilton's August offensive, because by this time Russia's collapse was complete, and the legions of the Central Powers which had been flooding Poland, Grodno and Volhynia, impeded by sparsity of communications rather than by the resistance of the Grand Duke Nicholas's ammunitionless army, had become available for operations in a new direction. The portents all pointed to an attack upon Serbia. If Serbia was to receive effective aid at the hands of the Western Powers, that aid must be well in motion before the enemy hosts should gather on the northern and western frontiers of our threatened Ally, otherwise the aid would assuredly be late owing to the difficulty of moving troops rapidly from board ship in Salonika roads, up to the theatre of operations. Hopes still existed, on the other hand, at least in the minds of some of the members of the Dardanelles Committee, that by sending additional reinforcements to Sir I. Hamilton a success might be obtained even yet in that quarter. The French for a week or two contemplated despatching four divisions which were to operate on the Asiatic side of the Hellespont; but the situation on the Western Front put an end to this design. There were two stools, the Dardanelles and Salonika, and among us we contrived to sit down between them. For while all this was in debate the danger to Serbia grew apace, and intelligence sources of information now made it certain that the German Great General Staff had not only planned, but had already made nearly all the preparations for, a great stroke in the direction of the western Balkans.

In this distressing state of affairs Bulgaria was always the uncertain factor. Her attitude could not be gauged with certainty, but it was extremely suspicious throughout. A pro-Bulgar element had for some months been listened to by our Foreign Office with greater respect, than it deserved, although nobody, pro-Bulgar or anti-Bulgar, entertained any trust in Tsar Ferdinand's integrity. Had Serbia even at this late hour been willing to relinquish Macedonia, it is conceivable that Bulgaria might have remained neutral, and that Ferdinand might have broken such engagements as he had secretly entered into with the Central Powers. But utter distrust and bitter hatred of Bulgaria prevailed in Serbia. Our Ally perhaps hardly sufficiently realized that national aspirations ought rather

M

to direct themselves towards the Adriatic and the regions inhabited by Serb stock under Austro-Hungarian rule, than towards districts peopled by mixed races on the shores of the Aegean. Be that as it may, the idea of delivering up Macedonia to the traditional Eastern enemy was scouted at Belgrade. We hoped that at the worst Greece would, in accordance with treaty obligations, take sides with Serbia should Bulgaria throw in her lot with the Central Powers against the Serbs. Then came the attack of the German and Austro-Hungarian forces, synchronizing with the mobilization of the Bulgarian army.

The Nish Government—Belgrade had been quitted by this time—entertained no illusions whatever regarding Bulgarian intentions, and wished to assume the offensive promptly eastwards while this very suspicious mobilization was still in progress. Our Government—I am not sure what attitude the French, Russian, and Italian Governments took up—realized that Serbia's seizing the initiative put an end to all hopes of Greece lending a hand, and they virtually vetoed the project, as has already been mentioned in Chapter IV. That, as it turned out, was an unfortunate decision, because it fatally injured the Serbian prospects of preventing their territory being overrun before the French and we could intervene effectively, while it did not secure Greek adhesion. We virtually staked on King Constantine, and we found too late that our King was a Knave.

Just at this awkward juncture Lord Kitchener instructed me to be prepared to proceed to Salonika, and all the necessary steps for starting on the journey were promptly taken ; but it was not clear what capacity I was going in. It seemed a mistake, although one was naturally heartened at the prospect of activities in a new sphere, even if these were only to be of a temporary character. But, as it turned out, the Dardanelles Committee (or the War Council, I am not sure of the exact date when the Dardanelles Committee deceased) intervened, wishing me to remain at my post. In view of what followed, one was well out of intimate contact with the Macedonian imbroglio on the spot, because, as everybody knows now, the Franco-British forces arrived too late to save Serbia from reverses which amounted to an almost overwhelming disaster at the hands of the great hosts which the Central Powers and Bulgaria threw into the scale.

We and the French had, judged by results, made a hideous mess of things between us. The Allies were late at a critical juncture—and in war that is the unpardonable sin. Sir E. Carson, who had for a brief period proved himself a tower of strength on the Dardanelles Committee, resigned from the Cabinet in disgust. Lord Milner, independent man of affairs at the time, spoke out strongly on the subject in the House of Lords. But although the opinion of either of them is well worth having on most questions, and although both know their own minds, I doubt whether they, either of them, had any clear idea then as to what ought to have been done to avert the catastrophe, and I doubt whether they, either of them, have a clear idea now. Subsequent to May we were confronted with a horribly complex military and political situation in the Near East (and by that time military forces were already committed to the Dardanelles venture); because it was only then that the position of affairs on the Eastern Front and in the Near East became transformed owing to the Russian *débâcle*—a *débâcle* which turned out to be considerably greater than the available information as to our Ally's munition difficulties had led us to anticipate.

It is easy to say now, after the event, that we ought to have come away from the Dardanelles in June, and to have transferred the force there, or part of it, to Serbia, which was obviously placed in peril by Russia's collapse. But in June reinforcements were already earmarked for the Gallipoli Peninsula, and Sir I. Hamilton was confident of achieving a substantial success after they should arrive. It is easy to say now, after the event, that, immediately the offensive from Anzac and Suvla in August miscarried, we ought to have come out of the Gallipoli Peninsula and to have transferred the force there, or some of it, to Serbia. But in the latter part of August the French were disposed to send a substantial contingent to the Asiatic side of the Straits, we were supposed to have troops to spare for that part of the world, and it was not until early September that all this was dropped in view of events on the Western Front. It is easy to say now, after the event, that the Entente ought to have foreseen that King Constantine would throw Serbia over in any case, and that therefore we ought not to have prevented the Serbs from attacking Bulgaria while she was still mobilizing. But we trusted a King's word, and we knew that M. Venizelos was heart and soul on our side. It is easy to say now that we ought to have insisted on Serbia buying off Bulgar hostility by handing over Macedonia. But Serbia might have refused despite our insisting, and, when all is said and done, Serbia has succeeded in keeping Macedonia after all. Ought we to have come out of the Dardanelles in September, as soon as it was decided that neither the French nor British would send reinforcements thither, and to have transferred the troops to Salonika ? Assuredly we ought then to have come away from the Gallipoli Peninsula. But the evacuation must have been a ticklish business, and to have aggravated its difficulties by despatching its war-worn garrison simultaneously to Salonika and Serbia, just when great enemy contingents were gathering on the Danube and the Save, would have thrown a tremendous strain upon staff, upon troops, and upon the shipping resources of all kinds actually on the spot.

No. Leaving out of consideration the blunder of having drifted into the Dardanelles enterprise at all, the real mistake lay in not abandoning that enterprise when it became apparent that the troops originally detailed could not accomplish their purpose, when it became apparent that gaining a footing on the Gallipoli Peninsula meant gaining a footing and no more and that no aid was to be expected from Bulgaria or from Greece. It was just at that juncture that Russia began to give out and that the tide turned in favour of the Central Powers on the eastern side of Europe. The matter was primarily one for H.M. Government, because the French were not deeply committed to the effort against the Straits; but H.M. Government at that moment happened to be in a state of flux. The staff at G.H.Q., St. Omer, were no doubt not absolutely unprejudiced judges; but I was hearing constantly from General H. Wilson between August 1914 and the end of 1915, and he always wrote in the same strain about the Dardanelles from April onwards: " Cut your losses and come out."

Some mention has already been made of M. Briand's inclination for Entente efforts based on Salonika. In the autumn of 1915 that eminent French statesman was head of the Government in Paris, and his Cabinet took up a very strong line indeed over this question. We all agreed that neither the city, linked as it was by railway with Central Europe, nor yet its spacious land-locked haven must fall into enemy hands. Our naval authorities were in full agreement with the French naval authorities on that point. But when it came to projects for planting down large military forces in this area, with the idea of ultimate offensive operations northward ever in the background, we of the General Staff at the War Office demurred, and we were, at all events in principle, supported by the majority of the War Council. Lord Kitchener left for the Aegean at this time; but both before going and after his return he always, as far as I know, deprecated locking up fighting resources in Macedonia. Our Allies across the Channel were, however, somewhat insistent. Two conferences took place: one, a military one at Chantilly at the very end of October, and a more authoritative one a few days later in Paris, both of which I attended. More will be said about these *réunions* in Chapter XII. General Joffre, with some of his staff, also paid a visit to London in connection with the matter. The upshot was that the French practically forced us into the policy of maintaining a large force about Salonika. But H.M. Government were placed in a difficult position in the matter, seeing that their pet project (or at all events the pet project of the pre-Coalition Government), that of attacking the Dardanelles, had so completely failed.

One could not altogether escape from the impression at the time that, in the determined attitude which our friends over the water adopted on this point, they were at least to some small extent actuated by anxiety to maroon General Sarrail, who had been sent off in command of the French troops already despatched, and also to keep him quiet by investing him with the supreme command in this new theatre of war—as was later arranged. Why the strong political support enjoyed in certain French quarters by this prominent, and in the opening days of the war highly successful, soldier should have been taken so seriously, it was hard for anybody on our side of the Straits of Dover to understand. One wonders whether M. Clemenceau might not have been somewhat less discomposed on the subject had he been at the head of affairs. But the attitude adopted on the point became extremely inconvenient at a later date when, after an offensive on a large scale undertaken on the Salonika front had miscarried completely, owing largely, if not entirely, to a lamentable lack of co-ordination between the various contingents engaged, a change in the chief command did not instantly follow. Unsatisfactory as was the policy of interning large bodies of British and French troops that were badly wanted at the decisive point, in a sort of cul-de-sac in the Near East, it was made all the more unsatisfactory by the way the military situation was dealt with locally for more than a year and a half.

In view of certain criticisms of the General Staff to which the lack of information concerning the Gallipoli Peninsula when it was needed in 1915 has given rise, it is worth mentioning that at my suggestion General Joffre sent one of his trusted staff-officers over from Chantilly in November 1915 to put up with us for a few days, particularly in connection with Macedonian problems. This representative of the French General Staff was astonished to find that we possessed numbers of detailed military reports concerning that part of the world, with full information as to railways and communications, and he was most complimentary on the subject. " Your England is an island, my general," he remarked to me ; " you have not had the eastern frontier always to think of like France. How could we devote attention to Macedonia ? " It was not here a question of reconnaissance work or of costly back-stairs methods in a carefully watched fortified area of prime strategical significance like the environs of the Hellespont. Getting information about Macedonia had merely been a matter of sending out experienced military observers to look about them and to report.

When I left the General Staff at the War Office at the end of the year, the position of affairs at Salonika was a thoroughly unsatisfactory one, although the General Staff could fairly claim that for this it was not responsible. A great Allied army was collected in this quarter, inert and virtually out of the game. Our antagonists had very wisely abandoned all idea of attacking, and of thereby justifying the existence of, that great Allied army. The Bulgars had, with some assistance from German and Austro - Hungarian troops, secured possession of the mountainous region of the Balkans ; and the Central Powers had thus acquired just that same advantageous strategical and tactical position on the Macedonian Front as they had for a year and a half been enjoying on the Italian borders—the advantageous position of having roped in Nature as a complaisant ally. The Entente had had an uncommonly difficult hand to play in the Near East, but, as things turned out, the Governments concerned had played it about as badly as was feasible.

Except in the matter of equipping the Greek forces at a very much later date, I was not directly concerned in what followed for weary months on the Salonika Front. During the few weeks when I was acting temporarily as Deputy C.I.G.S. in 1917, things happened to be pretty well at a standstill in Macedonia, except that just at that time one British division was transferred from that theatre to Palestine, where there was some prospect of doing something. I remained in touch with the General Staff, however, until the end of the war, and throughout was to a great extent behind the scenes.

Only one valid military excuse can be put forward for imprisoning a great field army for three years in the Salonika area, a plan to which the General Staff was consistently opposed from the outset. It enabled our side to employ some 150,000 Serbian and Greek troops, whom it might have been difficult to turn to good account elsewhere ; at the very end the Greek contingents were, moreover, being substantially increased. In what was to a great extent a war of attrition this was a point of some importance. But that great field army was for all practical purposes immobilized for the whole of the three years. It was immobilized partly by inferior bodies of troops—mainly Bulgarian, whom the German Great General Staff would have found it hard to utilize in other theatres. It was immobilized partly by having before it a wide zone of rugged uplands which were in occupation of the enemy, and which forbade the employment of masses of men. That great field army never at any time pulled its weight, and its presence in Macedonia threw a severe and unwarranted strain upon our naval resources owing to the difficulty of safeguarding its communications against submarines in a water area exceptionally favourable for the operations of such craft.

At the end of the three years that great field army did carry out a remarkably successful offensive, in which the Serbs played a gallant and prominent part. But, without wishing to disparage the fine work performed by the various contingents in that offensive of September 1918—British, French, Italian, Serb and Greek—the fact remains that the Bulgars were defeated not in Macedonia but in Picardy and Artois. Exhausted by years of hostilities—they had been at it since 1912—they knew that the game was up before the offensive ever started, knew that their side had lost the war, knew that there was no hope of succour from Germany. Considering the hopelessness of the situation from the point of view of the Central Powers, it is surprising that the Sofia Executive did not throw up the sponge at a somewhat earlier date.

The Macedonian side-show is a typical example of the kind of side-show which cannot be justified from the broad point of view of military policy. In the next chapter a number of other side-shows which had their place in the Great War will be touched upon. In it the fact will be pointed out that side-shows are sometimes unavoidable, and it will be suggested that most of those on which the British Government embarked between 1914 and the end of the war were justifiable, even when they were not absolutely unavoidable.

CHAPTER IX

OTHER SIDE-SHOWS

Three categories of side-shows—The Jackson Committee—The Admiralty's attitude—The Pacific, Duala, Tanga, Dar-es-Salaam Oceania, the Wireless Stations—Kiao Chao—The Shatt-el-Arab—Egypt—Question whether the Australasian forces ought to have been kept for the East—The East African operations—Our lack of preparation for a campaign in this quarter—Something wrong—My own visit to Tanga and Dar-es-Salaam in 1908—The bad start of the campaign—Question of utilizing South African troops to restore the situation—How this was managed—Reasons why this was a justifiable side-show—Mesopotamia—The War Office ought to have interfered—The question of an advance on Baghdad by General Townshend suddenly referred to the General Staff—Our mistake—The question of Egyptian defence in the latter part of 1915—The Alexandretta project—A later Alexandretta project propounded by the War Cabinet in 1917—Its absurdity—The amateur strategist on the war-path—The Palestine campaign of 1918 carried out almost entirely by troops not required on the Western Front, and therefore a legitimate side-show—The same principle to some extent holds good with regard to the conquest of Mesopotamia—The Downing Street project to substitute Sir W. Robertson for Sir C. Monro, a miss-fire.

" THERE must have been a baker's dozen of them," writes Lord Fisher in his *Memories* in reference to what he calls the " wild-cat expeditions " on which troops were engaged while he was First Sea Lord in 1914–15. There were a baker's dozen of them, and more, if the occupation by Australasian contingents of certain islands in the Indian Archipelago and the Pacific are included. But a correct appreciation of the merits and of the demerits of our numerous side-shows of those and later days is not covered by ejaculatory generalizations. Some of the very greatest of soldiers—Marlborough, Frederick the Great,

Napoleon, and Wellington—all countenanced side-shows that were kept within limits.

The truth about side-shows is that they may be divided up roughly into three categories: (1) The necessary, (2) the excusable, (3) the unjustifiable and mischievous. But there is no sharp dividing-line between the three categories. Of those for which we made ourselves responsible in the Great War, the majority undoubtedly come within the first category. Most of the remainder may, upon the whole, be classed as excusable. Unfortunately the small number which come under the third heading were just those which absorbed the greatest military effort, and which were the only ones that really reckoned as vital factors in influencing the course of the conflict as a whole. Amongst the necessary and un-avoidable side-shows were those which were undertaken, at all events in the first instance, in the interests of sea power. Amongst the side-shows which may be regarded as justifiable, although not unavoidable, may be mentioned the continuation of the Cameroons operations after the taking of Duala, the continuation of the operations in " German East " after the capture of Tanga and Dar-es-Salaam, and the continuation of the operations in " German South-West " after the great wireless station had been dealt with ; in each of these cases the forces and resources of various kinds absorbed were, for various reasons, of no great relative importance, and the conquest of the Boche territories involved was desirable. Two unjustifiable side-shows have already been discussed, the Dardanelles and Salonika ; another that comes within this third category was Mesopotamia subsequent to the securing of the Shatt-el-Arab and the Karun oil-fields, and yet another is represented by the excessive resources which were devoted to Palestine operations during certain periods of the war.

A special interdepartmental committee, an offshoot of the Committee of Imperial Defence, was set up on the outbreak of the war, virtually as an expansion of the

already existing Colonial Defence Committee.   By a stroke
of good fortune, its chairman was Admiral Sir Henry
Jackson, who was attached to the Admiralty for special
service at the time ; the Colonial Office and the India
Office, as well as the Admiralty were represented on it,
and I was the War Office delegate.   It was on the recommendations of this body that the operations against
Togoland, the Cameroons, and " German East " were
initiated, that every encouragement was given to the
projects set on foot by the Australasian Governments
for the conquest of German New Guinea, the Bismarck
Archipelago, Samoa, and other localities in Oceania, and
that similar encouragement was given to the Union
Government of South Africa in respect to its plans for
wresting " German South-West " out of the hands of its
possessors and oppressors.   The Admiralty attached extreme importance to Duala, and considerable importance
to Dar-es-Salaam and Tanga, as also to some of the ports
in Oceania owing to the presence of Von Spee's squadron
of swift cruisers in the Pacific.   They likewise were anxious
that the German wireless stations of great range and
power in Togoland, the Cameroons, " German South-
West," and " German East " should be brought to
nought.

Then there was also Kiao Chao.   The capture of that
enemy naval stronghold in the Far East was regarded as
eminently desirable ; and although the Japanese were
ready and willing to take the thing on alone it seemed
expedient that we should contribute a small contingent
to assist, very much on the same principle as the French
and Italians liked to have small contingents fighting under
the orders of General Allenby during his triumphant
operations in Palestine and Syria.   Our military garrisons
at Tientsin and Hong-Kong could easily find a couple of
battalions, and from our British point of view this contribu-
tion may be set down as coming within the category of an
excusable, if not an unavoidable, side-show.   Apart from
East Africa, none of these minor sets of operations absorbed

more than insignificant military forces, which in most cases were composed largely of Colonial coloured troops who were hardly fitted for fighting on the Western Front at that stage. In almost all of them, except " German East " and Kiao Chao, the object had been achieved within a few weeks of the outbreak of hostilities, and even the bitterest foes of the side-show in the abstract will admit that the end justified the means.

The question of an expedition to the Shatt-el-Arab was first raised by the India Office. Such an undertaking could indeed hardly suggest itself during the first few weeks of the war, seeing that the Ottoman Empire did not become involved until some weeks had elapsed. The object of this Mesopotamia side-show, which ultimately developed into one of the greatest campaigns ever undertaken by a European Power in a region beyond the seas, was, to start with, simply the seizure of the water-way for the length that this is navigable by ocean-going ships together with the port of Basrah, and to secure the safety of the oil-fields of the Karun. The operation incidentally could hardly fail to exercise considerable political effect around the Persian Gulf, which was all to the good, and the project did not call for the employment of a large force to effect the purpose that was in view at the start. Most military authorities would surely class this as a thoroughly justifiable, if perhaps not an absolutely necessary, side-show.

Then, thrusting itself into prominence about the same time as the Shatt-el-Arab affair developed, came the question of Egypt. The Turks would assuredly contrive a stroke at the Khedive's dominions from the side of the Isthmus of Suez sooner or later, the attitude of the tribes in the vast regions to the west of the Nile valley could not but give grounds for some anxiety, and there was a fair chance of effervescence within the Nile Delta itself. Maintaining the security of Egypt was hardly more a side-show than was the provision of garrisons for India ; but the defence of Egypt at a later stage more or less merged into offensive operations directed against Palestine.   The question of giving that defence a somewhat active form by undertaking expeditionary enterprises in the direction of the Gulf of Alexandretta came to be considered quite early in the war, as has already been mentioned in Chapter III.   But during the first six months or so Egypt only in reality absorbed military resources which for various reasons could not appropriately have been utilized elsewhere.   The British regulars were withdrawn from Cairo and Khartum and helped to form divisions for the Western Front, considerable bodies of Native Indian troops were transported to Suez from Bombay and Kurrachee, the East Lancashire Territorial Division was sent out from home, and the newly constituted contingents from the Antipodes secured a temporary resting-place in a region which climatically was particularly well suited for their purpose.   Anxiety as to Egypt was as a matter of fact in great measure allayed in January 1915, owing to the Osmanlis pressing forward to the Suez Canal, sustaining a severe rebuff near its banks at the hands of the defending force, and disappearing eastwards as a beaten and disorganized rabble.

The Palestine operations will be touched upon later ; but there is a subject in connection with the contingents from the Antipodes, referred to above, which, although it has nothing to do with the principle of side-shows in the abstract, may perhaps not inappropriately be discussed here.   Was it right ever to have employed those contingents on the Western Front, as they were employed from an early date in 1916 onwards to the end of the struggle ?   The result of their being so disposed of was that, covering a space of nearly three years, troops from the United Kingdom were perpetually passing eastwards through the Mediterranean while Australasian troops were perpetually passing westwards through the Mediterranean.   Military forces belonging to the one belligerent Empire were, in fact, crossing each other at sea.   This involved an avoidable absorption of ship-tonnage, it

threw an avoidable strain upon the naval forces of the
Entente, and it imposed an avoidable period of inaction
upon the troops concerned. Look upon the Anzacs
simply as counters and upon the Great War as a
Kriegspiel, and such procedure becomes ridiculous.
Whatever there is to be said for and against the Dardanelles, Salonika, Palestine, and Mesopotamia side-
shows, they did undoubtedly absorb military forces in
excess of those which Australia and New Zealand placed
in the field, and they provided active work in eastern
regions far nearer to the Antipodes than was the Western
Front.

This, however, entirely ignores sentiment, and sentiment can never justly nor safely be ignored in military
matters. The Anzacs would have bitterly resented
being relegated to theatres, of secondary importance so
to speak. Their Governments would have protested had
such a thing been even hinted at, and they would have
protested in very forcible terms. No other course than
that actually followed was in reality practicable nor, as
far as I know, ever suggested. As a matter of fact, however, none of the Australasian mounted troops, apart
from some quite minor exceptions, ever did proceed
west of the Aegean. After performing brilliant service
in the Gallipoli Peninsula acting as foot soldiers, the
Anzac Horse spent the last three years of the war in
Egypt, where they seized and made the most of opportunities for gaining distinction under General Allenby
such as would never have been presented to them in
France.

I was a good deal concerned in the operations in East
Africa during the first year and a half of the war, a period
of scanty progress and of regrettable misadventures.
We enjoyed the advantage, when this question came
before Admiral Jackson's committee, of having Lieut.-
Colonel (now Major-General Sir A. R.) Hoskins present,
who at the time was Inspector-General of the King's
African Rifles and was consequently well acquainted

with our own territories in that part of the world. From the outset, Hoskins was disinclined to regard operations in this quarter as a sort of picnic, and the event proved that he was right. It was, however, settled that the whole business should be handed over in the main to India to carry out, and that the commander and staff for the contemplated offensive, as well as the reinforcements needed for the purpose, should come across the Indian Ocean from Bombay.

At a very early stage it became apparent that our information concerning the enemy districts nearest to the frontier between German territory and British East Africa was defective, while information as to the districts on our own side was not all that might be wished, and I gathered from Hoskins at the time (and also later on from Colonel G. Thesiger, Hoskins' predecessor, who brought home his battalion of the Rifle Brigade from India during the winter of 1914–15 and who was killed when commanding a division at Loos in the autumn of 1915) that the prosecution of active intelligence work had received little encouragement from home during their terms of office. That is the worst of a corps like the King's African Rifles being under the Colonial Office instead of under the War Office, although there are adequate reasons for that arrangement ; but I cannot help thinking that if the General Staff had pressed the matter, not much difficulty would have been encountered in altering the Colonial Office's point of view, and that both no doubt were to blame. It may also be remarked incidentally that the Colonial Office probably has no secret service funds at its disposal. Still, be that as it may, there was something amiss.

Here we were, with British soil actually in contact with an extensive province in the hands of a potential enemy and known to be garrisoned by a considerable body of native troops. Everything pointed to the need for extensive reconnaissance work in the borderland districts with a view to possible eventualities. Numbers of active, intelligent, and adventurous young British officers, admirably fitted for acquiring military information, were stationed on our side of the frontier. And yet when the storm broke we were unprepared to meet it. We had plans worked out in the utmost detail for depositing the Expeditionary Force at its concentration points in French territory. Our naval policy was to all intents and purposes framed with a German war as its ultimate goal. The probability of a conflict with the Boches had for some years past virtually governed our military policy. But in East Africa we were in a measure caught napping.

There had been lack of foresight. I had been guilty of this myself, so that I have the less hesitation in referring to it; for I had been at both Tanga and Dar-es-Salaam early in 1908. At the first-named port our ship only spent a few hours, so that any kind of reconnaissance work would have been out of the question. But we lay for four days on end in Dar-es-Salaam harbour, and yet it never occurred to me to examine the place and its immediate surroundings from the point of view of possible attack upon it in the future—this, moreover, after having just given over charge of the strategical section in the War Office. Even allowing for the fact that war with Germany was not looming ahead to the same extent in 1908 as it was from 1909 onwards, there was surely something wrong on that occasion.

The start that was made in East Africa in 1914 can only be described as deplorable. Following a custom which to my mind is more honoured in the breach than in the observance, the mortifying results of the attempted maritime descent upon Tanga which ushered in the hostilities, were for a long time kept concealed from the public. That reverse constituted a grave set-back—a set-back on a small scale perhaps, but as decided a one as we met with during the war. Our troops not only lost heavily in casualties, but they also suffered appreciably in *moral*. For months subsequent to that untoward event we were virtually on the defensive in this theatre of war, although we unquestionably enjoyed the advantage

N

in actual numbers, and although the maritime communications were open to our side and closed to that of the enemy. The enemy enjoyed such initiative as there was. Bodies of hostile troops used to cross the border from time to time and inflict unpleasant pin-pricks upon us. The situation was an eminently unsatisfactory one, but what was to be done ?

That " German East " was just the very place to utilize South African troops in, became apparent at a comparatively early stage of the proceedings. Even before General Botha and his men had completed his conquest of " German South-West," one had already begun to dream dreams of these same forces, or their equivalent, coming to the rescue on the farther side of the Dark Continent, and of their getting our Indian and native African contingents, with their small nucleus of British regulars, out of the scrape that they were in. Being in constant communication with General C. W. Thomson, who was in command of the exiguous body of British soldiers left at the Cape, I was able to gauge the local feeling out there fairly correctly, and became convinced that we should be able to rely on securing a really high-class contingent of improvised units for " German East " out of South Africa, of units composed of tough, self-reliant, experienced fighting men who might not be disposed to undertake service on the Western Front. The special character of the theatre of war in East Africa, the nature of the fighting which its topography imposed on the contending sides, its climate, its prospects for the settler, and its geographical position, were all such as to appeal to the dwellers on the veldt. But when the subject was broached once or twice to Lord K. during the summer of 1915 he would have nothing to do with it. Once bitten twice shy. The War Minister looked on side-shows with no kindly eye. Nor could he be persuaded that this was one which would only be absorbing resources that could hardly be made applicable to other quarters.

Mr. Bonar Law, who was then Colonial Minister, was

very anxious to have the military situation in this part of the world cleared up, and I rather took advantage of Lord K.'s absence in the Near East in November to bring the whole thing to a head. Sir A. Murray quite agreed that South Africa ought to be invited to step in and help. So it came about that the business was practically settled by the time that the Chief came back from the Dardanelles, and although he was by no means enthusiastic, he accepted the situation and he chose Sir H. Smith-Dorrien for the command. Whether this was, or was not, a justifiable side-show is no doubt a matter of opinion. But a very large proportion of the troops who eventually conquered " German East " under Generals Smuts, Hoskins and Van Deventer would scarcely have been available for effective operations in any other theatre, and the demands in respect to artillery, aircraft, and so forth were almost negligible as compared to the resources that were in being even so early as the winter of 1915–16. Perhaps the most powerful arguments that could be brought forward against the offensive campaign that was initiated by General Smuts in German East Africa were its cost and the amount of ship-tonnage that it absorbed. The primary object for which operations in this region were undertaken, the capture of Tanga and Dar-es-Salaam so as to deprive the enemy of their use for naval purposes, had rather dropped out of consideration owing to the seas having been cleared of enemy non-diving craft in the meantime.

The Mesopotamian operations during the first year and a half were conducted entirely by the India Office and India, and, up till after Sir W. Robertson had become C.I.G.S., we had no direct responsibility in connection with them in the War Office. I had a subsection that dealt entirely with Indian matters ; this kept watch, noted the telegrams, reports, and so forth, dealing with what was going on on the Shatt-el-Arab and beyond, and it could at any moment supply me with general information as to the situation. From time to time I used to ask how the operations were progressing, and, without ever going carefully into the matter, was disposed to look somewhat askance at the procedure that was being adopted of continually pressing forward from place to place—like the hill-climber who on reaching one crest ever feels himself drawn on to gain the next—far beyond the zone which had in the first instance been regarded as the objective of the Expeditionary Force. The meteor of conquest appeared to be alluring " D " Force too far. Without examining the position of affairs closely, it was obvious that the farther our troops proceeded up the Tigris the longer became their line of communications, the shorter became that of the Turks, and the greater must inevitably become the contingents put in the field by our side. What had started as a limited-liability and warrantable side-show was somehow imperceptibly developing into a really serious campaign in a remote region.

Looking back upon those months in the light of later experience, the attitude which one felt disposed to assume, the attitude that as this was an India Office business with which the War Office had nothing to do it was their funeral, was a mistaken one. The War Office could not, of course, butt in unceremoniously. But Lord Kitchener was a member of the Government in an exceptionally powerful position in all things connected with the war, and had one represented one's doubts to him, he would certainly have gone into the question and might have taken up a strong line. I, however, have no recollection of ever speaking to him on the subject of Mesopotamia during the period when " D " Force was working right up into Irak, moving first to Amarah, then to El Gharbi, and then on to Kut, thus involving the Empire in a regular offensive campaign on an ambitious scale in the cradle of the world.

Then came that farther advance of General Townshend's from Kut to Azizieh, the project for an advance right up to Baghdad assumed shape at Army Headquarters on the Tigris, in Simla, and at the India Office, and it was then that the General Staff, now with Sir A. Murray in charge, was suddenly called upon to give a considered opinion concerning this ambitious scheme for the information of the War Council. Now it is an interesting fact that just at that very same time we were called upon to give a considered opinion on the subject of the best plan of rendering Egypt secure, and that this necessarily raised the question whether the plan should favour an active form of defence involving an expedition to Alexandretta or thereabouts, or whether it should take a more passive form of holding positions away back near the Suez Canal. The two Memoranda were as a matter of fact printed in the one secret document.

As regards Alexandretta we had no doubts whatever, although, as already mentioned on p. 79, Lord K. and the experts in connection with Egypt favoured operations in that direction. We made up our minds without the slightest difficulty, and pronounced dead against a forward policy of that kind at such a time. But in reference to Baghdad we all of us, I think, felt undecided and in a quandary. Unacquainted with General Townshend's views, assuming that the river transport upon which military operations up-Tigris necessarily hinged was in a reasonably efficient condition, ignorant of the obstacles which forbade a prompt start from Azizieh, we pictured to ourselves a bound forward at a very early date. Actually the advance did not materialize for more than a month, and in the meantime the Turks were gathering reinforcements apace. The city might have been occupied had General Townshend been able to push forward at once; for an army (favoured, it is true, by incomparably more effectual administrative arrangements) did sixteen months later reach the place within seven days of quitting Azizieh, although strongly opposed. But so exiguous an expeditionary force could not have maintained itself in that isolated situation in face of swelling hostile numbers. In falling back to his advanced base its leader would have been faced with nearly double the distance to cover that he compassed so successfully in his retreat from Ctesiphon. The little army would almost certainly have been cornered and compelled for lack of supplies to surrender in some advanced position in Irak five months earlier than, as it turned out, Kut hauled down the flag.

But, be that as it may, we made ourselves to some extent responsible for the disaster which occurred to General Townshend's force, owing to our not taking a decided line on the subject and not obeying the elementary principle that resources must not in war be wasted upon unnecessary subsidiary enterprises. Whether it was or was not feasible to get to Baghdad at the time was a matter of some uncertainty. But that the whole business of all this pouring of troops into Mesopotamia was fundamentally unsound scarcely admitted of dispute. That ought to have determined our attitude on the minor Baghdad point.

Egypt gave rise to little anxiety during the spring and summer of 1915 in consequence of the signal discomfiture which the Turks had suffered on the Canal early in the year ; the arid tract known as the Sinai desert indeed provided a satisfactory defence in itself during the dry months. But as autumn approached, the prospect of Ottoman efforts against the Nile Delta had to be taken into serious consideration, the more so that neither the Dardanelles Committee nor the War Council which took its place could disguise from themselves that the abandonment of the Dardanelles enterprise was at least on the cards, and that this would liberate Osmanli forces for efforts in other directions. There had been a school of thought in Egypt all along that the best defence of that region against Turkish invasion was by undertaking operations on the Syrian or Palestine coast, based on the Gulf of Iskanderun for preference, but possibly based on Beirut or Haifa. As the situation in the Near East grew rapidly worse during September, the War Council began to dream of diversions in new directions, quite apart from the Gallipoli Peninsula and Salonika, and some of them pitched upon the shores of the Gulf of Iskanderun, the strategical importance of which was unquestionable. A force landed in that quarter would give the enemy something to think about, would afford excellent protection to Egypt, and would indirectly assist our troops, which had been gradually penetrating along the Tigris right up into Mesopotamia.

On this project the General Staff was called upon to report, as already mentioned in Chapter IV. and as stated above, and the General Staff rejected the project without hesitation. This was a very different scheme from that which had been regarded with approval in the winter of 1914–15. Then the enemy resources in these environs had been insignificant, the Turkish communications leading thither had still been interrupted by the Taurus Mountains, and there had been no U-boats in the Mediterranean. Now the enemy was fully prepared in this quarter and would be on the look-out for our troops, the tunnels through the Taurus had been completed, and warships and transports could not possibly have lain moored in the roadstead of Alexandretta for fear of submarines. The landing would have had to take place in the inner portion of the Gulf of Iskanderun, Ayas Bay, where there were no facilities, where the surroundings were unhealthy, and where it would be particularly easy for the Turks to put up a stolid resistance. Our view was that for any operation of this kind to be initiated with reasonable safety, a very large body of troops would be necessary, that as far as Egypt was concerned the Nile Delta could be rendered absolutely secure with a much smaller expenditure of force, and that the inevitable result of embarking on a campaign in this new region would be to withdraw yet more of the Entente fighting resources from the main theatre of war in France. It would have been a side-show for which very little could be said and the objections to which seemed to us manifest and overwhelming. The War Council took our advice and dropped the scheme, although Lord Kitchener, who was out in the Aegean, favoured it. Any anxiety that prevailed as to Egypt settled itself shortly afterwards owing to the Gallipoli troops, so skilfully withdrawn from Anzac, Suvla and Helles, all assembling in the Nile Delta, where they were refitted and obtained some rest after their terribly arduous campaign in the Thracian Chersonese. This practically synchronized with the time of my leaving the War Office for the time being and proceeding to Russia.

As will be mentioned in Chapter XIV., one heard more about Alexandretta while out in that country. I, moreover, became indirectly concerned in that same old question again at a considerably later date. For, early in October 1917, the War Cabinet hit upon a great notion. On the close of the Flanders operations a portion of Sir D. Haig's forces were to be switched thither to succour Generals Allenby and Marshall in their respective campaigns, and were to be switched back again so as to be on hand for the opening of active work on the Western Front at the beginning of March 1918—a three months' excursion. This scheme seems to have been evolved quite *au grand sérieux* and not as a joke. At all events, a conference (which I was called in to attend as knowing more about the Dardanelles business from the War Office end than anybody else) assembled in the Chief of the Imperial General Staff's room one Sunday morning— the First Sea Lord and the Deputy First Sea Lord with subordinates, together with General Horne who happened to be over on leave from his First Army, and prominent members of the General Staff—and we gravely debated the idiotic project.

Nobody but a lunatic would, after Gallipoli experiences, undertake serious land operations in the Alexandretta region with less than six divisions. To ship six divisions absorbs a million tons. There were United States troops at this time unable to cross the Atlantic for want of tonnage, and, allowing for disembarkation difficulties on the Syrian coast, two soldiers or animals or vehicles could be transported from America to French or English ports for every one soldier or animal or vehicle that could be shifted from Marseilles or Toulon to the War Cabinet's fresh theatre of operations, given the same amount of shipping. Our Italian allies were in sore straits over coal for munitions and transportation purposes, simply because sufficient tonnage could not be placed at their disposal. Our own food supplies were causing anxiety, and the maintenance of the forces at Salonika afforded constant proof of the insecurity of the Mediterranean as a sea route. But fatuous diversion of shipping represented quite a minor objection to this opera-bouffe proposal. For, allowing for railing troops from the Western Front to the Côte Azure and embarking them, and for the inevitable delays in landing a force of all arms on a beach with improvised piers, the troops at the head of the hunt would already have to be re-embarking in Ayas Bay by the time that those at the tail of the hunt came to be emptied out on the shores of the Gulf of Iskanderun ; otherwise the wanderers would miss the venue on the Western Front.

Had this been suggested by a brand-new Ministry—a Labour Cabinet, say, reviewing the military situation at its very first meeting—nobody could reasonably have complained. People quite new to the game naturally enough overlook practical questions connected with moving troops by land and sea, and do not realize that those questions govern the whole business. Any third-form boy, given a map of Turkey-in-Asia and told of campaigns in Palestine, and Mesopotamia, and Armenia, and of the bulk of enemy resources being found about Constantinople and in Anatolia, who did not instantly perceive how nice it would be to dump an army down at Alexandretta, would, it is earnestly to be hoped, be sent up to have his dormant intelligence awakened by outward applications according to plan. Quite knowledgeable and well-educated people call this sort of thing " strategy," and so in a sense it is—it is strategy in the same sense as the multiplication table is mathematics. If you don't know that two added to two makes four, and divided by two makes one, the integral calculus and functional equations will defeat you ; if it has never occurred to you that by throwing your army, or part of it, across the route that your opponent gets his food and his ammunition and his reinforcements by you will cause him inconvenience, then your name is not likely to be handed down to posterity with those of the Great Captains. But the War Cabinet of October 1917 contained personages of light and leading who had been immersed up to the neck in the conduct of hostilities ever since early in 1915.

The Royal Navy could always be trusted to play the game on these occasions. When you cannot get your own way in the army, you beslaver the local martial Esculapius with soft words and prevail upon him to back you up. " Oh, if the medical authorities pronounce it necessary," thereupon declare the Solons up top who have been sticking their toes in, "it's of course got to be done." Similarly, when the amateur strategist gets out of hand, you appeal to the sailors to save the situation. "Just look at what these owls are after now," you say; "they'll upset the coach before they've done with it. *You* won't be able to do your share in the business, and we——" "Not do our share in the business ? Why not ? Of course we——" "Yes, yes, I know that; but you really must help us. One of those unintelligible masterpieces of yours all about prostitution of sea-power, and periscopes and that sort of poppy-cock with which you always know how to bluff the lubbers." "Well, we'll see what we can do"—and the extinguisher is dexterously and effectually applied. Co-operation between the two great fighting services is the master-key opening every impeditive doorway on the path to victory.

The operations which brought about the occupation of Palestine and Syria constituted a side-show on a very important scale indeed, and they at one period swallowed up contingents of British troops that were somewhat badly needed on the Western Front, just as the Salonika business did. Troops of that character, troops fit to throw against the Hindenburg Line, however, represented quite an insignificant proportion of the forces with which General Allenby achieved his startling triumphs in the year 1918. The urgent need of increasing our strength in France and Flanders during the winter of 1917–18 was fully realized by the General Staff at the War Office, and efforts were made to induce the War Cabinet to consent to withdraw some of the British troops from Palestine. But nothing was done in the matter until after the successful German offensive of March, when the enemy almost drove a wedge through the Allies' front near Amiens. After that the bulk of General Allenby's British infantry were taken from him and rushed off to France, native troops from India which had been created by Sir C. Monro since he had taken up the chief command there in 1916, together with some veteran Indian companies from Mesopotamia, being sent in their place. The brilliant offensive which carried our flag to Damascus and on to Aleppo after utterly defeating the Turks was executed with a soldiery of whom the greater part could be spared from the decisive theatre. The conquering army was composed almost entirely of mounted men for whom there was little scope in France, or of Indian troops. Even had the results been infinitely less satisfactory to the Entente in themselves than they actually were, a side-show run on such lines was a perfectly legitimate undertaking.

The same principle to some extent holds good in respect to the conquest of Mesopotamia by Sir S. Maude and Sir W. Marshall. The troops which won such striking successes in that theatre of war included a considerable proportion of units which would not have been employed on the Western Front in any case. The army was to a large extent a native Indian one, and latterly it included its quota of the freshly organized units which General Monro had created. The fact remains, however, that from April 1916 (when Kut fell) until the end of the war, a considerable force of British white troops was continuously locked up in this remote region, engaged upon what can hardly be called a necessary side-show.

In connection with the remarkably successful efforts made by the Commander-in-Chief in India to expand the local forces during the last two years of the conflict, there is a matter which may be mentioned here. That the victorious campaigns in Palestine and in Mesopotamia in 1917 and 1918 were in no small degree attributable, indirectly, to what General Monro had accomplished by energy and administrative capacity, is well known to all who were behind the scenes, and has been cordially acknowledged by Lord Allenby and Sir W. Marshall. Especially was this the case in Palestine in 1918, when brand-new native Indian regiments took the place of British troops belatedly summoned to the Western Front after our line had been broken at St. Quentin. Nevertheless, a Downing Street intrigue was set on foot about the end of April 1918 to substitute Sir W. Robertson for the commander of the forces in India who had accomplished so much since taking over charge.

Not that there was any desire to remove Sir C. Monro. The object of the shuffle was simply to get Sir W. Robertson out of the country, in view of the manner in which his warnings in connection with strengthening our forces in France had been disregarded and of his having proved to be right. Sir William would no doubt have made an excellent Commander-in-Chief in India ; but if ever there was an example of ill-contrived swapping of horses while crossing a stream, this precious plot would have provided the example had it been carried into execution. There would have been a three months' interregnum while the new chief was on his way out and was picking up the strings after getting out—this in the middle of the final year of the war ! The best-laid plans of politicians, however, gang aft a-gley. Sir C. Monro had stipulated, when reluctantly agreeing to give up command of his army on the Western Front in the autumn of 1916 and to proceed to Bombay, that this Indian appointment was to be a permanent one, and not a temporary one such as all other appointments came to be during the war. He did not feel disposed to fall in with the Downing Street project when this was broached. Is it to be wondered at that military men regard some of the personnel that is found in Government circles with profound suspicion ?

CHAPTER X

THE MUNITIONS QUESTION

WHO reads the platform addresses of political personages, even the most eminent and the most plausible ? Some people evidently do, or such utterances would not fill the columns of our newspapers. If one had ever felt tempted to peruse the reports of these harangues in the piping times of peace, one assuredly had neither the inclination nor yet the leisure to indulge in such practices during the early days of the Great War. To skim off the cream of the morning's news while at breakfast was about as much as a War Office mandarin could manage in the way of reading the daily papers during that super-strenuous time. One morning, however—it must have been the morning of the 22nd of April 1915—I met an assistant with a journal in his hand, as I was making my way along the corridor to my room in the War Office. " Seen this what Squiff says about the shell, general ? " he asked, handing me the paper with his finger on the passage in the Prime Minister's Newcastle speech, denying that there was an ammunition shortage.

The report of that discourse took one flat aback. For weeks past letters from G.H.Q., as also the fervent representations made by visitors over on duty or on leave from the front, had been harping upon this question. Lord Kitchener had informed the House of Lords on the 15th day of March that the supply of war material was " causing him considerable anxiety." There was not the slightest doubt, even allowing for the tendency of men exposed to nerve-racking experiences or placed in positions of anxious responsibility to find fault, that our army in France and Flanders was at a terrible disadvantage as compared to that opposed to it in the matter of artillery ammunition. The state of affairs was perfectly well known, not merely to the personnel of batteries constantly restricted in respect to expenditure, but also to the infantry and to other branches of the service deprived of adequate gun support. Into the controversies and recriminations which have taken place over the subject of how this extraordinary statement came to be made at Newcastle, it is not proposed to enter here. There is at all events no controversy as to whether the statement was true or not, in substance and in fact. It is common knowledge now, and it was indeed fairly common knowledge at the time, that the statement was in the highest degree misleading. It did a great deal of mischief amongst the troops in the war zone, and it caused serious injury to those who were responsible for the provision of munitions in this country.

A pronouncement of that kind, published as it was in all the newspapers, was bound to arouse comment not merely at home, but also amongst officers and men confronting the enemy between Dixmude and the La Bassée Canal. These latter, who were only too well aware of the realities of the case, resented such a mis-statement of facts, and they were also inclined to jump to the conclusion, not altogether unnaturally, that the serious ammunition shortage, the crying need for additional heavy ordnance, and so forth, were being deliberately ignored by those responsible for supply at home. The inferiority of our side in the field in respect to certain forms of munitions as compared to the enemy, came to be attributed to indifference and to mismanagement on the part of the Master-General of the Ordnance's department and of Lord Kitchener. Even the majority of artillery officers had not the slightest conception of what an expansion of output of munitions on a huge scale involved. Still less were staff officers in general and officers of other branches of the service in a position to interpret the situation correctly. They did not realize that before you can bring about any substantial increase of production in respect to shell, or fuses, or rifles, or machine-guns, or howitzers, you have to provide the machinery with which the particular form of war material is to be manufactured, and that you probably have to fashion some extensive structure to house that machinery in. It takes months before any tangible result can be obtained, the number of months to elapse varying according to the nature of the goods.

Dwellers in great cities will often note what happens when some ancient building has been demolished by the house-breaker. The site is concealed by an opaque hoarding. For months, even sometimes for years, nothing seems to follow. The passer-by who happens to get an opportunity of peeping in when some gate is opened to let out a cart full of debris, only sees a vast crater at the bottom of which men, like ants, are scurrying about with barrows or are delving in the earth. All the time that the ground is being cleared and that the foundations are being laid, those out in the street know nothing of what is going on, and they wonder why some effort is not made to utilize the vacant space for building purposes. Then one day, quite unexpectedly, scaffolding begins to rear its head. A few weeks later bricklayers and their work begin to show above the hoarding ; and from that moment things at last are obviously on the move. The edifice grows from day to day. Within quite a short space of time workmen are already putting on the roof. Then down comes the scaffolding, windows are put in, final touches are given to the interior, and, within what seems to be no time at all from the day when the scaffolding first was seen, the building is ready for occupation. So it is with the manufacture of munitions—experience in the United States in connection with output for us and also in connection with output for Russia, was exactly the same as in the United Kingdom in this respect. An interminable time seems to elapse before the output begins ; but once it has fairly started it grows by leaps and bounds.

At the time of the Newcastle oration, and for some months subsequently, the work of expansion on a colossal scale which the Master-General of the Ordnance had undertaken was still, speaking generally, rather on the footing of the building of which the foundations are only beginning to be laid even if the excavations have been completed and the debris has been cleared away. There was as yet comparatively little to show. The results did not begin to make themselves apparent until a date when the Ministry of Munitions had already come into being some time. That Department of State gained the benefit. Its Chief took the credit for work in connection with which it had for all practical purposes no responsibility beyond that of issuing what predecessors had arranged for. The full product of the contracts which the Master-General of the Ordnance had placed, of the development he had given to existing Government establishments, and of the

O

setting up of entirely new ones by him, with Lord
Kitchener ever using his driving power and his fertility
of resource in support, only materialized in the winter of
1915–16, at a stage when the Ministry of Munitions had
been already full six months in existence.

If the army in general failed to understand the position,
it is hardly to be wondered at that Parliament and the less
well-informed section of the Press should not understand
the position, and that the public should have been
deceived. Very shortly after the Newcastle speech, and
no doubt largely in consequence of it, the Northcliffe Press
stunt of May 1915 on the subject of shell shortage was
initiated. Up to a certain point that stunt was not only
fully justified, but was actually advantageous to the
country. It made the nation acquainted with the fact
that our troops were suffering severely from insufficiency
of munitions. It stirred the community up, and that in
itself was an excellent thing. But it succeeded somehow
at the same time in conveying the impression that this
condition of affairs was due to neglect, and in consequence
it misled public opinion and did grave injustice. We
must assume that, owing to fundamental ignorance of the
problems involved, to a neglect to keep touch with
industrial conditions, and to lack of acquaintance with
the technicalities of munitions manufacture, these newspapers (which usually contrive to be extremely well
informed, thanks to the great financial resources at their
back) were totally unaware that a sudden expansion of
output on a great scale was an impossibility; to suggest
that this aspect of the problem was deliberately suppressed
would be highly improper. The Northcliffe Press had
also maybe failed to become acquainted with the great
increase that had taken place in the forces at the front,
as compared to the strength of the original Expeditionary
Force which had provided the basis of calculation for
munitions in pre-war days, an increase for which there
was no counterpart in the armies of our Allies or of our
enemies. Or the effect that this must have in accent-

uating munitions shortage may have been overlooked, obvious as it was.   Be that as it may, the country readily accepted the story as it stood, and was in consequence grievously misinformed as to the merits of the question. The real truth has only leaked out since the cessation of hostilities, and it is not generally known now.[1]

After the Government had decided to create a Munitions Ministry with Mr. Lloyd George at its head, one of the first incidents that occurred was an unsavoury one. In the course of the discussions in the House of Commons over the Bill setting up this new Department of State, Sir H. Dalziel, a newspaper proprietor and a politician of long standing, delivered on the 1st of July a violent diatribe directed against Sir S. von Donop, the Master-General of the Ordnance.   The honourable member no doubt quite honestly believed that the lack of munitions was due to neglect on the part of the War Office since the beginning of the war.   It is clear that he was totally unqualified to express an opinion on the subject, and that he was ignorant of the manufacturing aspects of the problem.   He had heard stories of mistakes made here and there, such as was inevitable at a time of tremendous stress.   He probably had not the slightest conception that the primary cause of the shell shortage was the neglect of the Government of pre-war days (which had recognized his party services by conferring on him the dignity of a Privy-Councillorship) to give support to the establishments for manufacturing armaments that existed in the

---

[1] So late as the 21st of April 1920 *The Times* included the following passage in a leading article: " Every gunner officer on the Western Front during the winter of 1914–15 knows that there was a grave and calamitous deficiency of shells, and that no satisfactory attempt was made to rectify it until the matter was exposed in *The Times*." Dragging in the " gunner officer " at the front (who could not possibly tell what steps were being taken to rectify the deficiency) does not alter the fact that this passage amounts to an accusation that no satisfactory attempt was made to rectify the deficiency until after the Northcliffe Press stunt. *The Times* may have been so ill-informed as to the actual facts in 1915 as to suppose that this was true. *The Times* cannot have been so ill-informed as to the actual facts in 1920 as to suppose that it was true.

country. It is not with his performance on this occasion that one feels a disposition to quarrel, but with that of the newly created Minister of Munitions.

Mr. Lloyd George could not plead ignorance of the facts. He had been installed for a month or so. He must have known that it had been totally impossible to produce, within ten months of the outbreak of the war, the munitions that were required for an army in the field three or four times greater than had ever been thought of prior to mobilization.[1] He had actually given some pertinent information with regard to manufacturing difficulties when he was introducing the bill, which clearly demonstrated that he had grasped the general principles governing the problem of munitions output. But what was his attitude? Instead of following the honourable and chivalrous course, the course sanctioned by long-established precedent and practice on the part of Ministers of the Crown, of protecting, or trying to protect, the public servant who had been assailed, he contented himself with pointing out that the public servant ought to be given an opportunity of stating his side of the question—which was manifestly impossible in time of war—and that the onslaught was unexpected! There is not a man in the United Kingdom better able to protect himself, or anybody else, in speech and in argument in face of sudden attack than Mr. Lloyd George. Had he been willing to do so he could have disposed of Sir H. Dalziel, who in reality had no case, with the utmost ease.

But that line apparently did not suit the book of the Minister of Munitions. He must have been well aware that a great improvement in output was already beginning to take place, and that, thanks entirely to the labours of the Ordnance Department of the War Office and of Lord Kitchener, the output would within a few months reach huge figures. If it were represented to the House, and

---

[1] On the 1st July we had 23 divisions (exclusive of Indian divisions) in the field, and one on the water. The "Expeditionary Force" consisted of six divisions, but a vague sort of organization for a seventh had also existed on paper.

through the House to the country, that this question of munitions had been grossly neglected up to the time that he took charge, and if it became apparent subsequently that from the hour of his becoming Munitions Minister a rapid improvement set in, then the thanks of the nation would go out to him and he would be canonized. This is the only explanation that I can find for a most discreditable incident. For he made no attempt to meet the attack, and he contrived to convey the impression by his remarks that the attack was fully justified. I have, moreover, good reason for believing that on that day there was present on the Treasury bench a representative of the War Office, not a Cabinet Minister, who was ready and willing to defend the Master-General of the Ordnance and who was acquainted with the facts, but that the Minister of Munitions, being in charge of the House, refused to sanction his speaking. Happily such occurrences are rare in the public life of this country.

That reply of Mr. Lloyd George's on the 1st of July 1915—anybody can look it up in Hansard—left an uncommonly nasty taste in the mouth. The taste was made none the less nasty by his unblushing assumption on later occasions of the credit for the improvement in munitions output that took place from the summer of 1915 onwards. In my own case, although I was nowise concerned with munitions output then, neither pleasant association with Mr. Lloyd George at later dates in connection with various war problems, nor yet the admiration for the grit and courage displayed by him during the last three years of the great contest which is felt by us all, could wholly remove that nasty taste.

Much misapprehension—a misapprehension fostered by reckless and ignorant assertions made on the subject in Parliament and in the Press—exists in regard to the state of preparedness of our army for war in the matter of armament. Rightly or wrongly—most people probably now think wrongly—H.M. Government of pre-war days merely contemplated placing in the field for offensive purposes a force of six, or at the outside, seven divisions, with their complement of mounted troops. Leaving the Germans out of consideration, our Expeditionary Force of six divisions was upon the whole as well equipped in respect to armament (apart from ammunition reserves) as any one of the armies that were placed in the field in August 1914. It only failed in respect to two items, heavy ordnance and high-explosive shell for the field-guns, and in respect to field-howitzers and heavy field-guns (the 60-pounders) it was better off than any, including the German forces.

It will perhaps be urged that we were deplorably badly-off for machine-guns, and so in a sense we were. But what were the facts? The Expeditionary Force was better fitted out with this class of weapon than any one of the embattled armies at the outset of the war, with the exception of the German. Ex-Kaiser William's hosts enjoyed a tremendous advantage in respect to machine-guns, but they enjoyed that advantage to an even greater extent over the French and Russian legions than over ours. No action on the part of the German Great General Staff before the conflict reflects greater credit upon their prescience, than does their recognition in the time of peace of the great part that the mitrailleuse was capable of playing in contemporary warfare. The quantities of these weapons with which our principal antagonist took the field was a complete surprise to all; these were far in excess of the " establishment " that had been acknowledged and which was the same as our own. As a matter of fact we were better off for them, relatively, than the French, or Austro-Hungarians, or Russians. To say that the question of machine-guns had been neglected by us before the war either from the point of view of tactics or of supply, is almost as unfair as it would be to allege that the question of Tanks had been neglected by the Germans before the Battle of the Somme. In the course of the debate in the House over the Munitions Bill in the early summer of 1915, Sir F. Cawley stated that we were short of machine-guns at the beginning of the war, and that none had been provided ; the first charge was made under a misapprehension, and the second charge was contrary to the fact because a number of entirely new units had been fitted out with the weapons. Mr. Lloyd George's statement, made a week before, that it takes eight or nine months to turn out a machine-gun from the time that the requisite new machinery is ordered, was ignored.

This brings us to the question of heavy ordnance and of high-explosive ammunition for field-guns, and in this connection it is necessary to refer to the violent attacks made upon the War Office in respect to the supply of munitions, which find place in Lord French's "*1914*." The Field-Marshal has not minced matters in his references to this subject. He says of Mr. Lloyd George's work that it " was done in the face of a dead weight of senseless but powerful opposition, all of which he had to undermine and overcome." He speaks of the " apathy of a Government which had brought the Empire to the brink of disaster," although his attitude towards the head of that Government hardly betrays this. He devotes his last chapter to " making known some of the efforts " that he " made to awaken both the Government and the public from the apathy which meant certain defeat." His book appeared in the summer of 1919, three and a half years after he had returned from France, three and a half years which had given him ample time to examine at home into the justice of views which he had formed during critical months when confronting the enemy. His attitude relieves one of many scruples that might have otherwise been entertained when discussing the statement which he has made.

"*1914*," possibly unintentionally, leaves it to be inferred in respect to heavy howitzers and similar ordnance, that the question of supplying artillery of that type was first raised by Lord French himself during the Battle of the Aisne. For the absence of any such pieces from the Expeditionary Force when it started, no one, .in my opinion, was more responsible than the Field-Marshal. Plenty of gunner officers were advocates of the employment of such ordnance in the field, although none probably fully realized the importance of the matter ; but what evidence is there of encouragement from the Inspector-General of the Forces of 1907–12 and C.I.G.S. of 1912–14, who had been controlling the manœuvres of the regular army for the half-dozen years preceding August 1914 ? The question was taken up within the War Office three or four weeks before the commencement of the Battle of the Aisne—as soon, in fact, as the effect of the German heavy howitzers against Liége and Namur came to be realized. I spoke to Sir C. Douglas on the subject myself—I believe before the retreat from Mons began. A Committee was set up, to which I contributed a member from amongst the gunners in my branch. The immediate construction of a very large—although not nearly large enough—number of 8-inch, 9·2-inch and 12-inch howitzers was recommended by this body. Lord Kitchener approved its recommendations on the spot, and the Master-General of the Ordnance started work. All this, I believe, took place before Sir J. French raised the question at all. But past neglect could not be overcome at a moment's notice. Experiments had to be carried out, and designs had to be approved. To construct a big howitzer with its mounting takes time even after you have the machinery available, and in 1914 the machinery had to be got together in the first instance. How the ex-First Member of the Army Council comes to be unaware of the extent to which the factor of time enters into the construction of armament, I do not pretend to understand.

To a retired officer of artillery who had kept himself acquainted with military progress, it did seem strange that after the Balkan War of 1912–13, which had clearly demonstrated the value of high-explosive ammunition with field-guns, the War Office should continue to depend entirely upon shrapnel for our 18-pounders, instead of following the example of all other European countries that spent any considerable sums on their armies. No very intimate acquaintance with technical details was needed to realize that there were difficulties in the way, and that high-explosive is awkward stuff to deal with— a gun of my own 5-inch battery in South Africa was, shortly after I had left the unit to take up other work, blown to pieces by a lyddite shell detonating in the bore, with dire results to the detachment. To secure detonation is more difficult in a small, than in a big shell; but other countries had managed to solve the problem in the case of their field-guns somehow.

On joining at the War Office on mobilization, and before any fighting had taken place, I asked about the matter, but was not wholly convinced that there was adequate excuse for our taking the field without what our antagonists and our Allies alike regarded as a requisite. Ever since I joined the Army in 1878—and before—there had been a vein of conservatism running through the upper ranks of the Royal Artillery. (When my battery proceeded from India to Natal to take part in the first Boer War in 1881, we actually had to change our Armstrong breech-loading field-guns for muzzle-loaders on the way, because breech-loaders had been abandoned at home and there was no ammunition for them.) Of late years a progressive school had come into being—technically described as "Young Turks"—who had tried hard to secure the introduction of four-gun batteries and other up-to-date reforms, but without having it all their own way by any means. Whether the Young Turks favoured high-explosive or not, I do not know; but its absence somehow did rather smack of the reactionary, and, with the exception of one of its members, the personnel of the Expeditionary Force appeared to have some grounds for complaint at its field-batteries having none of this form of ammunition. The one exception was, in my opinion, its commander-in-chief.

Lord French's account of his achievements in this matter is artless to a degree. He informs his readers that he was always an advocate for the supply of high-explosive shell to our horse and field artillery, but that he got very little support ; that such support as he got was lukewarm in the extreme, and, finally, we are told that the " Ordnance Board was not in favour of it." Here we have the Chief of the Imperial General Staff and First Military Member of the Army Council advocating the adoption in our army of what practically all other armies had already adopted or were adopting, the adoption of a form of munitions the value of which had been conclusively demonstrated in encounters of which the General Staff must have had full cognizance, and he is turned down by the " Ordnance Board " ! If this represents the Field-Marshal's conception of the position and the duties of the General Staff and its head, then it is not surprising that, under another chief, Tanks were dismissed with ignominy by a technical branch of the War Office in January 1915 without the General Staff ever having been consulted. The pre-war C.I.G.S. was in a dominating position amongst the Military Members of the Army Council in virtue of his high rank and his distinguished antecedents. He was very much more than a *primus inter pares.* He was a field-marshal while the Master-General of the Ordnance was a colonel with temporary rank of major-general. Surely, if he had pressed this matter before the Army Council, he would have received support ? I feel equally sure that, supposing the Army Council had refused to listen to his urgings, he would have received satisfaction on representing the matter to the Committee of Imperial Defence.

As a matter of fact, it was only after more than one representation made by General von Donop that G.H.Q. agreed to take some high - explosive ammunition, and so it was introduced—in small quantities —very soon after fighting began, and when the urgent need of it had become apparent. But the output was necessarily very restricted for a long time, and no amount of talk and of bounce, such as the Minister of Munitions was wont to indulge in from the summer of 1915 onwards for several months, would have increased it. Here was a case of an entirely new article, for the provision of which no steps had been taken before the war. There happened to be special technical difficulties in the way of producing the article, *e.g.* the hardness of the steel necessary for this type of shell, and devising a safe and effective fuse. There is, moreover, one matter in connection with this question of high-explosive for our 18-pounders which should be mentioned, but to which no reference finds a place in " *1914.*"

Some months after this ammunition first came to be used in the field it began to give serious trouble. Something was wrong. The shell took to bursting in the bore of the gun and to bulging, or wholly destroying, the piece, although these disasters fortunately did not generally involve loss of life. Between August and October 1915, no less than sixty-four of our 18-pounders were thus rendered unserviceable—very nearly double the number lost during the retreat from Mons, and considerably more than the complement of one of our divisions. We could not comfortably afford this drain upon our supply of field-guns at a time when New Army divisions were still in some cases gun-less, and when the Territorial division were still armed with the virtually obsolete 15-pounder. Accidents of this character, moreover, have a bad effect upon the personnel of batteries, for the soldier does not like his weapon, be it a rifle, or a hand-grenade, or a sabre that crumples up, to play tricks on him. The difficulty was not got over until elaborate experiments, immediately set on foot by the War Office (which still dealt with design and investigation, although actual manufacture was by this time in the hands of the Ministry of Munitions), had been carried out. But before the end of the year it had been established that the failures were due to faults in manufacture, and from that time forward these *contretemps* became extremely rare in the case of the 18-pounder.

The question caused acute anxiety at G.H.Q. and in the War Office for some weeks ; the French had had a very similar experience, but on an even worse scale. The difficulty arose just after the Ministry of Munitions became responsible for manufacture, and I do not suggest that the destruction of the guns was the fault of that department, for the ammunition used in the field during that period and for many months later was ammunition ordered by the Master-General of the Ordnance. But similar trouble arose later in the case of the field howitzer ; there were no less than 25 of these damaged between April and June 1916, nearly a year after the Munitions Ministry had been set up.

It should be mentioned that some other statements regarding munitions which appear in "*1914*" are inaccurate. In discussing Lord Kitchener's memorandum written at the beginning of January 1915, which intimated that H.M. Government vetoed the Belgian coast project, Lord French declares that two or three months later, viz. in March and April, "large train-loads of ammunition—heavy, medium, and light—passed by the rear of the army in France *en route* for Marseilles for shipment to the Dardanelles." The Admiralty may possibly have sent some ammunition by that route at that time, but it is extremely unlikely. As for munitions for Sir I. Hamilton's troops, the Dardanelles force did not land till the end of April, and its war material was sent by long sea from the United Kingdom ; very little would have been gained, even in time, by adopting the route across France. No great quantities of ammunition were sent from the United Kingdom across country at any juncture· to the Gallipoli Peninsula, but G.H.Q. in France was once called upon to sacrifice some of its reserve, and Lord French makes especial reference to this incident.

He says that on the 9th of May—the date on which he launched his political intrigue—he was directed by the Secretary of State for War to despatch 20 per cent of his reserve supply of ammunition to the Dardanelles.

Now, what are the facts ?   Sir I. Hamilton had urgently demanded ammunition for a contemplated offensive.   A vessel that was loading up at Marseilles would reach the Aegean in time.   To pass the consignment through from the United Kingdom (where a large supply had just come to hand from America) would mean missing the ship. G.H.Q. were therefore instructed to forward 20,000 field-gun rounds and 2000 field-howitzer rounds to the Mediterranean port, and were at the same time assured that the rounds would straightway, over and above the normal nightly allowance sent across the Channel, be made good from home.   Sent off by G.H.Q. under protest, the field-gun rounds were replaced *within twenty-four hours* and the others within four days, but of the engagement entered into, and kept, by the War Office, " *1914* " says not one word.   Lord French was evidently completely misinformed on this matter.

It should be added that the amount of heavy artillery included in the Dardanelles Expeditionary Force was negligible, and that the amount of medium artillery was relatively very small.   Large train-loads of ammunition for such pieces were never required, nor sent.   Inaccurate statements of this kind tend to discredit much of Lord French's severe criticism of Lord Kitchener and the department of the Master-General of the Ordnance, for which there is small justification in any case.

One point made in the " Ammunition " chapter in " *1914* " deserves a word of comment.   Lord French mentions that the supply of shell received at the front in May proved to be less than half of the War Office estimate. That kind of thing went on after supply had been transferred from the War Office to the Ministry of Munitions. I had something to say to munitions at a subsequent period of the war, as will be touched upon later, and used to see the returns and estimates.   The Munitions Ministry was invariably behind its estimates (although seldom, if ever, to the extent of over 50 per cent) right up to the end.   There you have our old friend, the Man of Business, with his intolerable swank.   Some old-established private factories, as well as some new factories set up during the war, were in the habit of promising more than they could possibly perform.   Certain of them were, indeed, ready to promise almost anything.   Their behaviour, I happen to know, caused some of our Allies who placed contracts with them and were let in, extreme annoyance.   The names of one or two of them possibly stink in the nostrils of certain foreign countries to this day, although that sort of thing may also be common abroad.   Those in authority came to realize in the later stages of the war how little reliance could be placed on promises, and they became sceptical.   The Ministry of Munitions, one can well imagine, discounted the estimates that they got from their manufacturing establishments.   The War Office certainly discounted the estimates that it got from the Ministry of Munitions.   Commanders-in-chief in the field consequently no longer miscalculated what they might expect, to the same extent as Sir J. French did in May 1915.

I only became directly associated with armament questions in the summer of 1916, and then came for the first time into contact with the Ministry of Munitions. Such questions are matters of opinion, but it always seemed to me that this Department of State would have done better had it stuck to its proper job—that of providing what the Army and the Air Service required. The capture of design and inspection by the Ministry may have been unavoidable, seeing that this new organization was improvised actually during the course of a great war and under conditions of emergency ; but the principle is radically wrong.   It is for the department which wants a thing to say what it wants and to see that it gets it.   As a matter of fact, the Munitions Ministry occasionally went even farther, and actually allocated goods required by the Army to other purposes.   When a well-known and popular politician, after spending some three years or so at the front with credit to himself, took up a dignified appointment in Armament Buildings, the first thing that he did was to promise a trifle of 400 tanks to the French without any reference to the military authorities at all. Still, who would blame him ? His action, when all is said and done, was merely typical of that " every man for himself, and the devil take the hindmost " attitude assumed by latter-day neoteric Government institutions. But even the most phlegmatic member of the community will feel upset when the trousers which he has ordered are consigned by his tailor to somebody else, and on this occasion the War Office did gird up its loins and remonstrate in forcible terms.

With regard to the War Office and munitions, it only remains to be said again in conclusion that the country was never told the truth about this subject until some months after the armistice, when the nation had ceased to care. Never was it told till then, nor were the forces which had been fighting in the field told, that the great increase in the output of guns, howitzers, machine-guns, and ammunition, which took place from the autumn of 1915 onwards up to just before the Battle of the Somme, was the achievement, not of the Ministry of Munitions but of the War Office. The Munitions Ministry in due course did splendid work. Chancellor of the Exchequer become lord-paramount of a great spending Department of State, its chief was on velvet. " Copper " turned footpad, he knew the ropes, he could flout the Treasury— and he did. But it is a pity that unwarrantable claims should have been put forward on behalf of the department in not irresponsible quarters at a time when they could not be denied, claims which have tended to bring the department as a whole into undeserved disrepute amongst those who know the facts.

CHAPTER XI

COUNCILS, COMMITTEES, AND CABINETS

The responsibilities of experts at War Councils—The Rt. Hon. A. Fisher's views—Discussion as to whether these meet the case—Under the War Cabinet system, the question does not arise—The Committee of Imperial Defence merged in the War Council early in the conflict—The Dardanelles Committee—Finding a formùla —Mr. Churchill backs up Sir I. Hamilton—The spirit of compromise—The Cabinet carrying on *pari passu* with the Dardanelles Committee—Personal experiences with the Cabinet—The War Council which succeeded the Dardanelles Committee—An illustration of the value of the War Cabinet system—Some of its inconveniences—Ministers—Mr. Henderson—Sir E. Carson—Mr. Bonar Law—The question of resignation of individuals—Lord Curzon—Mr. Churchill—Mr. Lloyd George.

BEFORE proceeding to refer to a few personal experiences in connection with the Ministerial pow-wows at which the conduct of the war was decided, there is one matter of some public importance to which a reference will not be out of place. That matter is the question of responsibility imposed upon experts at gatherings of this kind. Are they to wait until they are spoken to, no matter what folly is on the tapis, or are they to intervene without invitation when things become serious ? My own experience is that on these occasions Ministers have such a lot to say that the expert is likely to be overlooked in the babel unless he flings himself into the fray.

The point is suggested by the " Conclusions " in the " First Report " of the Dardanelles Commission. The Commissioners gave it as their opinion that at the time of the initiation of the venture against the Straits, "the Naval Advisers should have expressed their views in

Council, whether asked or not, if they considered that the project which the Council was about to adopt was impracticable from a naval point of view." The Commissioners also gave the decision on this point in other words, but to the same effect, in another paragraph. Mr. Fisher, who represented the Commonwealth of Australia on the Commission, while subscribing to the Report in general, emphatically demurred to the view taken by his brother Commissioners on this point, and Sir T. Mackenzie, who represented New Zealand, agreed with Mr. Fisher although he did not express himself quite so forcibly on the subject. Mr. Fisher wrote : " I dissent in the strongest terms from any suggestion that the departmental advisers of a Minister in his company at a Council meeting should express any views at all other than to the Minister and through him, unless specifically invited to do so. I am of opinion it would seal the fate of responsible government if servants of the State were to share the responsibility of Ministers to Parliament, and to the people on matters of public policy." Which view is the right one, that of the seven Commissioners representing the United Kingdom, or that of the two Commissioners representing the young nations afar off ?

The answer to the question can perhaps best be put in the form of another. Does the country exist for the Government, or does the Government exist for the country ? Now, if the country merely exists for the Government, then Mr. Fisher's contention is unanswerable. Whether it receives the opinion of the expert or not, the Government is responsible. For a Minister to have an expert, within his own Department of State and therefore his subordinate, blurting out views contrary to his own is likely to be a sore trial to that Minister's dignity, and this is not altered by the fact that the expert is likely to be infinitely better qualified to express opinions on the subject than he is. Supposing that the War Council, or the Cabinet, or whatever the body happens to be, ignores

P

or is unaware of the opinion of the experts, and that it lands the country in some hideous mess in consequence, it can always be called to account for the lapse. The doctrine of responsibility which is regarded as of such paramount importance will be fully upheld—and what more do you want? Gibbets can be erected, the Ministers who have got the country into the mess can be hanged in a row, and a fat lot of good that will do towards getting the country out of the mess.

But if, on the contrary, the Government merely exists for the country, then in times of emergency it is the bounden duty of everybody, and particularly is it the duty of those who are really competent to do so, to help the Government and to keep it out of trouble if they can. One feels cold inside conjuring up the spectacle of a pack of experts who have been called in to be present at a meeting of the War Council or the Cabinet, sitting there mute and inarticulate like cataleptics while the members of the Government taking part in the colloquy embark on some course that is fraught with danger to the State. *Salus populi suprema lex.* Surely the security of the commonwealth is of infinitely greater moment than any doctrine of responsibility of Ministers, mortals who are here to-day and gone to-morrow. Indeed—one says it with all respect for a distinguished representative of one of the great British dominions overseas—it looks as though Mr. Fisher did not quite realize the position of the expert, and assumed that if the expert gave his advice when asked it made him responsible to the country. The expert is present, not in an executive, but in a consultative capacity. He decides nothing. The Ministers present decide, following his advice, ignoring his advice, failing to ask for his advice, or mistakenly imagining that the expert concurs with them as he keeps silence, according to the circumstances of the case. Naturally, the expert should try to induce the head of his department to listen to his views on the subject before the subject ever comes before the Cabinet or the War Council. But if the Minister takes a contrary view, if the matter is one of importance and if the Minister at the meeting fails to acquaint his colleagues that he is at variance with the expert, or again if the question crops up unexpectedly and the expert has had no opportunity of expressing an opinion, then the duty of the expert to the country comes first and he should say his say. It may be suggested that he ought to resign. Perhaps he ought to—afterwards. But the matter of vital importance is not whether he resigns, but whether he warns the Government of the danger. The country is the first consideration, not the Government nor yet the expert.

One great advantage of the War Cabinet system introduced by Mr. Lloyd George was that there was none of this sort of flapdoodle. At a War Cabinet meeting the expert never hesitated to express his opinion, whether he was asked for it or not. The work that I was doing in the later stages of the war did not involve me in problems of major importance, but when summoned to a War Cabinet meeting I never boggled over giving my views as to what concerned my own job. I have heard Sir W. Robertson, when he thought it necessary to do so, giving his opinion similarly concerning questions of great moment, and nobody dreamt of objecting to the intervention.

The Director of Military Intelligence was, more or less *ex officio*, a member of the Committee of Imperial Defence in pre-war days, and consequently I attended one meeting of this body shortly after mobilization. There was a huge gathering—the thing was a regular duma—and a prolonged discussion, which as far as I could make out led nowhere and which in any case dealt with matters that nowise concerned me, took place. Those were busy times, and, seeing that Lord Kitchener and Sir C. Douglas attended these meetings as a matter of course, I asked to be excused thenceforward. The Committee of Imperial Defence was obviously not a suitable assemblage to treat of the conduct of the war, seeing that it was only invested with consultative and not with executive functions, and that it bore on its books individuals such as Mr. Balfour and Lord Esher, who were not members of the Government, nor yet officials. It therefore at a comparatively early date gave place to the War Council, which captured its secretariat (a priceless asset), and which later on became transformed into the Dardanelles Committee. The Government did not, however, wholly lose the benefit of Mr. Balfour's experience and counsel. One day—it must have been in December—there was an informal discussion at the War Office in Lord Kitchener's room, he being away in France at the time, in which General Wolfe-Murray and I took part, and besides Mr. Lloyd George, Mr. Churchill and Sir E. Grey—I do not think that Mr. Asquith was there—Mr. Balfour was present.

Up till the early days of May, I attended no War Councils. Very soon after that, the Coalition Government was formed, and thereupon the War Council, which had been quite big enough goodness knows, developed into the Dardanelles Committee of twelve members, of whom, excluding Lord Kitchener, six were members of the former Liberal Government, and five were Unionists. Sir E. Carson only came in in August, making the number of representatives from the two factions equal and raising the total to the lucky number of thirteen. What object was supposed to be fulfilled by making the War Council such a bloated institution it is hard to say. Almost the only members of the Cabinet who counted and who were not included on its roll were Mr. Chamberlain and Mr. Long. Be that as it may, the result was virtually to constitute the Dardanelles Committee the Cabinet for general purposes of the war, and to lead to its dealing with many matters quite distinct from the prosecution of the campaign for the Straits. I have a vivid recollection of one meeting, which probably took place late in June (Lord Kitchener was not present), and at which the attitude to be assumed by us with reference to Bulgaria and Greece, particularly Bulgaria, was discussed. Sir

E. Grey wanted a " formula " devised to indicate to the Sofia Government what that attitude was ; as neither he nor anybody else knew what the attitude was, it was not easy to devise the formula. Formula is an odious word in any case, recalling, as it does, algebraical horrors of a forgotten past ; but everybody present wrote out formulae, and dialecticians had the time of their lives. Mr. Balfour's version was eventually chosen as the most felicitous. But the worst of it was that this masterpiece of appropriate phrase-mongering did not bring in the Bulgars on our side. The triumphant campaign of the Central Powers on the Eastern Front somehow proved a more potent factor in deciding Tsar Ferdinand as to what course to pursue, than a whole libraryful of formulae could ever have effected.

At another meeting, at which Lord Kitchener likewise was not present, a marked and disagreeable tendency to criticize Sir I. Hamilton for his ill-success made itself apparent. I was the only representative of the army present, and it was manifestly impossible for an officer miles junior to Sir Ian to butt into a discussion of that kind. But Mr. Churchill spoke up manfully and with excellent effect. The gist of his observations amounted to this : If you commit a military commander to the undertaking of an awkward enterprise and then refuse him the support that he requires, you have no business to abuse him behind his back if he fails. That seemed to me to fit the situation like a glove ; it did not leave much more to be said on the point, and no more was said, thanks to the First Lord's timely remonstrance.

There was any amount of chatter at these musters ; but on the other hand one seldom seemed to find oneself much forrarder. That is the worst of getting together a swarm of thinkers who are furnished with the gift of the gab and are brimming over with brains. Nothing happens. If a decision was by any chance arrived at, it was of a non-commital nature. The spirit of compromise asserted itself and the Committee adopted a middle course, a course which no doubt fits in well with many of the problems with which governments in ordinary times have to wrestle, but which does not constitute a good way of conducting war.

The full Cabinet of twenty-three was carrying on *pari passu* with the Dardanelles Committee. It did undoubtedly take some sort of hand in the prosecution of the war from time to time, because one day I was summoned to stand by at 10 Downing Street when it was sitting, soon after the Coalition Government was formed and when Lord Kitchener happened to be away, on the chance of my being wanted. They were hardly likely to require my services in connection with matters other than military. After an interminable wait — during the luncheon hour, too—Mr. Arthur Henderson, who was a very recent acquisition, emerged stealthily from the council chamber after the manner of the conspirator in an Adelphi drama, and intimated that they thought that they would be able to get on without me. In obedience to an unwritten law, the last-joined member was always expected to do odd jobs of this kind, just as at some schools the bottom boy of the form is called upon by the form-master to perform certain menial offices *pro bono publico.*

The mystery observed in connection with these Cabinet meetings was not unimpressive. But the accepted procedure—without a secretary present to keep record of what was done and with apparently no proper minutes kept by anybody—was the very negation of sound administration and of good government. Such practice would have been out of date in the days of the Heptarchy. Furthermore it did not fulfil its purpose in respect to concealment, because whenever the gathering by any accident made up its mind about anything that was in the least interesting, everybody outside knew all about it within twenty-four hours. And in spite of all the weird precautions, I actually was present once for a very brief space of time at one of these momentous sittings. It came about after this wise. On the rising of a Dardanelles Committee meeting, one of the Ministers who had attended drew me into a corner to enquire concerning a point that had arisen. There was movement going on in the room, people coming and going, but we were intent on our confabulation and took no notice. Suddenly there was an awe-inspiring silence and then Mr. Asquith was heard to lift up his voice. " Good Lord ! " ejaculated my Minister (just like that—they are quite human when taken off their guard), " the Cabinet's sitting ! " and until back, safe within the War Office portals, I almost seemed to feel a heavy hand on my shoulder haling me off to some oubliette, never more to be heard of in the outer world.

A less teeming War Council than the Dardanelles Committee was substituted for that assemblage about October 1915, and I only attended one or two of its meetings : Sir A. Murray was by that time installed as C.I.G.S., and things were on a more promising footing within the War Office. It was this new form of War Council which was thrown over by the Cabinet with reference to the evacuation of the Gallipoli Peninsula, as related on pp. 103, 104. As far as one could judge, when more or less of an outsider in connection with the general conduct of operations but none the less a good deal behind the scenes, this type of War Council, constituted out of the Ministers who were directly connected with the operations, besides the Prime Minister, Foreign Minister and Chancellor of the Exchequer, with the First Sea Lord and C.I.G.S. always in attendance, worked very well during the greater part of 1916. But Mr. Lloyd George's plan of a War Cabinet, in spite of certain inevitable drawbacks to such an arrangement, was undoubtedly the right one for times of grave national emergency. Its accessibility and its readiness to deal with problems in a practical spirit are illustrated by the following incident within my own experience.

We had got ourselves into a condition of chaos in

connection with the problem of Greek supplies at the beginning of 1918. There was an extremely vague agreement with the French, an unsigned agreement entered into in haste by representatives on our side of little authority, under which we were supposed to provide all sorts of things for the Hellenes. But the whole business was extremely irregular and it was in a state of hopeless confusion—it will be referred to again in a later chapter. In the War Office alone, several departments and branches were concerned, including my own up to a certain point. The Ministries of Munitions and Shipping were in the affair as well, together with the Board of Trade, the Foreign Office, and last but not least, the Treasury. But what was everybody's business was nobody's business. Each department involved declared that some other one must take the matter up and get things unravelled, and at last in a fit of exasperation, although my branch was only a 100 to 3 outsider in the matter, I took the bull by the horns and wrote privately to Sir M. Hankey, asking him to put the subject of Greek Supplies on the Agenda for the War Cabinet on some early date and to summon me to be on hand, which he did. When the matter came up, Mr. Lloyd George enquired of me what the trouble was. I told him that we were in a regular muddle, that we could not get on, that several Departments of State were in the thing, but that it hardly seemed a matter for the War Cabinet to trouble itself with. Could not one of its members take charge, get us together, and give us the authority we required for dealing with the problem? Mr. Lloyd George at once asked Lord Milner to take the question up, not more than five minutes of the War Cabinet's time was wasted, and within a very few hours Lord Milner had got the business on a proper footing and we all knew where we were.

Now, supposing that instead of the War Cabinet it had been a case of that solemn, time-honoured, ineffectual council composed of all the principal Ministers of the

Crown, gathered together in Downing Street to discuss matters which the majority of those present never know any more about than the man in the moon, what would have happened? We of the War Office might among us, with decent luck, have managed to prime our own private Secretary of State, and might have sent him off to the Cabinet meeting with a knowledge of his brief. But, unless the Ministers at the heads of the other Departments of State concerned had been got hold of beforehand and told what to do and to say, they would among the lot of them have made confusion worse confounded. If by any chance a decision had then been arrived at, it would almost inevitably have been a perfectly preposterous one, totally inapplicable to the question that was actually at issue.

A summons to attend a War Cabinet meeting was not, however, an unmixed joy. There was always an agenda paper; but it was apt to turn out a delusion and a snare. The Secretariat did their very best to calculate when the different subjects down for discussion on the paper would come up, and they would warn one accordingly. But they often were out in their estimate, and they had always to be on the safe side. Some quite simple and apparently straightforward subject would take a perfectly unconscionable time to dispose of, while, on the other hand, an apparently extremely knotty problem might be solved within a few minutes and so throw the timetable out of gear. The result was that in the course of months one spent a good many hours, off and on, lurking in the antechamber in 10 Downing Street.

Still, there was always a good fire in winter time, and one found oneself hobnobbing, while waiting, with all sorts and conditions of men. There would be Ministers holding high office but not included in the Big Five (or was it Six?), emissaries just back from some centre of disturbance and excitement abroad, people who dealt with wheat production and distribution, knights of industry called in over some special problem, and persons

purporting to be masters of finance—which nobody understands, least of all the experts. Who could possibly,
under any circumstances, be angry with Mr. Balfour?
But he was occasionally something of a trial when one
was patiently awaiting one's turn. Although the Agenda
paper might make it plain that no subject was coming
up with which the Foreign Office could possibly be in
the remotest degree connected, he would be descried
sloping past and going straight into the Council Chamber,
as if he had bought the place. Then out would come one
of the Secretary gang. The Foreign Minister had turned
up, and was setting them an entirely unexpected conun-
drum inside; the best thing one could do was to clear
out of that, as the point which one had been summoned
to give one's views about had not now the slightest chance
of coming before the Cabinet that day.

At the various forms of War Council at which the
prosecution of the war was debated, one was necessarily
brought into contact with a number of politicians and
statesmen, and was enabled to note their peculiarities
and to watch their methods. I never to my knowledge
saw Lord Beaconsfield; but in the late 'eighties and
early 'nineties Mr. Gladstone was sometimes to be met in
the streets, and, even if one thought that he ought to be
boiled, one none the less felt mildly excited at the spectacle.
That aphorism, " familiarity breeds contempt," does put
the point a little crudely; but the fact remains that when
you are brought into contact with people of this kind,
about whom there is such a lot of talk in the newspapers,
they turn out to be very much like everybody else.
Needless to say, they will give tongue to any extent,
but, apart from that, they may even be something of a
disappointment to those who anticipate great things of
them. Still, it is only right to acknowledge that the
majority of Ministers met with during the Great War
were sensible enough in respect to military matters.
The amateur strategist was fortunately the exception in
these circles, and not the rule. Most of them picked up

the fundamental facts in connection with any situation that presented itself quite readily; they grasped elementary principles when these were explained to them and they were able to keep those principles in mind. But there were goats as well as sheep. You might just as well have started dancing jigs to a milestone as have tried to get into the heads of one or two of them the elementary fact that the conduct of war cannot be decided on small-scale maps but is a matter of stolid and unemotional calculation, that imagination is a deadly peril when unaccompanied by knowledge, and that army corps and divisions cannot be switched about ashore or afloat as though they were taxi-cabs or hydroplanes.

Mr. Henderson shaped well when military matters were in debate; he looked portentous and he held his tongue. Then there was Sir E. Carson who, during the few weeks that he figured on the Dardanelles Committee, was an undeniable asset. His interjections of " Mr. Asquith, we really must make up our minds," uttered with an accent not unfamiliar to one who had passed youthful days in the vicinity of Dublin, and accompanied by a moody stare such as his victim in the witness-box must find rather disconcerting when under cross-examination at the hands of the famous K.C., had no great effect perhaps. But the motive was unexceptionable. He and Mr. Bonar Law used to sit together and to press for decisions, and it was unfortunate that Sir Edward resigned when he did. Mr. Bonar Law was within an ace of resigning likewise very shortly afterwards. He invited me to go over to the Colonial Office to see him and to talk over matters, and I expressed an earnest hope that he would stick to the ship. An artist in letter-writing (as was shown in his momentous epistle written on behalf of the Unionist leaders when Mr. Asquith's Cabinet were in two minds at the beginning of August 1914), his memorandum which is quoted in the " Final Report " of the Dardanelles Commission, and in which he insisted upon the advice of the military authorities with reference to the evacuation of the Gallipoli Peninsula being followed, indicates how fortunate it was that he remained at his post.

The truth is that resignations of the individual Minister seldom do any good from the point of view of the public interest, except when the individual Minister concerned happens to be unfit for his position—and then he generally seems immune from that " unwanted doggie " sort of feeling from which less illustrious persons are apt to suffer when they are *de trop*. The cases mentioned on p. 144 in connection with the Army Council stood on an entirely different footing. When a body of officials resign, or threaten to resign, their action cannot be ignored ; in the second case mentioned the mere threat sufficed. Lord Fisher paid me one of his meteoric visits on the morning that he submitted his resignation to Mr. Asquith, and he confided his reasons to me ; the reasons were good, but it seemed doubtful whether they were quite good enough to justify the taking of so drastic a step.

There was no more edifying and compelling personality amongst the party who were in the habit of taking the floor in 10 Downing Street in 1915 than Lord Curzon. He, Mr. Churchill, and Mr. Lloyd George might almost have been called rivals for the rôle of *prima ballerina assoluta*. The remarks that fell from his lips, signalized as they ever were by a faultless phraseology and delivered with a prunes, prisms and potatoes diction, seldom failed to lift the discussion on to a higher plane, to waft his hearers on to the serene hill-tops of thought, to awaken sublime sensations in all present such as the spectacle of some noble mountain panorama will summon up in the meditations of the most phlegmatic. Mr. Churchill, ever lucid, ever cogent, ever earnest, ever forceful, was wont to be so convincing that he would almost cause listeners to forget for the moment that, were the particular project which just then happened to be uppermost in his mind to be carried into execution, any small hopes which remained of our ever winning the war would inevitably be blotted out for good and all. As for Mr. Lloyd George in drab days before he became First Minister of the Crown in spite of his superhuman efforts to avoid that undesired consummation, he always loved to make his voice heard, and he always succeeded—just as a canary will in a roomful of chattering women.

CHAPTER XII

SOME INTER-ALLIES CONFERENCES

THE first meeting of importance with representatives of the Allies at which I was present took place in Paris at the end of April 1915, and has already been referred to on p. 63. Sir H. Jackson and I were sent over, as representing respectively the Admiralty and the War Office, to take part in a secret conference that was to be held between French, Russian, and British naval and military delegates on the one side, and Italian naval and military delegates on the other side in connection with Italy's entry into the war as an associate of the Entente. That Italy was to join the Allies had already been arranged secretly between the four governments, and it was understood that she was to open hostilities in the latter part of May. The purpose of the Conference was to permit of the situation being discussed, and formal naval and military conventions were to be drawn up between the contracting Powers. Sir Henry and I were accompanied by small staffs, and we put up at the Ritz in the Place Vendôme.

M. Millerand, who was French War Minister at the time, presided at the Conference which assembled in the War Office, and he made an ideal chairman—the French are always admirable at managing such functions. The principal French military delegate was General Pellé, General Joffre's Chief of Staff ; the Russians were represented by their Military Attaché in Paris, Colonel Count Ignatieff, and the principal Italian military delegate was a colonel (whose name I cannot recall), a most attractive and evidently an extremely capable soldier, who unhappily was killed within a few months when in command of a brigade in one of the early fights near Gorizia. In so far as framing the military convention was concerned, that part of the proceedings gave little trouble. The Italian representatives, it is true, were anxious that the Allies should undertake to embark upon an offensive on the greatest possible scale practicable, simultaneously with the Italian army crossing the frontier about the Isonzo ; but General Pellé and I could give no guarantee to that effect, the more so seeing that a Franco-British offensive had already, as it was, been decided upon to start in the Bethune-Vimy region within a few days and before the Italian army would be ready. One had a pretty shrewd suspicion that there was no opening whatever for an offensive on the Eastern Front in view of our Russian Allies' grave munitions difficulties, although the French seemed strangely unaware of the nakedness of the land in that quarter ; still, it was no part of the game to hint at joints in our harness of that kind to the Italian representatives. Ignatieff, bluff and cheery, was careful not to commit himself on the subject. The end of it was that our military convention amounted to little more than an agreement that we were all jolly fine fellows, accompanied by cordial expressions of good-will and of a determination on the part of the four contracting Powers to do their best and to stick together. The naval side of the problem, on the other hand, was beset by pitfalls, and that part of the business was not satisfactorily disposed of for several days.

Even to a landsman like myself, it was apparent that the Italian conception of war afloat in the year of grace 1915 was open to criticism. Our new friends contemplated employing their fleet very freely as an auxiliary to their army in its advance along the littoral towards Trieste, a theory of naval operations which came upon one with something of a shock at the very start. Pola and other well-sheltered bowers for under-water craft lie pretty handy to the maritime district in which King Victor's troops were going to take the field. For battleships and cruisers to be pottering about in those waters serving out succour to the soldiers on shore, succour which would in all probability be of no great account in any case, suggested that those battleships and cruisers would be transmogrified into submarines at a very early stage of the proceedings. One wondered if the Ministry of Marine away south by the Tiber had heard the tragic tale of the *Hogue*, the *Cressy* and the *Aboukir*. Nor was that all. The Italian naval delegates put forward requests that fairly substantial assistance in the shape of war-craft of various types should be afforded them within the Adriatic by the French and ourselves.

All this struck even an outsider like myself as somewhat unsatisfactory, and that was clearly the view which Sir H. Jackson took. For, in some disorder, he let slip an observation to the effect that it looked like the recently acquired collaborator with the Entente being rather a nuisance than otherwise. The rendering of this expression of opinion of the Admiral's into French at the hands of our Naval Attaché in Paris (Captain Hodges) was a masterpiece of diplomatic camouflage. In the end the Italian sailors were obliged to ask for an adjournment to allow of their communicating with Rome, and, if I recollect aright, the principal one of them had to proceed home to discuss the question at headquarters. All this took up time, and we did not finally get the conventions signed for nearly a fortnight.

M. Millerand gave a banquet at the War Office in honour of us delegates, at which we met M. Viviani, the Prime Minister, together with other members of the French Cabinet. I enjoyed the good fortune of sitting next to M. Delcassé, and so of making the acquaintance of one of the great Foreign Ministers of our time. Paris is at its best in spring, and had it not been war-time and had one not been in a fidget to get back to Whitehall, a few days of comparative idleness spent in *la ville lumière* after nine months of incessant office work, while the international sailor-men settled their differences, would have been not unwelcome. The pause, however, provided an opportunity for motoring down to St. Omer and spending a couple of days in the war zone—my first visit to the Front. Two points especially struck me on this trip. One was the wonderful way that the women and children of France (for scarcely an adult male was to be seen about in the rural districts) were keeping their end up in the fields. The other was the smart and soldier-like bearing of the rank-and-file amongst our troops, in striking contrast to the go-as-you-please methods which prevailed in South Africa, and to which, indirectly, some of the " regrettable incidents " which occurred on the veldt were traceable. It gave one confidence. Sir J. French and some of G.H.Q. were at advanced headquarters at Hazebrouck as offensive operations were impending, and Sir John, on the afternoon that I saw him, was greatly pleased at a most successful retirement of our line in a portion of the Ypres salient which General Plumer had brought off on the previous night. On getting back to Paris it transpired that the naval trouble was not yet settled.

One morning, sitting with Admiral Gamble who was

over to help Sir H. Jackson, in the long alley-way of the Ritz where one enjoys early breakfast if that meal be not partaken of in private apartments, Commodore Bartolomé, the First Lord's " Personal Naval Assistant," was of a sudden descried in the offing and beating up for the Bureau. " Good God ! " exclaimed the Admiral, horror-stricken. " Winston's come ! " He had, so we learnt from Bartolomé; but what he had come for nobody could make out. Telegraphic communication exists between Paris and London, and Sir H. Jackson was in constant touch with our Admiralty. However, to whatever cause the visit was to be attributed, there was Mr. Churchill as large as life and most anxious to get busy ; and I personally was glad to see him, because he told me all about what had been going on in the Gallipoli Peninsula since the landing of a few days before. One did not gather that the French were any more delighted at his jack-in-the-box arrival, and at his interventions in the Conference discussions, than were our naval representatives who had been officially accredited for the purpose. A satisfactory agreement was, however, at last arrived at over the Adriatic, the conventions were signed with due pomp and circumstance, and our party returned to England. While in Paris I had paid one or two visits to General Graziani, who was the Chief of the General Staff at the French War Office ; but we in Whitehall never could make out exactly what were the relations between the military authorities in Paris and those at Chantilly. The very fact that General Joffre's Chief of Staff had been French military representative at our Conference, and not General Graziani or his nominee, seemed odd.

Some six months later, early in November, I again went over to France, this time with Sir A. Murray, to attend a discussion with General Joffre at Chantilly concerning Salonika. Admiralty representatives, including Admiral Gamble and Mr. Graeme Thomson, Director of Naval Transport, were of the party. Sir J. French with Sir W. Robertson, his Chief of the General Staff, and Sir H.

Wilson came up from St. Omer. It was by no means a satisfactory meeting. We from the War Office in London desired to circumscribe British participation in this new side-show to the utmost, and to keep the whole business as far as possible within limits ; but we got uncommonly little support from G.H.Q. Sir W. Robertson expressed no opinion, nor was he called upon to do so ; he would have found it awkward to dissent from his commander-in-chief. But the result was that when a much more important conference over the same subject took place a few days later, this time between the two Governments, Sir J. French was not present while Sir W. Robertson was. These things do arrange themselves somehow.

As the discussion took place at Chantilly late in the afternoon, G.H.Q. and we put up at Amiens for the night. On our discovering that General Joffre contemplated crossing the Channel next day to have a chat with our Government, the C.I.G.S. prevailed upon Admiral Gamble to hurry on in his motor to Boulogne next morning so as to catch the packet there, to cross to Folkestone, and to get up to London in time to warn our people of the somewhat expansive Salonika programme which " Grandpère " had up his sleeve. The Silent Navy, it is hardly necessary to say, fairly rose to the occasion, for the Admiral was off under forced draught in the dog-watch. Chancing things, however, when weathering a promontory off Montreuil, he contrived to pile up his craft on a shoal in a bad position, and he would have missed trans-shipment at Boulogne altogether had he not got himself taken off in a passing craft which was under charge of soldier-officers who were likewise making for the packet. So he got across all right in the end and he flashed up to town, only to find that old man Joffre had not played the game. " Grandpère " had slept peacefully in the train, had boarded a destroyer at some unearthly hour of the morning, and was already in Whitehall before our staunch, precipitate emissary had cast off from Boulogne.

On the occasion of that next pow-wow mentioned

above, Messrs. Asquith, Balfour (now First Lord), Lloyd George and Sir Edward Grey crossed over as our representatives. Sir H. Jackson (now First Sea Lord), Sir W. Robertson, who had been summoned over to London, and I accompanied them, as well as Colonel Hankey and some others. We travelled by specials and a destroyer and took the Boulogne route. Our warship tied up to the *East Anglia*, hospital ship, at Boulogne, and as we passed across her some of us had a few words with nurses and wounded on board, little anticipating that she would be mined next day on the passage over to England, with most unfortunate loss of life. Eventually we arrived at the Gare du Nord about midnight, to be welcomed by a swarm of French Ministers and Lord Bertie, and to find all arrangements made for us with typical French hospitality.

The Conference took place at the Foreign Office on the Quai d'Orsay, M. Briand presiding. Several members of the French Government were present, besides Generals Joffre, Gallieni and Graziani ; and with our party, as well as interpreters, secretaries and others, there was quite a gathering. After M. Briand had welcomed us cordially and in felicitous terms, Mr. Asquith got a charming little speech in French off his chest ; it may perhaps have had a whiff of the lamp about it and had probably been learnt by heart, but the P. M. undoubtedly managed to serve up a savoury *appétitif*, and we felt that in the matter of courtesy and the amenities our man had held his own. In the course of the discussion that followed, Sir E. Grey's minute-gun process of turning our host's delightful language to account afforded all present ample time to take in the drift of his cogent, weighty arguments and to appraise them at their proper worth. Had it been any one else, Mr. Lloyd George would have been voted an unmitigated nuisance on all hands. As a result of prolonged residence in the Gay City at a somewhat later date, the Right Honourable Gentleman is now, it is understood, in the habit of bandying badinage with the *midinettes* in the *argot* of the Quartier Latin. But at the time that I speak of his acquaintance with the Gallic tongue was strictly limited (although he did put forward claims to be able to understand " Grey's French "), and he kept from time to time insisting upon the proceedings being brought to a halt while a translation of something that had been said was furnished for his benefit, generally selecting some particularly unprofitable platitude which had been uttered by one of those present for the purpose of gaining time.

The French took up a strong line over Salonika. In a sense they drove our side into a corner, and the responsibility for hundreds of thousands of French and British troops being interned in Macedonia for years rests with them, and it was in great measure the outcome of that day's debate. Sir W. Robertson was called upon to state his views. He knows French perfectly well, but he absolutely refused to speak anything but English, and his remarks were translated, sentence after sentence, by a young French officer with a perfect command of the latter tongue. After each successive sentence had been rendered into French, Sir William, who was sitting beside me, would murmur, " Infernal fellow, that's not what I said," as though repeating the responses, the poor interpreter having in reality done his duty like a man. The gist of his remarks was what might have been expected, viz. that the Germans were the real enemy and that the proper course for the Allies to pursue was to concentrate force against them and not to be hunting about for trouble in the uttermost parts of the earth. Views of that kind, enunciated bluntly and with considerable emphasis, were very likely not wholly palatable to M. Briand ; but it seemed to me that they were not regarded with disfavour by General Joffre, nor yet by General Gallieni, although those distinguished soldiers when invited to give expression to their views contrived merely to say nothing at considerable length. The end of it all was that we were committed to dumping down three

more divisions at Salonika in addition to the two already
there or disembarking, and that we were, moreover, committed to sending them thither without delay. When
they got there it took ages to get their impedimenta
ashore owing to lack of landing facilities—as we had fully
foreseen. The amateur strategist imagines that you can
discharge an army out of a fleet of transports and freight-
ships just anywhere and as easily as you can empty a
slop-pail.

We dined with the President and Mme. Poincaré at
the Elysée that night, and most of the French Cabinet,
as well as Generals Joffre and Gallieni, were likewise
invited. Our Big Four were in some doubt as to what
garb to appear in, seeing that it was not to be a full-dress
function, sporting trinkets; and they eventually hit upon
dinner-jackets with black ties. So Sir W. Robertson and
I decided to doff breeches, boots and spurs, and to don
what military tailors refer to as "slacks" but what in
non-sartorial circles are commonly called trousers. The
French civilians all wore frock-coats, so that there was
an agreeable lack of uniformity and formality when we
assembled. I sat next to M. Dumergue, the Colonial
Minister, and between us we disposed of the German
Colonies in a spirit of give and take—or rather take,
because there was none of that opera-bouffe "mandate"
which has since then been wafted across from the Western
Hemisphere, included in our arrangements. In the
course of the evening I managed to obtain General Joffre's
views concerning the feasibility of withdrawing from the
Gallipoli Peninsula without encountering heavy loss, a
subject that one had constantly in mind at that time.
Père Joffre's opinion was that, subject to favourable
weather and to the retreat taking place at night, the
thing could be managed; and he emphasized the fact
that the conditions of trench warfare rather lent themselves to secret withdrawals of that nature.

We made our way back to London on the following
day, leaving Paris in the forenoon, and were to embark

at Calais ; but owing to some misunderstanding our special ran into Boulogne and out on to the jetty, where numbers of troops were assembled as a leave-boat was shortly to cross. This afforded me an opportunity of experiencing how very engaging Mr. Lloyd George can make himself when dealing with a somewhat critical audience. For the whole party got out, glad to stretch their legs, and I wandered about with the Munitions Minister. We got into conversation with some of the men, he was recognised, and a crowd speedily gathered round us. He questioned them, and it is hardly necessary to say that, being British soldiers, they did not forget to grumble ; they were particularly eloquent on the subject of the quality and the quantity of hand-grenades. But Mr. Lloyd George handled them most skilfully, got a great deal of useful information out of them, delighted them with his cheery manner and apt chaff, and when we had to hurry off as our train was about to move on, the men cheered him to the echo. " Sure he's a great little man intoirely," I heard a huge lump of an Irish sergeant remark to a taciturn Highlander, who removed his pipe from his mouth to spit in unqualified acquiescence.

They say that a destroyer represents an invaluable form of fighting-ship, and no doubt she does ; but it is ridiculous to pretend that she makes an agreeable pleasure-boat—at all events not at night and with all lights out. In the first place there is nothing whatever to prevent your falling out of the vessel altogether, and as the gang-ways which pretend to be the deck are littered with anchors, chains, torpedoes, funnels, ventilators, and what not, you dare not, if you have been so ill-advised as to remain up top, roam about in pitch darkness even in harbour, let alone when the craft is jumping and wriggling and straining out in the open. Having tried the high-up portion of the ship at the front end, where the cold was perishing and the spray amounted to a positive outrage, on the way over, I selected the wardroom aft on the way back and found this much more inhabitable. There was a nice open stove to sit before, a pleasant book to read, and there was really nothing to complain about except the rattle and whirr of the propellers. Sir W. Robertson is a very fine soldier, but he does not cut much ice as a sailor ; although it was as settled as the narrow seas can fairly be expected to be in late autumn, he lay perfectly flat on his back on a bunk with his hands folded across his chest like the effigies of departed sovereigns in Westminster Abbey, and he never moved an eyelid till we were inside the Dover breakwaters. All the same, he stayed the course, and that is more, I fear, than the First Lord of the Admiralty did. For the Ruler of the King's Navy made a bee-line for the Lieutenant-Commander's own private dug-out the moment he came aboard at Calais, and he remained in ambuscade during the voyage.

There used to be a ditty sung at a pantomime or some such entertainment when I was at Haileybury—music-halls were less numerous and less aristocratic in those days than they are now—of which the refrain was to the effect that one must meet with the most unheard-of experiences ere one would " cease to love." We used to spend an appreciable portion of our time in form composing appropriate verses, as effective a mental exercise perhaps as the labours we were supposed to be engaged on. Mr. Goschen had recently been appointed First Lord of the Admiralty, and one distich in the official version ran : " May Goschen have a notion of the motion of the ocean, if ever I cease to love." It is to be apprehended that Mr. Balfour acquired a better notion of the motion of the ocean than he cared for, on these destroyer trips in which he was in the habit of indulging ; for when we fetched up on this side of the Channel and made our way to the attendant dining-car, where the trained eye instantly detected the presence of glasses on the tables of that peculiar shape that denotes the advent of bubbly wine (none of your peasant drinks when the taxpayer is standing treat), the First Lord rolled up swathed in a shawl, a lamentable bundle, and disappeared like a transient and embarrassed phantom into a corner, to be seen no more until we steamed into Charing Cross.

The run up to town from Dover by special was edifying and was not uninstructive, for it threw some light upon the mystery that is connected with the frequent leaking-out of matters which upon the whole had better be kept secret. A train composed of only a couple of cars makes less noise than the more usual sort, and our dining-car happened to be a particularly smooth-running one. The consequence was that almost every word that was said in the car could be heard by anybody who chose to listen. The Big Three (Mr. Balfour had deserted as we have seen) sat together at one table, whilst we lesser fry congregated close at hand at others. The natural resilience following upon the conclusion of the Conference and the happy termination of cross - Channel buffetings may perhaps have been somewhat stimulated by draughts of sparkling vintage ; but, be that as it may, the Prime Minister and the Minister of Munitions were in their most expansive mood, and after a time their conversation was followed by the rest of us with considerable interest. To the sailors present, as also to one or two of the junior soldier-officers, it was probably news—and it must surely have been news to the waiters—to learn that Sir J. French was shortly to vacate command of the B.E.F. in France. Nor could we be other than gratified at the discussions concerning Sir D. Haig's qualifications as a successor ; I was expecting every moment to hear Sir W. Robertson's suitability for the post freely canvassed ; he was sitting back-to-back with the Munitions Minister, but with the half-partition usual in our English dining-cars intervening. Cabinet Ministers certainly are quaint people.

I attended more than one Conference with the Allies on the subject of munitions and supplies at a later stage of the war. They had a rather inconvenient habit, some of them, of springing brand - new proposals upon one without any warning, and they would without turning a hair raise questions the discussion of which was wholl unforeseen and had not been prepared for. A good deal of trouble was, for instance, caused on a certain occasion owing to the question of armament for Russia being brought up at one of the Chantilly Conferences which used to take place from time to time, without our having a delegate present who was posted up in the actual situation with regard to this particular problem. The Russians had, shortly before, put forward requests that we should furnish them with a very big consignment indeed of heavy guns and howitzers—somewhere about 600 pieces of sorts. We had no intention of falling in with this somewhat extravagant demand; but we had more or less promised about 150. However, at a meeting of a Sub-Committee on munitions delegated by this particular Chantilly Conference, only General Maurice, who was not concerned in munitions details nor aware of the actual facts, represented us; and at this meeting the Russians and French mentioned in the course of the discussion that we had promised 600 pieces. Not fully acquainted with the position, General Maurice did not contradict the assertion. This caused some difficulty, because on later occasions the French and Russians would say, " But you agreed to furnish 600 at Chantilly," and would produce the protocol of the meeting. Similarly, we were regularly rushed into a Conference at Paris over Greek supplies in the autumn of 1917—the subject has already been mentioned on p. 216, and it will be referred to again farther on in this volume—without knowing what the business was about. Greek supplies and our connection with them were consequently in a shocking tangle for months to come.

There was one of these international gatherings, one that was held in Mr. Lloyd George's room in the War Office about November 1916 when he was Secretary of State for War, of which I have a vivid recollection. M. Albert Thomas and General Dall' Olio, the respective Munitions Ministers in France and Italy, had come over, accompanied by several assistants; and the Russian

Military Attaché from Paris with several representatives of the special Russian Commission in England were present, as well as the Head of the Roumanian Military Mission in France.   The Russians, Roumanians and Italians all, needless to say, wanted to get as much as they could out of us, and the French were quite ready to back the Russians and Roumanians up.   Mr. Lloyd George made a tip-top chairman, conciliatory and, thanks to ignorance of French, always unable to understand what was said when it happened to be inconvenient to grasp the purport. At one juncture M. Thomas and General Dall' Olio came rather to loggerheads over something or other, steel I think.   Had they been Britishers, one would have been preparing to slip under the table so as to be out of harm's way ; but Latin nations are more gesticulatory than we are, and this sort of effervescence does not mean quite so much with them as it does when it shows a head amongst us frigid islanders.   Just when the illustrious pair of Ministers were inclined to get a little out of temper, arguing of course in French, Mr. Lloyd George burst out laughing, threw himself back in his chair and ejaculated, " Now will some kind friend tell me what all that's about ! "   He had touched exactly the right note.   Everybody beamed.   The disputants burst out laughing too, harmony was completely restored, and the discussion was conducted thenceforward in friendliest fashion.

By far the most interesting feature, however, about this pow-wow, and several others, was provided by the interventions of M. Mantoux, the gifted interpreter who used to come over from Paris, and of whom I believe great use was made at Conferences at various times at Versailles.   His performance on such occasions was a veritable *tour de force*.   He never took a note.   He waited till the speaker had finished all that he wanted to say—and your statesman generally has an interminable lot to say—whether it was in French or in English.   He then translated what had been said into the other language—English or French as the case might be—practically word for word. His memory, quite apart from his abnormal linguistic aptitudes, was amazing. Nor was that all. He somehow contrived, almost automatically it seemed, to imitate the very gestures and the elocution of the speakers. M. Thomas is troubled with a rather unruly wisp of hair which, when he gets wrought up in fiery moments, will tumble down over his brow into his eyes, to be swept back every now and again with a thrust of the hand accompanied by a muttered exclamation, presumably a curse. Rendering M. Thomas into English, M. Mantoux would sweep back an imaginary wisp of hair with an imprecation which I am confident was a " damn ! " Then again, no man can turn on a more irresistibly ingratiating smile when he is getting the better of the other fellow than Mr. Lloyd George, and he has mastered a dodge of at such moments sinking his voice to a wheedling pitch calculated to coax the most suspicious and recalcitrant of listeners into reluctant concurrence. M. Mantoux would reproduce that smile to admiration, and his tones when translating Mr. Lloyd George's seductive blandishments into French were enough to cajole a crocodile.

CHAPTER XIII

A FIRST MISSION TO RUSSIA

Reasons for Mission—An effectual staff officer—Our distinguished representatives in Scandinavia—The journey—Stockholm—Lapps —Crossing the frontier at Haparanda—Arrival at Petrograd— Sir G. Buchanan—Interviews with General Polivanoff, Admiral Grigorovitch and M. Sazonoff—Imperial vehicles—Petrograd— We proceed to the Stavka—Improper use of the title " Tsar "— The Imperial headquarters—Meeting with the Emperor—Two disconcerting incidents—Nicholas II.—His charm—His admiration for Lord Kitchener's work—Conference with General Alexeieff— Mohileff—Service in the church in honour of the Grand Duchess Tatiana's birthday—Return to Petrograd—A rencontre with an archbishop—The nuisance of swords—Return home.

IN spite of the *débâcle* which had taken place in the early summer of 1915, the information coming to hand from Russia in the War Office later in the year was not wholly discouraging. It became apparent that a strenuous effort was being made to repair the mischief. Marked energy was being displayed locally in developing the output of munitions and war material of all kinds. This, coupled with the unequivocal confidence that was manifestly being displayed in Lord Kitchener by the Emperor, the Grand Duke Nicholas, and the leading statesmen of our great eastern Ally whether they belonged to the Government or not, gave promise that the vast empire, with its swarming population and its boundless internal resources, might yet in the course of time prove a tremendous asset on the side of the Entente.

We had, however, never established a very satisfactory understanding with the Russian General Staff. A number of British officers of high rank had gone out to pay more

237

or less complimentary visits, but rather more than that appeared to be needed. I had been thinking in the latter part of 1915 that some steps ought to be taken in this direction, and so, when it became known that Sir W. Robertson was shortly coming over to become C.I.G.S. at the War Office, which would assuredly mean other important changes of personnel, I wrote to him suggesting that I should go out and talk things over with General Alexeieff, the Russian Chief of the General Staff. After Sir William had taken over charge and had considered the matter, he agreed, and he gave me practically a free hand as regards making known our views, only stipulating that I should return promptly and report to him.

One of the many active and capable members on its rolls, Captain R. F. Wigram, was picked out from the Director of Military Operations' staff to perform the functions of Staff Officer and A.D.C. He possessed the merit amongst many others of being young and of looking younger, and he lost no time in exhibiting his remarkable fitness for the post. For without one moment's hesitation he bereft his club in Pall Mall of the services of a youth of seventeen, who by some mysterious process became eighteen then and there, whom he converted into a private of Foot, whom he fitted out with a trousseau extracted from the Ordnance Department that a Prince of the Blood proceeding to the North Pole might have coveted, and who thus, as by the stroke of a magician's wand, became transformed into an ideal soldier-servant. We made our way north-eastwards via Newcastle, Bergen and Stockholm, round the north of the Gulf of Bothnia, and thence on through Finland to Petrograd. Traversing the chilly northern waters between the Tyne and the Norse fiords, it became possible to appreciate to some very small degree what months of watching for a foe who could not be induced to leave port on the surface must have meant to the sister service and to its wonderful auxiliaries drawn from the Mercantile Marine. For if there is a more dismal, odious, undisciplined stretch of ocean on the face of the globe than the North Sea, it has not been my ill-fortune to have had to traverse it.

Our Foreign Office has served as a butt for a good deal of criticism of late years, some of which has perhaps not been wholly undeserved. But whether it was by design or was the result of some happy accident, Downing Street managed to be most efficiently represented at the courts of northern Europe during the epoch of the Great War. Sir G. Buchanan's outstanding services in Russia are now recognized on all hands—even apparently by H.M. Government. But the country also owes much to Sir E. Howard and to Sir M. Findlay, who represented us so worthily in Sweden and Norway during periods of exceptional stress and difficulty. It was a real pleasure when passing backwards and forwards through Scandinavia to meet these two strong men who were so successfully keeping the flag flying, to discuss with them the course of events, to be made acquainted with the peculiar problems that were constantly confronting them, to note the marked respect in which they were held on all hands, and to enjoy the hospitality of two typical English homes planted down in a foreign land. On one occasion Sir E. Howard was good enough to make special arrangements for me to meet the Russian and French Ministers at Stockholm and the French Military Attaché at luncheon at the Legation, thereby enabling us to examine into a number of points of common interest.

Bergen was reputed to be a regular hotbed of German spydom, and apparently with justice. A party of Russian officers coming over on a mission to this country and France some months later were taken off the Bergen-Newcastle packet by a U-boat. The commander of the U-boat had a list of their names, with ranks and everything in order, and he knew all about his prisoners. One officer was overlooked, and he brought news of the *contretemps* to this country; he had, as it happened, only joined the party at the very last moment as an afterthought, and the Boche agents at Stockholm and Bergen had evidently overlooked him on the way through. An idea prevailed over here that the Swedes in general were decidedly hostile to the Entente ; Stockholm, a cold spot in winter—almost as cold as, but without the blistering rawness of, Petrograd—was undoubtedly full of Germans, and the red, white and black colours were freely displayed. But partiality for the Central Powers seemed in the main to be confined to the upper classes and to the officers, and, even so, the Swedish officials were always civility itself. It was indeed much easier to get through the formalities at Haparanda on the Swedish side of the frontier, going and coming, than it was at Tornea on the Finnish side, although there we were honoured guests of the country with special arrangements made on our behalf. One could not but be impressed by the unmistakable signs of wealth in Stockholm, where hospitality was being exercised on the most lavish scale at the leading restaurants and at the palatial Grand Hotel—no bad place to stop at when you are travelling on Government service and can send in the bill. The good Swedes (who, like most other people, have an eye for the main chance) were making money freely out of both sides in the great contest, although they were always protesting against our blockading measures.

Travelling is particularly comfortable alike in Norway and in Sweden, for the sleeping - cars are beyond reproach ; owing to snowfalls, the time-table is, however, a little uncertain during the winter months. With their eternal pine-woods, Sweden and Finland are dismal enough regions to traverse in the cold season of the year, although on the Swedish side the line crosses a succession of uplands divided by deep valleys, which are probably very picturesque after the melting of the snows. It was noticeable that all the important viaducts in Sweden were protected by elaborate zeribas of wire entanglement although the country was neutral, a form of defensive measure which was much less noticeable in England and Russia although they were belligerents. Haparanda is close to the Arctic circle, and there the Lapps were very much *en evidence*, forming apparently the bulk of the population—the children astonishingly sturdy creatures, maybe owing to the amount of clothes that they had on. Lapps did all the heavy work in the way of sleigh-driving, porterage at the station, and so on; nor did they manifest much disposition to depreciate the value of their services when it came to the paying stage.

To the traveller without special credentials, the short journey from Haparanda to the railway-car at Tornea which is to bear him onwards must have been almost a foretaste of the Valley of the Shadow of Death. Even for the members of a military mission with " red passports," whose advent had been announced, it was one prolonged agony; and it would probably have been even worse when the intervening estuaries were not frozen over and when one had to take the ferry. All the formalities had to be gone through twice over because there was an island, although the Russian officials were the very pink of courtesy. One learns a great deal of geography on journeys of this kind; we had not realized the extent to which Finland, with its special money, its special language, and its special frontier worries, was distinct from Russia. The train took three days and nights between Stockholm and Petrograd, and one was supposed to fetch up at the terminus somewhere about midnight; but it always took two or three hours to get through the frontier station between Finland and Russia at the last moment, with the result that one might arrive at the capital at any hour of the early morning. When we at last steamed into our destination we found awaiting us on the platform Count Zamoyski, a great Polish landowner and A.D.C. to the Emperor, who had been appointed to attend me, with Colonel Knox, our Military Attaché, and we were driven off in Imperial carriages to the Hotel d'Europe.

Our object was to reach Mohileff, where Russian General Headquarters, known as the " Stavka," were stationed.

R

But the Emperor happened to be away from there just at the moment, so that we were obliged to wait in Petrograd for two or three days until His Majesty should have returned. Still, there was plenty to be done and seen in the capital. In the first place there were the official calls on the Imperial family to pay ; that, however, was merely a case of writing names in the books for the purpose. Then there was the Embassy to be visited, to enable me to make the acquaintance of Sir G. Buchanan and the Embassy staff. Sir George was not in the best of health, and he obviously stood in need of a rest and change of air—the climate of Petrograd is trying, making it an undesirable place for prolonged residence—but the unique position that he held in the eyes of the Russians of all shades of opinion made it almost impossible for him to leave the capital. Diplomats as a class are not generally popular in military circles abroad, and that was perhaps more marked in Russia than in most countries, but our ambassador was held in extraordinary esteem even amongst soldiers who only knew him by name. Properly supported from home, he would have proved a priceless asset when things were going from bad to worse in the latter part of 1916 and the early days of 1917.

I had interviews with General Polivanoff, the War Minister, Admiral Grigorovitch, the Minister of Marine, and M. Sazonoff, the Foreign Minister. General Polivanoff told me his plans, what he had already effected and what he still hoped to effect, confirming the favourable reports that we had received from General Hanbury-Williams and our Military Attachés as to the efforts that were being made to set the Russian army on its legs again ; he also explained that his friendly relations with a number of the leading Liberal men of affairs in the Duma were proving of great assistance in connection with his extending the manufacture of war material throughout the country, in which the " zemstvos " were lending willing aid. With M. Sazonoff I had a very long and interesting conversation, all the pleasanter owing to his complete command of

English. Like General Polivanoff, he was sanguine that, given time, Russia would yet play a great rôle in the war.

In the meantime we were being royally entertained and looked after. One had heard a great deal about Russia having " gone dry " by ukase ; but the drought was not permitted to cast its blight over guests of the nation, and our presence ensured that those at the feast would be enabled to abandon rigid temperance for the moment, an opportunity which was not missed. Who, after all, ever heard of a pleasant party round a pump ? Imperial carriages, with the servants in gorgeous yellow livery, all over eagles, were always at our disposal, and traffic was held up as we passed. This was all very well when you were heading for a Grand Duke's residence to leave cards, or proceeding to the Embassy ; but you felt rather the beggar on horseback when the object of the drive was merely to procure a razor-strop at a big store in replacement of one mislaid on the journey. Your desire was to purchase the cheapest one that was to be had ; but *noblesse oblige,* you simply had to buy the most expensive one there was, and it was a mercy that they had not got one set in brilliants. Zamoyski, most light-hearted and unconventional of companions, was quite happy to remain in Petrograd in preference to rushing off hot-foot to Mohileff, and he made everything extremely pleasant for us. Dining at the Yacht Club one night we met Admiral Phillimore, who had recently arrived on a naval mission ; having commanded the *Inflexible* at the Falkland Islands fight and afterwards in the Dardanelles (where he had spent some anxious hours after his ship had been holed by a drifting mine during the big fight of the 18th of March), few naval officers of his rank had enjoyed a more varied experience since the beginning of the war.

Petrograd is, or was then, in many respects a fine city, adorned by numbers of imposing buildings and churches ; while the view across the half-mile-wide Neva, with its stately bridges and the famous fortress of Peter and Paul on the far side, is very impressive. But its winter climate seemed detestable, cold and tempestuous, accompanied by intervals of thaw which converted even the most important streets into unspeakable slush, while the drip from the roofs was moistening and unpleasant. It has to be confessed that the exhibition of extravagance apparent on all hands in the capital of an empire large portions of which were in the hands of a foreign foe, was not altogether edifying ; the atmosphere was so different from that of Paris. Still, there were not wanting encouraging signs. The soldiers in the streets were smart, well-set-up, stalwart fellows garbed in excellent uniforms, and the training carried on on the Marsova Polye (Champ de Mars) near the Embassy struck one as carried out on excellent lines, particularly the bayonet work.

After three days' stay we proceeded to Mohileff, leaving at night and arriving on the following afternoon, to be put up at the hotel where Hanbury-Williams and the other foreign missions were housed. We dined and had luncheon at the Emperor's mess while at the Stavka, as always did the heads of the various foreign missions. Now that the glories of the House of Romanoff have suffered eclipse consequent upon the terrible end of Nicholas II. and his family, interest in it has no doubt to a great extent evaporated. But it may perhaps be mentioned here that our practice of referring to the Autocrat of All the Russias as the " Tsar " is incorrect, and the custom indeed seems to have been almost peculiar to this country. You never heard the terms " Tsar " and " Tsaritza " employed in Russia, not, at all events, in French ; they were always spoken of as " L'Empereur " and " L'Imperatrice," and in the churches it was always " Imperator." On the other hand, one did hear of the " Tsarevitch," although he was generally spoken of in French as " Le Prince Héritier "—rather a mouthful. How we arrived at that extraordinary misspelling, " Czar " (which is unpronounceable in English), goodness only knows.

The Emperor and his personal staff occupied a couple of fine provincial government buildings, which Davoust had made his headquarters at the time of the battle of Mohileff in 1812, standing in an enclosure which shut them off from the rather unattractive town and overlooking the Dneiper. The practice at meals was for the party to assemble in the antechamber; the Emperor would then come in from his private apartments, would go round the circle speaking a few words to some of those present, and would then lead the way into the dining-room. There, after we had partaken of the national " zakuska " preceded by a nip of vodka, he presided, sitting in the centre of the long table with General Pau, the senior foreign officer, generally on his right, and one of the other foreign officers taken by rote, or else a visitor, on his left. I understood that General Alexeieff had excused himself from these somewhat protracted repasts, on the ground that he really had not the time to devote to them; but one or two others of the Headquarters Staff were generally present, besides the Household. After the meal the Emperor would talk for a short time to some of those present in the antechamber, and would then retire to his own apartments while we of the foreign missions made our way back to our hotel.

I was presented to him while he was making his round before dinner on the first night. That clicking of heels business is highly effective on such occasions, but it is a perilous practice when you are adorned with hunting spurs; they have protuberances which have a way of catching. There is no getting over it—to find, when conversing with an Emperor, that your feet have become locked together and that if you stir you will topple forward into his arms, does place you at a disadvantage. An even worse experience once befell me when on the staff at Devonport a good many years ago. Our general liked a certain amount of ceremonial to take place before the troops marched back to barracks of a Sunday after the parade service at the garrison church; a staff officer collected the reports and reported to another staff officer, who reported to a bigger staff officer, and so on; there was any amount of saluting and of reassuring prattle before the general was at last made aware that everything was all right. One Sunday it was my turn to collect the reports and to report to the D.A.A.G. In those days cocked hats had (and they probably still have) a ridiculous scrap of ribbed gold-wire lace of prehensile tendencies at their fore-end—at their prow, so to speak. While exchanging intimate confidences with the D.A.A.G., the prows of our cocked hats became interlocked; so there we were, almost nose to nose, afraid to move lest one or both of us should part with our headgear. But he never lost his presence of mind. " Hold your infernal hat on with your hand, man," ·he hissed, and did the same. We backed away from each other gingerly, came asunder, and there was no irretrievable disaster; but the troops (who ought all to have been looking straight to their front) had apparently been watching our performance with eager interest, because there was a fatuous grin on the face of every one of them, officers and all. The colonel of the Rifle Brigade said to me afterwards that he trusted the staff did not mean to make a hobby of these knock-about-turns on parade, because if they did it would undermine the discipline of his battalion.

After dinner the Emperor summoned me into his room and we had a long conversation. He spoke English perfectly, almost without trace of foreign accent, and was most cordial, being evidently pleased at the possibility of a closer understanding being arrived at between his General Staff and ours. He expressed the hope that I would speak quite openly to General Alexeieff at the conference which we were to have on the following day. I sat next to him at dinner that next day after the conference and he was most anxious to hear my report of it, having previously seen General Alexeieff and heard what he had to say. The Emperor had the gift of putting one completely at one's ease on such occasions, and, being an admirable conversationalist, interested in everything and ready to talk on any subject, it was a pleasure to be with him. He spoke most affectionately of our Royal Family— His Majesty the King had been pleased to entrust me with a private letter to him—and, referring to the Prince of Wales and Prince Albert, he remarked what a fine thing it was that they were old enough to take their share in the Great War, whereas his boy was too young. The little Tsarevitch had been staying at the Stavka shortly before, and the foreign officers agreed that he was a bright, intelligent, mischievous youngster ; but the Emperor told me the boy was momentarily in disgrace. It appeared that they had on a recent occasion been going to some big parade at the front. At these ceremonials the Emperor, or whoever is carrying out the inspection, salutes the troops on reaching the ground by calling out " Good day, brothers " ; but the Tsarevitch had managed to get off before the flag fell and, slipping on in front, had appeared first and called out, " Good day, brothers," to which the troops had lustily responded. It had upset the whole business. " The young monkey ! " said the Emperor.

He expressed the utmost detestation of the Germans in consequence of their shameless conduct in Belgium and France, and he referred in indignant terms to their treatment of Russian prisoners. If I inquired of the Austro-Hungarian captives, of whom a number were employed on road-mending and similar useful labours in Mohileff, I would find, he said, that they were perfectly contented and were as well looked after in respect to accommodation and to food as were his own troops. Of Lord Kitchener and his work he spoke with admiration, and he asked me many questions about the New Armies, their equipment, their training, their numbers and so on. He talked with wonder of what our great War Minister had accomplished in the direction of transforming the United Kingdom into a first-class military Power in less than a year. In this respect he, however, merely reflected the opinion held in military circles right throughout

Russia ; one heard on all hands eulogy of the miracles that had been accomplished in this direction. His Imperial Majesty was also most appreciative of what our War Office was doing towards assisting the Russians in the all-important matter of war material, and he asked me to convey his thanks to all concerned for their loyalty and good offices.

General Alexeieff had likewise pronounced himself most cordially with regard to Lord Kitchener, his achievements and his aid to Russia, at the conference which Hanbury-Williams and I had had with him that afternoon. The general was not a scion of the aristocracy, as were so many of the superior officers in the Emperor Nicholas's hosts ; he could not talk French although he evidently could follow what was said in that language. He said he did not know German, so we had to work through an interpreter, an officer of the General Staff, employing French. Alexeieff was very pleasant to deal with, as he expressed himself freely, straightforwardly and even bluntly with regard to the various points that we touched upon. Our meeting was taking place late in January 1916, and at a moment when active operations on both the Western and the Eastern Front were virtually at a stand-still ; but he was anxious to know when we should be in a position to assume the offensive on a great scale, and he seemed disappointed when I said that, merely expressing my own personal opinion, I doubted whether we should be ready to do much before the summer, as so many of our New Army divisions were short of training and as we were still in arrear to some extent in the matter of munitions. As a matter of fact, the great German offensive against Verdun was rather to settle this question for us ; for it kept the French on the defensive and General Joffre was not obliged to call upon Sir D. Haig for aid, which allowed our troops just that comparative leisure (apart from holding the line) that enabled them to prepare for the Battle of the Somme.

Mohileff was reputed to be about the most Jewish

township in Russia, and, judging by the appearance of
the inhabitants, that reputation was not undeserved.
One had heard a lot about pogroms in the past, but they
would not appear to be of the really thoroughgoing
sort. It is an unattractive spot in the winter-time
in spite of its effective position, emplaced on a plateau
with the Dneiper winding round two sides of it in a deep
trough. Hanbury-Williams was a great walker, always
anxious for exercise, and each afternoon we wandered out
somewhere in the snow for a constitutional ; the Emperor
used to do the same, but he always motored a good way
out into the country before starting on his tramp. The
only exercise that the other foreign officers ever seemed
to take consisted in motoring backwards and forwards
between the hotel and the Imperial headquarters for meals.
It is wonderful how any of them survived.

The last forenoon that we spent there, a special service
took place in the principal church in honour of the Grand
Duchess Tatiana's birthday ; and the foreign missions
received a hint to go, it being understood that the Emperor
proposed to be present in person. This, however, proved to
be a false alarm. The service began at 10 A.M., and we
went at 11.30 A.M. and stayed till noon ; it was still going
on at that time, and we understood that they were only in
the middle of it. Even half an hour of this was something
of an ordeal, seeing that the church was overheated (as
Russian interiors always are), that we had our furs on,
and that we had to choose between standing or else
kneeling down on the stone floor. Services of the
Orthodox Church are not unimpressive even when one
cannot follow them ; the Chief Priest at Mohileff had a real
organ voice and made the very most of it ; he was almost
deafening indeed at times. The prayers appeared to be
devoted entirely to the welfare of the Imperial family;
at all events the names of the Emperor, of the Empress, of
the Empress Marie, of the Tsarevitch and of the Grand
Duchess herself were thundered out every minute or two
—they were the only words that I could understand

Listening to the priest's sonorous incantation reverberating through the building that morning, one little dreamt that within less than two years' time the winsome princess— her photograph was to be seen everywhere in the Petrograd streets and she seemed to be especially popular—whose day we were engaged in celebrating, would have been foully done to death by miscreants in some remote eastern spot of Russia.

We left for Petrograd in the evening, and shortly after the train got under way a message came to hand to say that the Archbishop of Petrograd was on board and hoped that I would pay him a visit in his compartment. At the first hint of this, Wigram, being a man of resource, went to sleep in self-protection ; so only Zamoyski and I proceeded to His Grace's lair. It turned out that the Archbishop could not speak French, so that conversation had to be carried on through Zamoyski. Our host, as is usual, sent for tea, and we spent about half an hour talking about the war, the Emperor, Lord Kitchener and other matters. His Grace, however, intimated that he was particularly interested in the possibility of a union being effected between the Orthodox and the Anglican Churches, and he expressed himself as most anxious to have my opinion on the subject. Now this was not a matter that I should have felt myself especially competent to debate at a moment's notice even in English ; but, seeing that the discussion was being conducted in French, with a Pole as intermediary who happened to be a Roman Catholic, the perplexities of the situation were appreciably aggravated. A safe line to take, however, was to declare that a union such as was proposed would be all to the good, and the Archbishop pronounced himself as much gratified to find that I was entirely in accord with him. He said something to his secretary, who disappeared and turned up again presently with a beautiful little gold pectoral cross and chain which His Grace presented me with, Zamoyski receiving a smaller replica. When we got back to our own carriage and the Staff Officer saw what we had carried off, he intimated his intention of keeping awake in future when high dignitaries of the Church were about.

Swords, it may here be mentioned, were a regular nuisance to British officers visiting the dominions of the Emperor Nicholas during all the earlier months of the war. The Russians had not, like the French, Belgians and Italians, copied our practice, acquired during the South African War, of putting away these symbols of commissioned authority for the time being. They were not worn actually at the front ; but officers were supposed to appear in them elsewhere just as used to be the invariable practice on the Continent in pre-war days. That our airmen should not possess swords took the Russians quite aback, a sabre being about as appropriate in an aeroplane as are spurs on a destroyer. Transporting a sword through Sweden was apt to stamp you as a belligerent officer, so that all sorts of dodges had to be contrived to camouflage an article of baggage that, owing to its dimensions, refuses to lend itself to operations of concealment. Wigram's absurd weapon gave us away as a matter of course, although no harm befell. I was all right on the journey, because General Wolfe-Murray, who had recently been out on a visit to present decorations, had left his at the Embassy at Petrograd for the use of any other general who might come along later. It, however, was one of the full-dress, scimitar-shaped variety that has been affected by our general officers ever since one of them brought back a richly jewelled sample, the gift of Soliman the Magnificent or some other Grand Turk for a service at Belgrade. It is not a pattern of sabre designed to fit readily into the frog of a Sam Brown belt, and it used to be a regular business getting my borrowed one off and on when one went to a meal in a club or a restaurant in Petrograd.

Most cordial invitations had been extended to us to visit the front. But this must have involved several days' delay. It was not always easy to get a move on in

Russia, and no great value was set upon the element of time ; so that, although such a trip would assuredly have been interesting and it might have been instructive, we were obliged to decline. Instructions ran that I was to return to London as soon as possible after visiting the Stavka. We consequently spent only twenty-four hours in Petrograd before taking the train back for Tornea, and thence via Stockholm and Christiania to Bergen ; we, however, stayed for a few hours in each of the Scandinavian capitals. Since quitting Bergen about three weeks earlier a sore misfortune had befallen the place, for a great part of the best quarter of the town had been destroyed in a disastrous conflagration which had obliterated whole streets. But the flames fortunately had not reached the railway station, nor yet the quays on the side of the harbour where the steamers berthed, so that transit was not appreciably interfered with. We were back at the War Office within four weeks of setting out, having only passed ten days actually within the Russian Empire.

CHAPTER XIV

A SECOND MISSION TO RUSSIA

WE made a fresh start for Russia by the same route about three weeks later, the party swelled by Captain Guy MacCaw, Hanbury-Williams' staff officer, who had been home on leave. Sir W. Robertson wished me to see

General Alexeieff again, and then to proceed to Tiflis to discuss the position of affairs with the Grand Duke Nicholas and his staff. H.M. the King desired that this opportunity should also be taken to present the G.C.M.G. to General Yudenitch, who a short time before had achieved a brilliant success in Armenia in the capture of Erzerum almost in midwinter, and also to the Minister of Marine in Petrograd.

The general military situation was not at this time wholly reassuring. It was known that a great German attack upon Verdun was imminent. We had our own special anxieties in Asia owing to the unfortunate turn taken by affairs in Mesopotamia. News had come of the failure of the attempt to relieve Kut by an advance on the right bank of the Tigris, and this, following upon a similar failure some weeks earlier on the left bank, rendered the conditions decidedly ominous. A study of the large-scale maps and of the available reports at the War Office, had served to indicate that the prospects of saving the beleaguered garrison were none too hopeful, even allowing for the fact that General Maude's division, fresh from Egypt and the Dardanelles, was bringing welcome rein-forcements to Sir P. Lake. Whatever plan should be adopted for the final effort, this must inevitably partake of the character of attacking formidable entrenchments with but limited artillery support, and of having to carry out a difficult operation of war against time. The Grand Duke Nicholas had expressed a readiness to help from the side of Persia ; but little consideration was needed to establish the fact that effective aid from that quarter was virtually out of the question. Situated as the Russian forces were in the Shah's territories, they would be in the position of having either to advance in consider-able strength and to be starved, or to move forward as a weak column and to meet with disaster at the hands of the Turks on the plains of Irak.

One read at Stockholm on the way through of the early successes gained by the Germans at Verdun, the news sounding by no means encouraging; so that it was a great relief on arriving in Petrograd to find that the heroic French resistance before the fortress had brought the enemy's vigorous thrust practically to a standstill. We met Sir A. Paget at Tornea on his way back from handing to the Emperor his baton of British Field-Marshal. There we also found Colonel Baron Meyendorff awaiting us, who had been deputed to accompany me during my travels. The Emperor was absent from the Stavka when we arrived at the capital, with the consequence that we were detained there for several days. As we were to make a somewhat prolonged stay in the country this time we fitted ourselves out with the Russian cap and flat silver-lace shoulder-straps; the Grand Duke Nicholas had indeed insisted, when he was Commander-in-Chief, upon foreign officers when at the front wearing these distinctive articles of Russian uniform as a protection. Cossacks are fine fellows, but they were apt to be hasty; their plan, when they came across somebody whose identity they felt doubtful about, was to shoot first and to make inquiries afterwards.

Meyendorff, who was married to an English lady and who spoke our language fairly well, looked after us assiduously and provided us with occupation and amusement during the stay at the capital. One day he took us to see trotting matches, a very popular form of sport in Petrograd although it struck me as rather dull. We dined at different clubs, went to the Ballet one night, and another night were taken to the Opera where we occupied the Imperial box in the middle of the house. In those days Russian society thoroughly understood the art of welcoming a guest of the country, for the different national anthems of the Allied Powers were played through before the Second Act, everybody standing up, and when it came to the turn of "God save the King," the entire audience wheeled round to face the Imperial box, our national anthem was played twice over, and I received a regular ovation although all that those present can have known, or cared, was that here was a British general turned up on some official business. One result of wearing what amounted to a very good imitation of Russian uniform was that officers and rank and file all saluted, instead of staring at one in some surprise ; it was the rule for non-commissioned officers and private soldiers when they met a general to pull up and front before saluting ; this looked smart, but it was rather a business when one promenaded along the Nevski Prospekt which always swarmed with the military. It was, moreover, the custom in restaurants, railway dining-cars, etc., for officers who were present when a general came in, not only to rise to their feet (if anywhere near where the great man settled down), but also to crave permission to proceed with their meal. This was a little embarrassing until one realized that a gracious wave of the hand to indicate that they might carry on was all that was called for.

The late Sir Mark Sykes had worked under me in Whitehall since an early date in the war ; his knowledge of the Near East was so valuable that I had been obliged to detain him and to prevent his going to France in command of his Territorial battalion, much to his disappointment. Latterly, however, he had been acting for the Foreign Office, although under the aegis of the War Office as this plan was found convenient. He was now in Petrograd in connection with certain negotiations dealing with the future of Turkey in Asia, and as it was desirable that he should visit the Stavka and also Transcaucasia, he attached himself to me for the time being.

One forenoon before leaving for Mohileff I proceeded, accompanied by our Naval Attaché, Meyendorff and Wigram, to the Admiralty to present the G.C.M.G. to the Minister of Marine and the K.C.M.G. to the Chief of the Naval Staff. It seemed desirable to make as much of a ceremony of the business as possible—British decorations were, indeed, very highly prized in Russia ; warning had therefore been sent that we were coming, and why.

On arriving we were met at the gates by several naval officers, and were conducted to outside the door of the Minister's room where the presentation was to take place. One then assumed the simper of the diplomatist, Wigram (who always managed to turn pink on dramatic occasions, which had a particularly good effect) bore the cases containing the insignia, the door was flung open, and we marched solemnly in. I addressed the recipients in my best French, saying that His Majesty had entrusted me with the pleasant duty, and so on, finishing up with my personal congratulations and by handing over the cases. The recipients replied in suitable terms, expressing their gratification and their thanks; we had a few minutes' conversation, and were introduced to the other officers present—there were quite a lot—and we then cleared out, escorted to our gorgeous Imperial carriages by some of the junior officers. The Naval Attaché spoilt the whole thing by remarking afterwards, " You know, general, those Johnnies know English just as well as you do." It was most inconsiderate of him, and he may not have been right ; Russian naval officers down Black Sea way did not seem to know English or even French.

On this second occasion we only spent twenty-four hours at Mohileff ; the interview with General Alexeieff was successfully brought off on the first afternoon, MacCaw accompanying me as he understood Russian thoroughly, although a General Staff Officer interpreted. I told Alexeieff that our chances of relieving Kut appeared to be slender, and that he ought to be prepared for its fall although there was still hope. He thereupon raised the question of our sending a force to near Alexandretta, so as to aid the contemplated Russian campaign in Armenia. Such a project was totally opposed to the views of Sir W. Robertson and our General Staff, and it had at the moment—late in March—nothing to recommend it at all, apart from the point of view of the Armenian operations. Although Lord Kitchener and Sir J. Maxwell had been a little nervous about Egypt during the winter,

S

the General Staff at the War Office had felt perfectly happy on the subject in view of the garrison assembled there after the evacuation of the Gallipoli Peninsula. Now that spring was at hand, any prospect of serious Turkish attempts across the Sinai Desert was practically at an end as the dry months were approaching. Troops sent to the Gulf of Iskanderun at this stage—to get them there must take some weeks—could not possibly aid Kut, even indirectly. Such side-shows were totally at variance with our General Staff's views concerning the proper conduct of the Great War. We wished the Russians well, of course, in their Armenian operations, and as they held the Black Sea there appeared to be every prospect of their achieving a considerable measure of success. But nothing that happened in that part of the world would be likely to exercise any paramount influence over the decision of the conflict as a whole.

Alexeieff suggested our transferring troops from Salonika to Alexandretta. I do not think that he fully realized what that kind of thing meant in time, shipping, and so on ; but it was pointed out to him that the French would disapprove of such a move owing to the importance they attached to the Macedonian affair, while, as for us, if we took away part of our forces from Salonika we would want to send them to France to fight the Germans, not to dissipate them on non-essentials. It was also pointed out that there were very serious naval objections to starting a brand-new campaign based on the Gulf of Iskanderun, that the tonnage question was beginning to arouse anxiety, and that Phillimore (who was at the Stavka at the time) would certainly endorse this contention. The Russian C.G.S. was not quite convinced, I am afraid. In the course of the discussion he made a remark, which was not translated by the interpreter but which MacCaw told me was to the effect that we could do what he asked perfectly easily if we liked. That was true enough. We could have deposited an army at Ayas Bay, no doubt, and could have secured its maritime communications

while it was ashore ; but we would have been playing
entirely the wrong game, wasting military resources, and
throwing a strain upon the Allies' sea-power without any
adequate justification. Still, our conference was throughout most amicable. Alexeieff expressed confidence as
regards effecting a powerful diversion on the Eastern
Front during the summer ; but he begged me to try to
extract some of our heavy howitzers for him out of our
War Office, as he was terribly handicapped, he said, for
want of that type of artillery. It was the last that I was
to see of this eminent soldier and patriot, who died some
time in 1918, broken down under the exertion and anxiety
of trying to save his country from the horrors of Bolshevik
ascendancy.

The Emperor, as I sat next to him at dinner in the
evening, referred to Alexandretta ; he had evidently seen
Alexeieff in the meantime. He also begged me to press
the question of heavy howitzers for Russia at home. He
asked a good deal about Sir W. Robertson, and he com-
mented on the fact that two soldiers who had enjoyed
no special advantages such as are not uncommon in
the commissioned ranks of most armies, Robertson and
Alexeieff, should have been forced to the front under the
stern pressure of war and should now be simultaneously
Chiefs of the General Staff in England and Russia. He
spoke of the possibility of Lord Kitchener visiting Russia
now that his labours at our War Office were somewhat
lightened. He told me that Sykes, who had had a long
discussion with the General Staff about Armenia and
Kurdistan, had enormously impressed those who had
heard him by his knowledge of the geography and the
people of those regions, and he asked why, when Wigram
and I were wearing the Russian shoulder-straps, Sykes
was not ; he evidently liked our doing so. The Grand
Duke Serge, who was Inspector-General of the Artillery,
was staying with the Emperor ; he also spoke about the
urgent need of heavy howitzers, saying that he hoped
within a few months to be on velvet as regards field-guns

and ammunition, but that aid with the heavier natures of ordnance must come from outside.

In conversations that we had at Mohileff, Hanbury-Williams expressed himself as somewhat anxious about the internal situation in Russia. General Polivanoff had recently been dismissed from his post as War Minister in spite of the good that he had effected within a very few months, and this was simply the result of a Court intrigue against an official who was known to have Liberal tendencies and was a *persona grata* with leading spirits in the Duma. That kind of attitude was calculated to arouse dissatisfaction, not merely amongst the educated portion of the community in general, but also in the ranks of the army; for in military circles the extent to which the troops had been sacrificed as a result of gross misconduct in connection with the provision of war material was bitterly resented. The losses suffered by the nation in the war already amounted to a huge figure, and although at this time the people at large probably held no very pronounced views on the subject of abandoning the contest, there undoubtedly was discontent. Under such circumstances, statesmanship imperatively demanded that mutual confidence should be maintained between the Court and Government on the one side, and the leaders of popular opinion on the other side. The removal of Polivanoff, who was doing so well, was just the kind of act to antagonize the educated classes and the military. Suspicion, moreover, existed that some of those in high places were not uncontaminated by German influence and were pro-German at heart.

No reasonable doubt has ever existed amongst those behind the scenes that the Emperor personally was heart and soul with the Allies; but that did not hold good, there is every ground for believing, amongst some of those with whom he was closely associated. No stranger brought into contact with Nicholas II. could help being attracted by his personal charm; but he was a reactionary surrounded by ultra-reactionaries and evil counsellors, who played upon his superstitions and his belief in the Divine Right of Kings and who brought him to his ruin together with his country. One had heard much in the past of the veneration in which Russians of all ranks and classes held their Sovereign as a matter of course. But, when brought into contact with Russian officers in 1916, one speedily realized that the Emperor Nicholas had lost his hold upon the affections of the army. Not that they spoke slightingly of him—they merely appeared to take no interest in him, which was perhaps worse. As for the Empress, there was little concealment in respect to her extreme unpopularity. Rasputin I never heard mentioned by a Russian in Russia ; but one knew all about that sinister figure from our own people.

Owing to a telegram that he received in connection with his special negotiations, Sykes left hurriedly that night, making straight for Tiflis, and I did not see him again in Russia. We, on the other hand, returned to Petrograd for a day or two. There were special entrances, with rooms attached, for the Imperial family at all the Petrograd stations and also at stations in important cities like Moscow and Rostoff ; we were always conducted to and from the trains through these, which was much pleasanter than struggling along with the crowd. For the journey to Transcaucasia we were provided with a special car of our own. In this we lived except when actually at Tiflis—a much more comfortable arrangement than going to hotels at places like Batoum and Kars ; we each had a double compartment to ourselves, and another was shared by our soldier-servant with one of the Imperial household, who accompanied us in the capacity of courier, interpreter and additional servant. There is no getting away from it, travelling under these somewhat artificial conditions has its points. As far as the Don we used the ordinary dining-cars ; but beyond that point dining-cars did not run, and meals were supposed to be taken at the station restaurants. For us, however, cook, meal and all used to come aboard our car and travel along to some station farther on, where the cook would be shot out with the débris ; it was admirably managed, however it was done, and was more the kind of thing one expects in India than in Europe. Although our soldier-servant had never been on parade in his life (I had taught him to salute when at Petrograd by making him salute himself in front of the big glass in my room, a plan worth any amount of raucous patter from the drill-sergeant), the very fact of his being in khaki seemed to turn him into a Russian scholar by that mysterious process adopted by British soldiers in foreign lands. Wigram had a grammar, and I had known a little Russian in the past ; but in the absence of Meyendorff and the courier neither Wigram nor I could get what we wanted, while the soldier-servant could.

Having seen nothing but everlasting dreary white expanses since quitting the immediate environs of Petrograd, except where the railway occasionally passed through some township, it was pleasant to find the snow gradually disappearing as one approached the Sea of Azov near Taganrog. Then, after crossing the Don at Rostoff, where extensive railway works were in progress and a fine new bridge over the great river was in course of construction, we found ourselves in a balmy spring atmosphere, although it was only the end of March. From there on to the Caspian the railway almost continuously traversed vast tracts of corn-land, the young crop just beginning to show above ground ; at dawn the huge range of the Caucasus, its glistening summits clear of clouds, made a glorious spectacle. In this part of the country oil-fuel was entirely used on the locomotives, and at Baku, where the petroleum oozes out of the sides of the railway cuttings, and beyond that city, the whole place reeked of the stuff. If you fell into the error of touching anything on the outside of the car, a door-handle or railing, you could not get your hand clean again any more than Lady Macbeth. We arrived at Tiflis late one afternoon, having taken within three or four hours of five complete days on the run from Petrograd. There we were met by a crowd of officers, and were conducted to a hotel.

Next morning we paid a number of formal visits. General Yanushkhevitch, Chief of the Staff, had held that same position when the Grand Duke Nicholas had been commander-in-chief at the Stavka. Tall, handsome and debonair, he was a man whom it was a pleasure to meet, although he may not perhaps intellectually have been quite equal to the great responsibilities placed on his shoulders in the early days of the war. This distinguished soldier of very attractive personality was murdered by revolutionaries while travelling by railway somewhere near Petrograd in 1917. General Yudenitch, we found, happened to be in Tiflis, and at the call that we paid him I arranged to present him with his order on the following morning.

I had a prolonged interview with the Grand Duke at the palace during the course of the day. He was not only Commander-in-Chief in Transcaucasia but was also Governor-General, and he told me that civil duties took up more of his time than military duties. Like Alexeieff, and probably by arrangement with the Stavka, he raised the question of our sending a force to near Alexandretta, and he put in a new plea for which I was not quite prepared. As he spoke at considerable length it, however, gave one time to think. He maintained that the right policy for the Allies to adopt was to knock the Turks out for good and to have done with them, expressing the opinion that it would not be difficult to induce them to make peace once they had undergone a good hammering. I replied that there appeared to be political problems involved in this which were quite outside my province, but that certain obvious factors came into the question. The prospects of prevailing upon the Sublime Porte to come to terms hinged upon what those terms were to be, and Constantinople seemed likely to prove a stumbling-block to an understanding. The Ottoman Government

might be prepared to part with Erzerum and Trebizond
and Basrah, and even possibly Syria and Palestine, but
Stamboul and the Straits were quite a different pair of
shoes. H.I.H. gripped my hand and pressed it till I
all but squealed. It was delightful to talk to a soldier
who went straight to the point, said he, but he dashed off
on another tack, asking what were our military objections to the Alexandretta plan ; so I went over much the
same ground as had already been gone over at Mohileff,
promising to let him have a memorandum on the subject.

He pronounced himself as most anxious to aid us in
Mesopotamia, did not seem satisfied with what his troops
in Persia had accomplished, and was concerned at my
rather pessimistic views with regard to Kut. Kut actually
held out for ten days longer than I had been given to
understand was possible at the War Office. He also
conveyed to me a pretty clear hint that in his view Major
Marsh, our Military Attaché with him, ought to have his
status improved. There I was entirely with him, but did
not say so ; there had been a misunderstanding with
regard to rank in Russia, for which I, when D.M.O., had
been in a measure responsible. The fact that there is
no equivalent to our grade of major in Russia had been
overlooked. The Military Secretary's department had
all along been ready enough to give subalterns the temporary rank of captain, or to improve captains into majors ;
but they had invariably humped their backs against
converting a major into a lieutenant-colonel for the time
being. The consequence was that there were a lot of
newly caught British subalterns doing special jobs who
had been given the rank of captain, and there were a
certain number of captains whom we called temporary
majors but who were merely captains in Russia. Marsh
was a real live major of some standing in the Indian army,
with two or three campaigns to his credit and a Staff
College man, and yet at Tiflis he was simply regarded as
a captain. This was put right by the War Office on
representation being made.

The Grand Duke spoke confidently as to the forth-coming capture of Trebizond, for which the plans were nearly ready. Good progress, he said, was being made by the force which was working forward along the coast, and he promised that the necessary arrangements should be made for us to visit the front in that quarter. He was most cordial, and he made many enquiries about Lord Kitchener for whom he expressed the highest regard. The interview was an extremely pleasant one, for the Grand Duke's manner, while dignified and impressive, was at the same time very winning, and he made it a strong point that I should discuss everything with him direct although also approving of my holding consulta-tions with his staff. Sykes' visit, he assured me, was highly appreciated both by himself and by his experts, who had been astonished at the knowledge of the country and the people which Sir Mark had displayed.

Next day the presentation of the G.C.M.G. to General Yudenitch was successfully brought off; that brilliant soldier was more at home in the field than in French, and he would probably have dispensed with all ceremony gladly enough. Scarcely had we got back to the hotel after the performance when he turned up to call, arrayed in all the insignia except the collar. He hoped that he had not done wrong in omitting this, and he was anxious to know when it was supposed to be put on. He rather had me there, because I did not know; but it was easy to say that the collar was only worn on very great occasions. Inside the case containing the Russian order which the Emperor had handed me at my farewell visit to him before returning home a few weeks earlier, there had been instructions in French with regard to the wearing of the different classes of the decoration; a similar plan might prove useful in these days when British orders are freely conferred upon foreign officers.

The city of Tiflis and the country around are worth seeing, and as we had a car at our disposal we made one or two short trips to points of interest. The Grand

Ducal entourage and the staff did all they could to make our stay pleasant.   No Allied general had visited Trans-caucasia since the outbreak of hostilities, so that we were made doubly welcome.   At luncheon at the palace we made the acquaintance of the Grand Duchess and of several young Grand Duchess nieces of the Grand Duke's, with whom Wigram proved an unqualified success ; in conversation with these charming young ladies it was only necessary to mention the name of the Staff Officer and they thereupon did the rest of the talking.   But after three or four days of comparative leisure, Meyendorff announced that all was ready for us to go on to Batoum, so we took up our residence in our railway-car again one evening after dinner and found ourselves by the Black Sea shore next morning.

We were most hospitably entertained at Batoum by the general in command and his staff, our railway-car being run away into a quiet siding.   We were driven out first to a low-lying coast battery in which a couple of 10-inch guns had very recently been mounted, and where we saw detachments at drill ; it appeared that the *Breslau* had paid a call some four or five months before, had fired a few projectiles into the harbour and the town, and had then made off ; it was hoped to give her a warm welcome should she repeat her tricks.   The emplacement between the two filled by the 10-inch was occupied by a huge range-finder, apparently on the Barr and Stroud principle, with very powerful lenses.   We afterwards drove up to one of the forts guarding the town on the land side, from which a fine view was obtained over the surrounding country.   Then we went on board the hospital ship *Portugal*.   A Baroness Meyendorff, cousin of our Meyendorff, was found to be matron-in-chief, and she took us all over the vessel, which was to proceed during the night to pick up wounded at Off, the advanced base of the force which was moving on Trebizond and which we were to visit next day.   In the afternoon we had a fine run along an excellently engineered road up the Tchorok valley, a deep trough in the mountains. The air in this part of the world seemed delightfully genial after the rigours of Scandinavia, Petrograd and Mohileff, reminding one of Algiers in spring ; the vegetation was everywhere luxuriant on the hillsides, the ground was carpeted with wildflowers, and oranges abounded in the groves around the town.

Up about 3 the next morning, we boarded a destroyer to make the run to Off, which was eighty-five miles away along the coast, and put off out of the harbour through the gap in the torpedo-net about dawn. It was a lovely morning without a breath of air ; this was as well perhaps, because the interior of the vessel, an old-type craft making a tremendous fuss over going, say, 18 knots, was not particularly attractive. The officers on board could not speak English or French, which struck one as odd ; but apparently the personnel of the Black Sea fleet rarely proceeded to other waters—to the Baltic, for instance, or the Far East. All went smoothly until we were within about a dozen miles of our destination when a wireless message was picked up announcing that the *Portugal* had just been torpedoed and was sinking close to Off, and asking for help. We cracked on all speed, the craft straining and creaking as if she would tumble to pieces, and I doubt if we were making much more than 25 knots then ; but by the time that we reached the scene of the disaster any of the personnel who could be saved were already on board other vessels and being landed. We learnt that several of the male personnel and two or three of the nurses, including the Baroness Meyendorff, had, unhappily, been drowned.

The *Portugal* was the second hospital ship that I had set foot on since the beginning of the war, and, like the *East Anglia* mentioned on p. 228, she had gone to the bottom within twenty-four hours of my visit. I determined to give hospital ships a wide berth in future if possible—I did not bring them luck. With her Red Cross markings she was perfectly unmistakable ; she had been attacked in broad daylight on an almost glassy sea, and the U-boat commander must have been perfectly well aware of her identity when he sank her. The tragic occurrence naturally cast a gloom over Off,. where we landed on the open beach and were met by General Liakoff, commanding the Field Force, with a numerous staff.

There had been a sharp combat by night some thirty-six hours before, when the Turks had delivered a most determined onset upon a portion of the Russian position ; it had, indeed, been touch-and-go for a time. General Liakoff proposed to take us up to the scene of the fight ; so the whole party mounted on wiry Cossack horses and cobs, and the cavalcade after crossing the little river near Off proceeded to breast the heights, our animals scrambling up the rugged hill-tracks like cats, till we reached the summit of a detached spur where the affray had been the most violent. The enemy had almost surrounded this spur, and the numerous bodies of dead Turks lying about on the slopes and in the gullies testified to the severity of the fight ; Wigram, whose experiences of the battlefield had hitherto been limited to a visit to the Western Front on a special job, was as delighted with these grim relics as a dog is who has found some abomination in the road. Quantities of used and unused cartridges, Turkish and Russian, were strewed about, and it was evident that the defenders had only managed to hold on by the skin of their teeth. General Liakoff told me that his troops were especially pleased at their success, as it had transpired that the assailants were Turks belonging to picked corps recently arrived from the Gallipoli Peninsula.

The Russian outposts were now on the next ridge, beyond a narrow valley, and all was quiet at the moment. The views from the spur were very fine, commanding the coast-line in both directions. Trebizond, some fifteen miles off but looking to be nearer, glistened white in the midday sunshine ; each patch of level was bright green with growing corn, the higher hills were still crowned with snow, and the littoral as a whole in its colouring and its features was the Riviera faced about and looking north. The general gave me to understand that he would be unable to advance for some days, as he had to make up his reserves of supplies ; but the Grand Duke had let me know that considerable reinforcements were to be brought across the Black Sea before the final attack upon Trebizond took place.

We spent the afternoon down at Off. With recollections of Afghan and South African accumulations of war material and condiments, one was struck with the very limited amount of impedimenta and stores which this Field Force carried with it. The advanced base of a little army comprising a couple of divisions, with odds and ends, scarcely exhibited the amount of transport and food dumps that one of our 1901–2 mobile columns on the veldt would display when it was taking a rest. The weather had been particularly favourable for landing operations for some days, we were told, and that afternoon a small freight ship, with a queer elongated prow that enabled her to run her nose right up on to the beach, was discharging her cargo straight on to the foreshore. But it was obvious that, with anything like a breeze blowing home, landing operations at Off would be brought to a standstill, and that the progress of the campaign was very dependent upon the moods of the Black Sea. A road was, it is true, being constructed along the shore from Batoum, and a railway was talked of ; but for the time being the Field Force had to rely almost entirely upon maritime communications. A different destroyer from the one we had come in took us back, several of the nurses saved from the *Portugal* also being on board, and we got ashore at Batoum after 9 P.M., to find the general and staff anxiously awaiting our arrival in anticipation of dinner which we travellers were more than ready for. We returned to Tiflis next day.

We had hoped to make a trip to Erzerum, so famous in the chequered annals of Russo-Turkish conflicts in

Asia ; but the thaw had set in on the uplands of Armenia, the staff at Tiflis said it would be almost impossible to get a car through the slush for the hundred miles from the railhead at Sarikamish, and we had no excuse for going other than curiosity ; so the idea was abandoned. It was arranged, however, that we should proceed to Kars and Sarikamish. A short time elapsed before we could start, and during this delay we were bidden to a gala dinner at the palace given in our honour, at which Marsh also was present. The palace is not a specially imposing building, but it has a fine broad staircase, and the effect of the Cossacks of the Guard lining this in their dark red cloaks was very striking. In his speech the Grand Duke expressed great satisfaction at our visit to Transcaucasia, as indicating that Russian efforts in this region were appreciated in England.

From Tiflis up to Kars means a rise of over 4000 feet, and the locomotives on the line were specially constructed for this climbing work, having funnels at either end. Whatever may be the case at other times, Armenia when the snows are melting is a singularly dreary region, almost treeless and seemingly destitute of vegetation ; some of the scenery along the line was grand enough in a rugged way, however, and near Alexandropol the railway traversed plateau land with outlook over a wide expanse of country. Studying the large-scale map, it looked as if one ought to be able to see Mount Ararat, eighty miles away to the south, but there was a tiresome hill in the way obstructing the view in the required direction.

Mention of Alexandropol suggests a reference to the pronunciation of Russian names, which we always manage to get wrong in this country. Slavs throw the accent nearer the end of words than we are inclined to do. Thus in Alexandropol they put the accent on the " dro," not on the " and " as we should. We always put the accent on the " bas " in Sebastopol, but the accent properly is on the " to." In Alexeieff the accent is on the second " e," and in Korniloff it is on the " i." You will not generally go far wrong if you throw the accent one syllable farther from the beginning of the word than you naturally would when speaking English.

Twenty-four hours were spent at Kars, a filthy, but on account of its associations and of the works being carried on, extremely interesting place ; unfortunately, I was not familiar with the story of Sir Fenwick Williams' great defence of the stronghold during the Crimean War, for the old battlements and outworks still existed, if in a ruinous condition. We were taken all round the place by car, were shown the elaborate magazines being excavated in the heart of a mountain, and fetched up at one of the outlying forts in which a large garrison resided. By this time I was getting quite accustomed to the ceremony gone through when one met troops on parade or in barracks. You called out, " Starova bradzye ? " which being interpreted apparently means " How are you, brothers ? " There followed an agonizing little pause during which you had time to think that you had got the thing wrong, had made an ass of yourself, and were disgraced for evermore. Then they all sang out in unison, " Wow wow wow-wow wow "—that, at all events, is what it sounded like. Goodness knows what it meant. One had too much sense to ask, because one might have got the two sentences mixed, which would have meant irretrievable disaster. The effect, however, when there were a lot of troops on the ground was excellent, as they always performed their share with rare gusto. The rank and file particularly appreciated a foreign officer giving them the customary greeting.

The size of the garrison of this outlying fort afforded evidence of the Russian wealth in man-power. There were a good many guns mounted, of no great value, and some machine-guns flanked the ditches ; but the amount of personnel seemed out of all proportion to the importance of the work or the nature of its armament. The men were packed pretty tight in the casemates, arranged in a double tier, the sojourners on the upper tier only having the bare boards to lie on. Afterwards we went out to an entirely new fort which was not yet quite completed, situated on the plain some six miles from the town. The Russians were making Kars into a great place of arms on modern lines, and one rather wondered why.

Continuing the journey in the afternoon, we were met at Sarikamish station by General Savitzky, commanding the Sixty-sixth Division and the garrison, with his staff and a swarm of officers. The place had been the frontier station before the war and was well laid out as an up-to-date cantonment, although owing to the thaw the mud was indescribable. The environs constituted almost an oasis in the bleak Armenian uplands owing to the hills being clothed in pine-woods, and Sarikamish had the reputation of making a pleasant summer resort, people coming out from Tiflis to spend a few weeks so as to escape the heat. We were treated with almost effusive cordiality, dined at the staff mess that night, and Cossacks gave an exhibition of their spirited dancing afterwards and sang songs. Of the large number of officers acting as hosts, only one, unfortunately, could speak French, so that Meyendorff was kept busy acting as an intermediary.

The idea prevalent in this country that Russians in general are good linguists, it may here be observed, is a delusion. The aristocracy, no doubt, all speak French perfectly. In the Yacht Club in Petrograd most of the members appeared to be quite at home in either French or English, and no doubt could have chattered away in German if put to it; but away from the capital and Moscow it was not easy to get on without a knowledge of Russian. The staff at Sarikamish were anxious that I should meet the Turkish officer prisoners interned there, as they believed that a couple of them were Boches and nobody able to speak German had come along for months; but as it turned out, there was no time for a meeting.

Next morning we started off in a blizzard to proceed by car some way in the direction of Erzerum along the high-road over the col which marked the frontier; the pass would be about 7600 feet above sea-level, as the elevation of Sarikamish was given as 6700. This high-road constituted the main line of communications of the Russian forces in the field beyond railhead, and the traffic along it was unceasing. With a long, stiff upward incline, there were the usual sights of broken-down vehicles and of dead animals on all hands ; but the organization appeared to be good, if rough and ready, and the transport was serviceable enough. Getting the cars along past the strings of vehicles and animals was no easy job, and it proved a chilly drive. But the weather brightened, and on the way back we got out and proceeded on foot to a hill-top of historic interest known as the " Crow's Nest," above Sarikamish. For it had been the site of headquarters on the occasion of those very critical conflicts in December 1914, when the Ottoman commanders had made a determined effort to break through into Russian Transcaucasia, and when their plans had only been brought to nought by a most signal combination of war on the part of the defenders.

There, on the scene of his triumph, Colonel Maslianikov of the 16th Caucasian Rifle Regiment described to a gathering of us fur-clad figures how, with his regiment and some other troops hastily scraped together, he had brought the leading Turkish divisions to a standstill, largely by pure bluff and by audacious handling of an inferior force, and so had prepared the way for the dramatic overthrow of three Osmanli army corps which transformed a situation that had been full of menace into one which became rich in promise. News of this dramatic feat of arms reached the War Office at the time, but without particulars. That the victor of this field, a field won by a masterpiece of soldiership, should remain a simple colonel, suggested a singular indifference on the part of authorities at the heart of the empire to what wardens of the marches accomplished in peace and war. That pow-wow in an icy blast amid the snow recalled the Grand Duke Nicholas's appeal to Lord Kitchener that we should make some effort to take pressure off his inadequate and hard-pressed forces in Armenia, an appeal which landed us in the Dardanelles Campaign ; and it further recalled the fact that the colonel's feat near Sarikamish had put an end to all need for British intervention almost before the Grand Duke made his appeal. The Russian victory, the details of which were explained to us that day by its creator, was gained on a date preceding by some weeks the Allies' naval attempt to conquer the Straits single-handed.

After a belated luncheon at the staff mess, following on this long programme, we had to hurry off accompanied by Savitzky and his staff to our railway-car. All the officers and a goodly number of the rank and file in Sarikamish seemed to have collected at the station to give us a rousing send-off, making it evident that our visit had been much appreciated. This was not unnatural. Here were Allies fighting in a region far removed from the principal theatres of war in which the armies of the Entente were engaged, and they were with justice desirous that their efforts should not remain wholly unknown. Like Off, Sarikamish conveyed a very favourable impression of the working of the Transcaucasian legions under the supreme leadership of the Grand Duke Nicholas, of whom officers all spoke with enthusiasm, and whose personality undoubtedly counted for much amongst the impressionable moujik soldiery. What one had seen in these forward situations inspired confidence in the future. Nor was that confidence misplaced, for the Russian forces in Armenia were to achieve great triumphs ere 1916 was out.

We had hoped to cross the Caucasus from Tiflis to Vladikavkas by the great military road over the Dariel Pass, but the staff would not hear of it, as there was still some risk from avalanches and as the route was not properly open. We had a farewell luncheon at the palace, and I had a long talk on military questions with the Grand Duke beforehand, at which he entrusted me with special messages to Lord Kitchener and Sir W. Robertson, and expressed an earnest desire for close co-ordination between his forces in Persia and ours in Mesopotamia. News had arrived of the repulse of the Kut Relief Force at Sannaiyat after its having made a promising beginning at Hannah, so that there was no disguising the fact that little hope remained of saving Townshend's force. I did not know what course might be adopted by our Government in this discouraging theatre of war, assuming that Kut fell ; but there could be no doubt that co-ordination was desirable, as we were bound to hold on to the Shatt-el-Arab and the oil-fields, whatever happened ; it was therefore quite safe to promise that we would do our best. Having made our farewells, our little party proceeded straight from Tiflis to Moscow.

In that famous city we were put up in the palace within the Kremlin, and we passed a couple of days mainly devoted to sight-seeing. What has become of all the marvels gathered together within the grim fortress walls in the heart of the ancient Russian capital ? Of the jewelled ikons, of the priceless sacerdotal vestments, of the gorgeous semi-barbaric Byzantine temples, of the galleries of historic paintings, of the raiment, the boots and the camp-bed of Peter the Great ? One wearied of wandering from basilica to basilica, from edifice to edifice and from room to room. Only the globe-trotting American keeping a diary can suffer an intensity of this sort of thing. But then we were taken out one of the afternoons by car to the Sparrow Hills ridge above the Moskva, about three miles outside the city and not far from where one morning in 1812 the Grand Army topped a rise and of a sudden beheld the goal which it had travelled so far to seek. From there we viewed the spectacle of a riot of gilded cupolas gleaming in the sun, a sight incomparably more striking in its majesty than that of the interiors and memorials of the past we had been reconnoitring at close quarters.

Another afternoon we drove out to a palace in the

outskirts, which had been converted into a military hospital and was being maintained by the Emperor out of his private purse. There are some writers of war experiences on the Western Front who have revelled in pouring ridicule upon the inspections that are ever proceeding at our hospitals in the field, although these functions furnish the humorist with just that opportunity which his soul craves for. My experience, however, is that in the military world doctors and nurses simply love to have their tilt-yard visited by people who have no business there. You could not meet with a Russian hospital-train on its journey, drawn up at some railway station, but you were gently, if firmly, coerced into traversing its corridors from end to end. When following the course of the Turko-Greek conflict in 1897 on the side of the Hellenes, where almost every known European nation had its Red Cross hospital, I was dragged round these establishments one and all. To have strangers tramping about staring at them must be an intolerable nuisance to wounded men who are badly in need of peace and quiet. One went through the " starova bradzye " game in each hospital ward visited in Russia, and the din of the " wow wow wow-wow wow-ings " reverberating through these halls seemed strangely out of place amidst surroundings of gloom and suffering, where many a poor fellow was nearing his end. Our acting Consul-General came to pay me a visit at the palace, and we had a long talk about the internal conditions of Russia, of which he took none too rosy a view; distrust and discontent were growing apace, he implied, for the Court was entirely out of touch with the people, and the Government seemed to be going the way of the Court. On the night that we were leaving we were taken to the ballet at the Opera House, and we went straight from the theatre to board the train, which left about midnight for Petrograd.

There we found Hanbury-Williams putting up at the Astoria, and I was able to have several conversations with him and also with Sir G. Buchanan and Colonel

Blair, our Assistant Military Attaché. From what I gathered from them and observations during the trip, it would be safe to report to the War Office that from the military point of view the outlook in Russia was distinctly promising. Even if there was little prospect of anything of real importance being effected on the Eastern Front this year, we might reasonably reckon upon the immense forces of the empire, adequately fitted out with rifles, machine-guns, field-artillery and ammunition, and with some heavy guns and howitzers to help, performing a dominant rôle in the campaign of 1917. And yet all was not well. The political conditions, if not exactly ominous, gave grounds for anxiety. The dim shadow of coming events was already being cast before. The internal situation required watching, and it was on the cards that the influence of the Allies might have to be thrown into the scale in order to prevent a dire upheaval.

While at the capital on this occasion we paid a visit to the British hospital, occupying a palace on the Nevski Prospekt, which was under the management of Lady Sybil Grey. The most interesting patient in this admirably appointed institution was a sturdy little lad of about fourteen, who had been to the front, had got hit with a bullet, and had been converted into a sergeant. He was evidently made much of, accompanying us round as a sort of assistant Master of the Ceremonies, and he seemed to be having a good time ; but he complained, so we were given to understand, that the nurses would insist on kissing him. If that was the only inconvenience resulting from a wound, it seemed to me to be a form of unpleasantness that one might manage to put up with.

When the time for departure came, Meyendorff was quite unhappy at my objecting to his accompanying us all the way to Tornea ; but we meant to travel through Finland disguised as small fry and in plain clothes. On the occasion of our previous heading for home, our leaving had been advertised in all the newspapers ; the Embassy had drawn the attention of the authorities to this, and the Press had been directed to make no mention in future of foreign officers starting for Scandinavia. Even if the enemy under-water flotilla was hardly likely to make special endeavours to catch us on the Bergen-Newcastle trip, there was no object in running unnecessary risks by letting them know that we were coming along.

We enjoyed a rare stroke of luck on the voyage across the North Sea this time. Our packet was plodding peacefully along on a hazy, grey forenoon, about half-way to the Tyne, when the faint silhouettes of a brace of destroyers were descried racing athwart our course a good many miles ahead. We were watching them disappear far away on the starboard bow, when others suddenly hove in sight looming up through the mist, all of them going like mad in the same direction, and then four great shadowy battle-cruisers showed themselves steaming hard across our front, four or five miles away. The armada, a signal manifestation of vitality and power and speed, was evidently making for Rosyth; it had no doubt been on the prowl about the Skagerrack, and it presumably meant to coal at high pressure and then to get busy again. Such a spectacle would naturally be an everyday occurrence to the Sister Service ; but to a landsman this assemblage of fighting craft going for all they were worth was tremendously impressive as a demonstration of British maritime might—far more impressive than interminable rows of warships, moored and at rest, such as one had seen gathered together between Southampton Water and Spithead for a Royal Review.

What surprised one most perhaps was the wide extent of the water-area which this battle-cruiser squadron covered, consisting as it did of only a quartette of capital ships after all, with their attendant ring of mosquito-craft keeping guard ahead, astern and on the flanks. The leading pair of destroyers cannot have been much short of twenty miles in advance of the two scouts which came racing up at the tail of the hunt. Our old tub had got well within the water-area by the time that these latter sleuths approached, and their track passed astern of us ; but at the last moment one of them pivoted round, just as a Canadian canoe will pivot round in the hands of an artist, and came tearing along after us—it may have been to look at us or it may merely have been to show off— passed us on the port hand not more than a cable's length off as if we were standing still, shot across our bows, and was off like a flash after her consort. Of those battle-cruisers that looked so imposing as they rushed along towards the Firth of Forth that forenoon, at least one was to meet her fate before many days had passed. The Battle of Jutland was fought about three weeks later.

CHAPTER XV

THE RUSSIAN BUNGLE

INCOMPARABLY the most grievous disaster met with by
the Entente during the progress of the Great War was
the Russian Revolution of March 1917. All the other
mishaps, great and small, which the Allies had to deplore
—the occupation of Belgium and of wide areas of France
by German hosts at the very outset, the collapse of the
Emperor Nicholas's legions in Poland in 1915, the Dardanelles failure, Bulgaria's accession to the ranks of our
enemies and the resultant overthrow of Serbia, the fall
of Kut, Roumania's unhappy experience—sink into in-
significance compared with the downfall of the Romanoffs
and what that downfall led to.

Had the cataclysmic upheaval in Russia been averted,
or at least been delayed until hostilities were at an end,

the war would have been brought to a successful conclusion before the close of the year 1917. Much loss of life would have been saved. The European belligerents, one and all and whichever side they fought on during the contest, would be in an incomparably less anxious economic position than they actually are in to-day. The Eastern Hemisphere would have settled its own affairs without intervention, other than naval and financial, from the farther side of the Atlantic. Peace would in consequence have been concluded within a very few months of the cessation of hostilities, instead of negotiations starting on a preposterous basis and being protracted for more than a year.

That the Revolution could have been prevented, or at all events could have been deferred until subsequent to the end of the war, I firmly believe. Our diplomacy has been severely criticized in connection with Near Eastern affairs in 1915 ; nor will any one maintain that it was successful, judged by results. But the situation in the Balkans was one of extraordinary perplexity in any case, and the problem was complicated by the fact that the Allies were not all of one mind as to what course to pursue on almost any single occasion. The position of affairs during the critical months leading up to March 1917 in Russia, on the other hand, was no puzzle, and the political situation had never been a puzzle since the outbreak of war. Our French and Italian friends, moreover, fully realized that this country, if it chose to do so, possessed the means of exerting a special and controlling influence within the governing clique holding· sway at the head of the empire, and they were most anxious that that influence should be exercised. But before touching on this question some comments on the military conditions within the territories of our whilom eastern Ally previous to, and at the time of, the catastrophe will not be out of place.

The potentialities of Russia for carrying on a war of first-class magnitude had been altogether overestimated at the outset in the United Kingdom and in France, alike by the public and by the military authorities—in France perhaps even more so than in this country. The armies of our eastern Ally did, it is true, accomplish greater things in some respects than had been anticipated, because they struck an effective blow at an earlier date than had been believed possible, and they thereby relieved pressure in the West at a critical juncture even if their enterprising and loyal action in East Prussia was later to lead them into a terrible disaster. During the first two or three months after the outbreak of hostilities their weakness in regard to equipment and to munitions was not, however, known, or at all events was only partially known. There was much talk in the Press about the " steam-roller " which was going to flatten the Central Powers out. We at the War Office had received warnings from our very well-informed Military Attaché, it is true ; but those warnings did not convey to us the full gravity of the position, a gravity which was probably not re-cognized even in high places in Russia for some time. Moreover, as far as we could judge, Paris had no idea that anything was seriously amiss beyond the Vistula, in spite of the Franco-Russian alliance having been in force for some years.

The first really alarming tidings on this subject that we received came to hand, oddly enough, from Japan ; and it bears testimony to the efficiency of our Far Eastern Ally's intelligence service that the Island Empire should have been so intimately acquainted with the military conditions in a State with which it had been at war only a very few years before. This information reached us, I think, in October 1914. But as far as I recollect, that warning, inexorable as it was, only touched the question of ammunition. We were told plainly that the Russians were likely to run out of this indispensable at an early date ; but the message did not mention rifles, although these already began to run short within eight months of the commencement of the struggle. How it came about that there should have been so deplorable a break-down in respect to war material can only be a matter of conjecture ; but we may hazard a pretty shrewd guess that the collapse which was to lead to such deplorable results in the early summer of 1915, was attributable to graft on a Homeric scale. For the Russian army budgets had for several years before the war been framed on lavish lines ; that for 1914, for instance, mounted up to 725,000,000 roubles, which represented a higher figure than the corresponding budgets in either Germany or France. General Sukhomlinoff, the War Minister on the Neva from 1910 to 1915, was, as is well known, disgraced in the latter year, and he was tried for his life after the Revolution.

The Russian victories in Galicia during the winter of 1914–15, followed as they were by the reduction of the important place of arms, Przemysl, caused unbounded satisfaction in this country. But those behind the scenes feared, with only too good reason, that such triumphs represented no more than a flash in the pan, and that, should the Germans decide to throw heavy forces into the scale, the Grand Duke Nicholas would speedily find himself obliged to abandon the conquests which looked so gratifying on paper. We in the War Office learnt, indeed, that the Russian generalissimo, who recognized that the munitions situation did not justify offensive operations on an ambitious scale, had been indisposed to undertake the capture of Przemysl, but that political pressure had been brought to bear on him.

Lord Kitchener was constantly watching the Eastern Front with anxiety during the early months of 1915, fearing that in view of the Russian weakness some great transfer of enemy forces from East to West might be instituted. A strategical combination on such lines on the part of the German Great General Staff would under the existing circumstances have been a very natural one to adopt. But it is conceivable (if not very probable) that the higher military authorities in Berlin were not fully aware of the condition of their antagonists in Poland. The fact, moreover, remains that in their accounts of the campaign of 1915 the numerous books on the war which have appeared in Germany ignore to a remarkable extent the munitions difficulties under which the Grand Duke Nicholas was suffering. That, however, may be attributable to a disinclination to admit that Hindenburg's successes were due, not to any outstanding brilliance in the handling of his troops nor to the gallantry and efficiency of those concerned in the operations under his orders, but simply to his opponent being almost bereft of armament. Be that as it may, Russia was in such evil plight for arms and ammunition from the summer of 1915 on to that of 1916 that she was wellnigh powerless, except in Armenia. She only became really formidable again during the period of quiescence that, as usual, set in during the winter of 1916–17.

Shortly after returning home in May 1916, I took over charge (under circumstances to be mentioned in the next chapter) of the War Office branch which dealt with munitions and supplies for Russia, and I am consequently familiar with this question. To show what strides were made towards fitting the military forces out for a strenuous campaign in 1917, some output figures may be given. (I have none for dates prior to January 1916.) It should be mentioned that the output of field-artillery ammunition had already, owing to General Polivanoff's exertions, been greatly expanded during the latter part of 1915, and there was no very marked increase in this during 1916 ; the French supplied large numbers of rounds, and it had been hoped that great quantities would come to hand from the United States, but the influx from this latter source hardly materialized before the winter of 1916–17. Seeing how greatly the Russian armies had suffered from lack of heavy artillery during the first year of the war, the huge increase in output of howitzer and 6-inch rounds is particularly worth noting.

	January 1916.	January 1917.
Rifles	93,000	129,000
Machine-guns	712	1,200
Small-arms ammunition	96,000,000 rounds	173,000,000 rounds
Field-guns . . .	169	407
Field-howitzers	33	62
Field-howitzer ammuni-		
tion . .	72,000 1ounds	369,000 rounds
6-inch guns and howitzers	1	17
6-inch gun and howitzer		
ammunition	32,000 rounds	230,000 rounds

By the early weeks of 1917 the empire was not dependent upon its own resources alone. Great contracts for rifles, machine-guns, small-arms ammunition, and field-gun ammunition had been placed in the United States under arrangements made by Lord Kitchener in the summer of 1915. The factories on the farther side of the Atlantic only began to produce during the summer of 1916, and they had not got into full swing before the latter part of the year; but by March 1917, 412,000 rifles, 12,200 machine-guns, 240,000,000 rounds of small-arms ammunition, and 4,750,000 rounds of field-gun ammunition had already been handed over, and great part of this armament had been shipped (the field-gun ammunition mainly to Vladivostok across the Pacific); and a great output was still in progress. Over 800 howitzers and heavy guns, with abundant ammunition for them, had also by that time been despatched to Russia from the United Kingdom and France, and nearly 6,000,000 rounds of field-gun ammunition from France. Such statistics could be multiplied. Suffice it to say that there was every reason to assume that the Emperor Nicholas's legions would be adequately supplied with most forms of munitions for the 1917 campaign, and that, thanks to the great increase in the numbers of rifles, machine-guns and pieces of artillery available, they would take the field in far stronger force numerically than at any previous period of the war.

From the purely military point of view the position of affairs in the winter of 1916–17 was, in fact, decidedly promising. A huge force was under arms and was coming to be well equipped. General Brusiloff's successes in the summer of 1916, even if they made no appreciable alteration in the general strategical situation, had afforded most satisfactory evidence that the stubborn fighting spirit of the Russian troops had suffered no eclipse consequent upon disasters of the past. Confidence reigned at the Stavka, and competent leaders had been forced to the front. But the internal situation, on the other hand, had become ominous in the extreme.

Some references were made in the last chapter to the discontent that was manifesting itself throughout the country even early in 1916, and to the attitude of marked indifference that was being displayed by the officers in respect to the Sovereign to whom they owed allegiance. But things had gone rapidly from bad to worse since that date. M. Sazonoff, the eminent Foreign Minister, to whose efforts before the war the satisfactory understanding between Great Britain and Russia was largely due and whose policy was uncompromisingly anti-German, had been got out of the way by the machinations of the Court clique. (The Emperor, it may be mentioned, had been almost cringingly apologetic to our representatives about this step, which he could not but realize would create a very bad impression in London and Paris.) Successive substitutions carried out amongst the personnel of the Executive had all tended towards introducing elements that were reactionary from the point of view of internal policy and were suspect from the point of view of the Entente. Dissatisfaction and loss of confidence had been growing apace amongst the public, and what had been merely indifference manifested amongst the officers towards the Autocrat at the head of the State was giving place to openly expressed dislike and even to contempt for a potentate who, however well-meaning he might be, was constantly affording evidence that he was in the hands of mischievous counsellors and possessed no will of his own.

A special Mission had come over to England from Russia in August, including amongst its numerous personnel the Finance Minister and the Chief of the General Staff at the Ministry of War. This Mission had obtained from us promises of financial assistance running into scores of millions sterling, to say nothing of an undertaking to furnish substantial consignments of war material. But in the understanding that was then arrived at, I never could detect any trace of conditions designed to check the dangerous policy which all who were behind the scenes realized the Emperor to be adopting. Who paid the piper never called one note of the tune. There was an ingenuousness about the proceedings on the part of our Government that was startling in its Micawberism and improvidence.

Now, our Cabinet was extraordinarily fortunate in the British representatives within the Russian Empire upon whom they depended or ought to have depended. They were admirably served on the Neva, at the Stavka and in the field. We had an ambassador who was trusted to an unprecedented extent by all ranks and classes in the realm which he was making his temporary home. The Head of our Military Mission, Hanbury-Williams, was a *persona gratissima* with the Emperor. Our Military Attachés—Knox, Blair, and Marsh—were masters of the Russian language, and, in common with several British officers especially accredited to the different armies, ever had their fingers on the pulse of military sentiment on the fighting fronts. How it came about that our Government —or rather Governments, because Mr. Lloyd George and his War Cabinet replaced Mr. Asquith and his sanhedrin of twenty-three just when things were becoming highly critical—shambled blindly along trusting to luck and did nothing, it is hard to say. But among them they nearly lost us the war.

Towards the end of the year 1916 the situation was

already becoming almost desperate, even if the putting away of the horrible Rasputin did seem for a moment to relieve the gloom. Officers high up in the army were imploring our military representatives for British intervention with their rulers. Our ambassador appears to have done everything that man could do, even remonstrating in set terms with the Emperor ; but he would not seem to have been accorded the strenuous support from home which he had a right to look for, and which would have given his representations that compelling weight demanded by an exceedingly precarious situation.

Owing to the nature of my duties in connection with supplies of all kinds for Russia, following upon visits to that country, I had been closely in touch with the situation for some months, heard from our military representatives from time to time, and saw Russians in an official position in London practically daily. By the end of the year the position seemed to me so fraught with peril that, on learning of the contemplated despatch of a special political and military Mission to Murmansk *en route* for the interior, I wrote a private letter to Mr. Lloyd George, and this was duly acknowledged with thanks by his Private Secretary. This communication warned the Prime Minister that Russia was on the brink of revolution owing to the reactionary tendencies of her government ; it pointed out that if a revolution were to break out the consequences must be disastrous to the campaign of 1917 on the Eastern Front, as all arrangements would inevitably be thrown out of gear ; and it proposed that we should play our trump card, that, backed by the express authority and enforced by the active intervention of the War Cabinet, we should turn to its fullest account the influence of our Royal House with the Emperor Nicholas. The remedy might not have produced the desired effect. The diagnosis at all events turned out to be correct.

One never anticipated, needless to say, that if the revolution which seemed to be imminent were actually to take place, the consequences would be quite so terrible as those which have actually supervened. One never dreamt of the executive power over great part of the vast dominions then under the sway of the Romanoff dynasty falling into the hands of wretches such as Peter the Painter, Trotzky and Lenin. But, even assuming a more or less stable form of reasonable republican government to replace the existing autocracy, it could not be other than obvious to all who were in any way conversant with the social conditions holding good in this enormous area, peopled as it was by illiterate and profoundly ignorant peasants, that a revolution was bound to produce a state of affairs for the time being bordering on chaos. What ought to prove the decisive year of the war was at hand. Revolution must be staved off at all costs.

The special Mission actually started for Murmansk some two or three weeks later. Although the list of its personnel made a good enough show on paper, it lacked the one element that was practically indispensable if its representations were to save the situation. They say that Lord Milner, on getting back, gave the War Cabinet to understand that all was going on fairly well in Russia, and that there was little or no fear of a *bouleversement.* This would have seemed to me incredible had I not met several of the members of the Mission when they turned up again, and had they not, one and all, appeared perfectly satisfied with the internal situation of the empire on which they had paid a call. Whom these good people saw out there, where they went, what steps they took to acquire knowledge in quarters other than official circles, how it came about that they returned to this country with no more idea of the state of affairs than a cassowary on the plains of Timbuctoo, furnishes one of those mysteries which cast such a recondite glamour over our public life. Why, the Babes in the Wood were prodigies of analysis and wizards of cunning compared with this carefully selected civilian and military party, which, it has to be acknowledged, spent a by no means idle time while sojourning in the territories of our eastern

U

Ally. For among them they promised away any amount more munitions and war material of all kinds. They went into the details of the contemplated deal with meticulous care and consummate administrative skill. They elaborated a programme which would undoubtedly have proved in the highest degree advantageous to Russia, had the conditions not undergone a complete metamorphosis owing to the outbreak of the Revolution in Petrograd a very few days after they landed, sanguine and reassuring, in this country on their return journey.

Had it not been for the *Hampshire* disaster, had Lord Kitchener succeeded in carrying out his mission in the summer of 1916, it is conceivable that, in virtue of that almost uncanny intuition that he possessed, he would have pieced together the realities of the situation, and would have managed to teach his colleagues in our Cabinet to understand them on his return. His personal influence might have made all the difference in the world in Russia. He would have gained touch with all sorts and conditions of men while out there, and would have got to the back of their minds by methods all his own. The very fact that Russians have so much of the oriental strain in them would have helped him in this. But it was not to be.

Of what followed after the Revolution much might be said ; but, in so far as the blunders committed by our Government are concerned, it has to be admitted that the situation was no easy one to grapple with. When you have been such an ass as to ride your horse into a bog, there is a good deal of excuse for your botching getting the beast out again, as that is in the nature of things a difficult job. The mischief was done when the Revolution was allowed to occur. After that it became a case of groping with a bewildering, kaleidoscopic, intangible state of affairs. Mr. Henderson's performances have excited much ridicule, but against his absurd belief in M. Kerensky must be set his prompt recognition of his own unfitness for the position of representative of the

British Government on the banks of the Neva. M. Kerensky, no doubt, may have meant well by the Allies after his own fashion ; but as he can claim so great a share in the work of destroying the discipline of the Russian army, he proved the kind of friend who in practice is more pernicious than are open and undisguised enemies. One of the most singular features, indeed, in the epoch-making events of 1917 in Eastern Europe was the fact that a windbag of this sort should ever have gained power, and that, having gained power, he should have retained it for the space of several months. Only in Russia could such a thing have happened. It must be added that the perplexities to which the Entente Governments were a prey in connection with the Russian problem subsequent to March 1917 were aggravated from the outset—and yet more so after Lenin's gaining the mastery—by the very divergent views which prevailed amongst them in connection with most of the awkward questions that arose.

This was illustrated by the strange happenings concerning Siberia and Vladivostok of the early part of 1918. Gathered together at the extreme eastern doorway into Russia were enormous accumulations of war material and of vital commodities of all kinds—most of them, it may be observed incidentally, being goods which had been procured in the United States by British credits on behalf of pre-Bolshevist governments, Imperial and republican. It was imperative that these should not fall into the hands of Lenin's warrior rabble that was spreading eastwards from beyond the Ural Mountains, and it was equally imperative that the progress of these tumultuary Bolshevist levies into Siberia should be stayed at the earliest possible moment. These were duties which, owing to the geographical conditions, naturally devolved upon the United States and Japan, and, seeing that the United States were hurrying soldiers in hot haste to the European theatre of war, the duties in reality properly devolved upon Japan. But it was now no longer a question of reconciling the views merely of London,

Paris, Rome, and Tokio.   A disturbing factor had cropped up.   President Wilson had entered the lists.

The fact that no decision as to Siberia and Vladivostok was arrived at for weeks, and that when it was arrived at it was an unsatisfactory one, was not the fault of the British, nor of the French, nor of the Italian, nor yet of the Japanese Government.   We have heard a good deal at times about " wait and see " ; but Mr. Asquith is a very Rupert compared to the Autocrat reigning in the White House in 1918.   Had Japan been given a free hand, with the full moral support of the Allies, and with some financial support and support in the shape of certain forms of war material, Bolshevism might have been stamped out even before the Central Powers were brought to their knees in 1918.   It would surely be to the interest of the United States, as it would undoubtedly be to the interest of Canada and Australasia, that the swelling millions peopling eastern Asia should be encouraged to expand westwards into the rich but sparsely populated regions lying north of Mongolia, rather than that they should be seeking to expand across the Pacific Ocean. As it was, Japan received scanty encouragement, and only received it after procrastination had been developed to the very utmost.

What occurred in connection with Siberia and Vladivostok on that occasion provided an unpleasant foretaste of the pathetic performance which was to go on for months and months in the following year at Versailles.   It moreover foreshadowed and furthered that untoward extension of Bolshevism far and wide which has since taken place. Some of us would willingly have made shift to get on without a League of Nations could we have been saved from the disastrous consequence of action on the part of civilization in Siberia in 1918 having been so unjustifiably delayed, and its having taken so perfunctory a form.

CHAPTER XVI

CATERING FOR THE ALLIES

ONE day early in the summer of 1915 Lord Kitchener sent for me to say that I must find him an artillery officer to take general charge of the arrangements that he was setting on foot for supplying the Russians with armament from the United States and elsewhere. I repaired to Colonel Malcolm Peake, who dealt with all questions of artillery personnel (he was killed on the Western Front very shortly after taking up an artillery command there), who asked what qualifications were needed. It was intimated that the officer must be something of an Admirable Crichton, must be a thoroughly up-to-date gunner of sufficient standing to be able to keep his end up when dealing with superior Russian officials, must be possessed of business capacity, must be gifted with tact and be a reservoir of energy, and ought to have a good working knowledge of French.

Peake asked for time, and next day proposed Colonel W. Ellershaw for the appointment. Ellershaw had just been ordered home from France to assume charge of an important artillery school on Salisbury Plain, and he was duly instructed to come and report himself to me. He was by no means enthusiastic on his being informed of the proposal to divert him from the work that he had arrived to take over and which particularly appealed to him, and he displayed a diffidence for which, it speedily became apparent, there were no grounds whatever, for he proved himself to be absolutely made for the Russian job. As a result of his practical knowledge, of his genius for administration, of his driving power and of his personal charm, he gained the complete confidence of Lord Kitchener and of all Russians who were brought into contact with him. I kept him in a manner under my wing till the end of the year, although his work was not, properly speaking, General Staff work ; but his little branch was transferred to General von Donop's department when Sir W. Robertson arrived and reorganised the General Staff arrangements at the War Office.

Ellershaw formed one of the party which accompanied Lord Kitchener on the ill-fated expedition that terminated off the Orkneys, and he was drowned with his Chief. His death, like that of Colonel Fitzgerald and Mr. O'Beirne, was a real loss to his country, and it was greatly deplored by the many highly placed Russians who had had dealings with him and who had been enormously impressed by his work on their behalf. For some weeks after the *Hampshire* catastrophe his place was not filled up ; but General von Donop eventually asked me to take charge of his branch, which I agreed to by no means willingly, the work being entirely out of my line and my technical knowledge being virtually non-existent. Ellershaw, however, had everything in such good order and had got together such efficient assistants that the duty of superintendence did not, as it turned out, prove so difficult as had seemed likely. General Furse, on succeeding General von Donop some months later, objected to having under him a branch which was not a supply branch, but a liaison branch between the Russians on the one hand and his department and the Munitions Ministry on the other hand, so it was then settled that we should come directly under the Under-Secretary of State—a very appropriate arrangement.

As all armament for Roumania had to pass through Russia, it became convenient that my branch should look after this as well, and we gradually came to be co-ordinating the supply of armament to all the Allies. Then, early in 1918, as a consequence mainly of the muddle that the War Office had got into over the question of supplies for Greece (of which armament only formed a small proportion), it was decided, somewhat late in the day, that we should deal with supplies of all kinds furnished by the War Office to the Allies. But it was arranged at the same time that my branch, instead of remaining under the Under-Secretary of State, its proper place, should be included in the new-fangled civilian department of the Surveyor-General of Supplies which had nothing to do with armament, a plan that set fundamental principles of administration at defiance inasmuch as the branch actually supplied nothing and merely acted as a go-between. It simultaneously acquired a title that constituted a very miracle of obscurantism and incongruity, warranted to bewilder everybody. Labours in connection with Russia and Roumania were by that time, however, virtually at an end, the importance of the branch had to a great extent lapsed, and it was afforded a not unedifying experience. For it became possible to compare the working of the military departments within the War Office with that of a department set up within that institution and run on the lines of the Man of Business, just as it had been possible before to compare the working of those military departments within the War Office with that of the Ministry of Munitions. If the military departments of the War Office came out with flying colours, it must in fairness be allowed that, as they were of the old-established and not the mushroom type, their competitors were giving away a lot of weight.

As a matter of fact, the branch had never in principle been supposed to deal direct with the representatives of the Allies, although in practice we were in close and constant touch with them. Official business transactions with them were carried out, accounts kept, and so forth, by the " Commission Internationale de Ravitaillement," and, until we became entangled with the Surveyor-General of Supplies people and were obliged to shift quarters, we were accommodated in the building occupied by the " Commission," which constituted a very important department, nominally under the Board of Trade but for all practical purposes independent. This C.I.R.—departments and branches are always described by their initials in official life ; the day would not be long enough nor would available stationery suffice to give them their full titles—was an admirably managed institution. It enjoyed the good fortune of being under charge of an experienced Civil Servant, Sir E. Wyldbore Smith, who had one or two of the same sort to help him, although the bulk of the staff were of the provisional type ; and, as the various foreign delegations dealing with supplies were housed under the same roof, this was manifestly the proper place for us to be. We were in close touch with the people we actually had to deal with. The foreign delegates could always look in on us and could discuss points of detail with us on the spot, thereby avoiding misunderstandings and friction. Consisting, as they did, for the most part of officers, they liked to have officers to deal with. A foreign officer of junior rank will take " no " for an answer from a general and be perfectly happy, whereas he may jib at receiving the same answer from a civilian or from an officer of his own standing. Points of that kind are apt to be overlooked in a non-military country like ours.

My branch had an extremely busy time in connection with the supply of the munitions which were promised to the Russians on the occasion of that mission of theirs which was sent to England just at the time that I took over charge, and which is mentioned on p. 287 in the last chapter. These munitions included war material of all kinds, but particularly field-howitzers and heavy artillery. The Russian delegation were quite ready to leave all the arrangements for getting the goods to Archangel from wherever they were turned out in this country, to the C.I.R. and us, working in conjunction with the Naval Transport Department of the Admiralty at first and afterwards with the Ministry of Shipping. They recognized their own administrative shortcomings and wisely left such matters under British control. Some difficulty did, however, arise in respect to the apportionment of tonnage space, as between the armament supplied by the War Office and commodities of other kinds which the delegates procured more or less direct from the trade through the C.I.R. Some regrettable delay occurred in the winter of 1916–17 in getting armament shipped which had been hurried from the factories to Liverpool, owing to its being shut out by goods of much less importance. It was imperative to get heavy artillery out as soon as possible in view of the coming campaign, and it was exasperating to have valuable howitzers idle at the docks which our own army in France would have welcomed. One had to take a high hand; but the Russians were easy to manipulate in such matters, and they never resented virtual dictation in the least so long as the iron hand remained concealed within the velvet glove. Relations were, indeed, always particularly pleasant.

Although the average standard of education was probably lower in Russia than in any other State which could be called civilized, the country has produced many scientists of the very foremost rank, and the Russian artillery included many highly scientific—almost too scientific—officers. It used to be a little trying to find them, after they had received a consignment of our own pattern armament (which the French or the Italians or the Belgians would have jumped at), picking it to pieces, so to speak, criticising the details of high-explosive shell or of fuses from every point of view, and showing greater disposition to worry over such points than to get the stuff into the field and to kill Germans with it. The technicalist, indeed, almost seemed to rule the roost, although this unfortunately did not lead to even reasonably good care being taken of war material that arrived in the country. The Russians had done wonders in respect to developing the port of Archangel; they had performed the miracle actually during the war. But if they had achieved a veritable administrative triumph in this matter, their methods were terribly at fault in assembling goods as they arrived and in getting the goods through to their destination in good order. If they undoubtedly were strong on the scientific side, they were correspondingly weak on the practical side, as is illustrated by the following experience.

I was taken down one afternoon to Hatfield Park to see a demonstration of a certain flame-producing arrangement, of which they had ordered large numbers. This was a pleasant outing, and the demonstration was interesting enough in itself ; but the elaborate contrivance seemed to me totally unsuited to the conditions on the Russian front, because the flame was only projected eighty yards —one was quite comfortable a hundred and fifty yards straight in front of the projector—and the device was only adapted to conditions such as had existed in the Gallipoli Peninsula and as held good at a very few points on the Western Front, where the opposing trenches happened to be quite close together. As a matter of fact, the contrivance had been found of very little use when tried by us in the field. Strong recommendations came to hand shortly afterwards from some of our officers accredited to the Russian armies that a goodly supply of trench mortars should be sent out, and particularly of the invaluable Stokes mortars; it was foreseen by the applicants that, once the pattern was available, these could easily be constructed locally in Russia. But one encountered the greatest difficulty in inducing the delegation in this country to have anything to say to the Stokes mortar, because of its comparatively short range. And yet the range of the very oldest pattern of Stokes mortar was five times that of the flame projector, upon which material and time and labour and tonnage were being wasted.

Then, again, there arose the question of tanks. Now a tank could not possibly at that time have been got along the Murmansk railway without squashing the whole track down for good and all into the marshes across which the permanent way was conveyed by precarious and provisional processes. Needless to say, we had no tanks to spare to be kept reposing idle for months at ports and congested junctions, awaiting transport to Vilna or Podolia. But as they could not get tanks, nor transport them if they were to secure some in this country, the Russians were anxious to procure drawings and specifications of these new-fangled engines of war. There was no reasonable likelihood of such a contraption ever being turned out in Russia owing to lack of raw material and to manufacturing difficulties, even supposing drawings and all the rest of it to be available. There were secrets in connection with the internals of a tank which must be zealously guarded. Under the circumstances, I suggested to the General Staff, when putting forward a request on behalf of the Commission for the paper stuff, that faked drawings and details should be furnished to keep the Russians quiet. This was done; but what was furnished would not have bluffed a novice in a select seminary for young ladies of weak intellect. So I sent the rubbish off to General Poole (who was representing this country out there in connection with the munitions that were arriving), telling him the facts of the case and leaving him to do as he thought fit. I was thus able to say, when pressed by the Commission, that this valuable documentary material had already been sent straight to Poole. No doubt he put it all in the wastepaper-basket. Sir A. Stern mentions in his book that he deemed it expedient to hand over a " child's drawing and incorrect details." It is satisfactory to find that he thought of adopting the exact course which I had proposed when originally putting forward the request on behalf of the Russians.

That reminds me of a droll incident that occurred in connection with a Russian delegate quite early in the war. We had no clear understanding with our Allies at that date with regard to the allocation of material between us, nor as to the imperative necessity of preventing anything in the shape of competition in the British markets amongst us partners. The War Office had a certain article in mind that was being produced somewhere up north—at Manchester, I think, but anyway we will call it Manchester. The Russians happened to be after the same thing, and, without our knowing it, one of their officers who was in this country was about to enter into negotiations with the people up north with a view to securing it, and in due course he proceeded to Manchester with the purchase in view. But he was of an inquisitive disposition ; he managed to get into some place or other to which he did not possess the entrée. So, being a foreigner, he was promptly run in, and he spent about twenty-four hours incarcerated in some lock-up before he could establish his credentials. During that very twenty-four hours a representative of the War Office appeared in Manchester and snapped up what the captive was after.

The Russian Military Attaché came to the War Office to enter a strong protest at the outrage of which his brother officer had been the victim. He evidently meant to kick up no end of a row, and he had just got into his stride and was going strong and well, when he suddenly went off into a tempest of giggles. He saw the humour of the situation. He was fully persuaded that we had deliberately arrested his friend so as to get him out of the way while we managed to push the deal through ourselves, and he evidently gave us gratifying credit for being so wide-awake. It was not the slightest use our explaining that this was one of those coincidences in real life which are stranger than fiction, that we had been wholly unaware that the Russian officer was even thinking about the article that we had secured, that we knew nothing whatever about him or his adventures. The Military Attaché was politeness itself ; but he evidently did not believe a word we said—who, under the circumstances, would ? Still, we had come out top-dog in the business, so we left it at that.

It must not be supposed that things never went wrong in spite of the elaborate system that we were adopting for transferring war material to Archangel under our control. Late in the autumn of 1916 I extracted out of von Donop a 9·2-inch howitzer and mounting all complete —he did not part readily with his goods—so as to send them on ahead and to afford the Russians an opportunity of learning the points of this ordnance, in anticipation of the arrival of a regular consignment of the weapons which had been promised for a later date. But part of the concern somehow found its way into one ship and the rest of it into another ship, and one of the ships managed to get rid of her propeller in the North Sea, drifted aimlessly for a whole month, was believed to have foundered, and was eventually discovered and towed ignominiously back to one of our northern ports. She was lucky not to meet with a U-boat during her wanderings. The result was that the Russians received either a howitzer and no mounting or a mounting and no howitzer, I forget which, and the whole bag of tricks was not assembled at its destination until after part of the regular consignment of 9·2-inch howitzers had arrived in Petrograd about April.

In connection with this business of shipping goods to our eastern Ally, it should be mentioned that the sealing up of the port of Archangel and of the White Sea in

general from about mid-November until well on in May—
the exact period varied in different seasons, and depended
to some extent upon the direction of the wind—complicated the problem. Some forty of our ships had been
embedded in ice for months in these waters in the winter
of 1915–16, and the Admiralty were taking no risks this
time. It was not a question merely of getting a vessel
to its destination, but also a question of getting her dis-
charged and out of the trap before it snapped-to. That
a railway had not been constructed to Murmansk years
before, illustrates the torpor and lack of enterprise of the
ruling classes in Russia. Although Archangel is ice-
bound somewhat longer, the Gulfs of Finland and Bothnia
likewise become impassable for navigation during the
winter; so that for some months of the year maritime
communication between northern portions of the empire
and the outer world was almost necessarily to a great
extent cut off. And yet all the time there existed a fine
natural harbour of great extent on the Arctic coast which
was never frozen over, simply asking to be made use of.
Not until a state of affairs, which ought to have been
foreseen, arose in actual war—the Baltic and exit from
the Black Sea barred by hostile belligerents—was anything
done. A British company was trying hard to obtain
powers to construct a railway to Murmansk at the time
of the outbreak of hostilities ; but a line was not completed
till more than two years had elapsed and was then of the
most ramshackle character.

It was not only from the United Kingdom and from
France that war material and other goods were being
conveyed by sea to Russia, but also from America ; and
it was infinitely preferable for these latter to take the
easterly route to the northern ports of the empire, than
for them to take the westerly route across the Pacific to
Vladivostok, involving a subsequent journey of thousands
of miles along a railway that was very deficient in rolling
stock. Matters in connection with Lord Kitchener's contracts in the United States were in the hands of Messrs.

Morgan on the farther side of the Atlantic, with a Russo-British Commission on the spot watching developments. Responsibilities in connection with the transactions in this country had come under charge of the Ministry of Munitions. My branch noted progress, kept the General Staff informed, and represented the War Office in connection with the subject when questions arose. Experience of these huge American contracts fully bore out what had occurred at home in connection with the expansion of munitions production on the part of the War Office after the outbreak of war—only in a somewhat exaggerated form. Whereas in this country output began to intensify rapidly within twelve months and the credit was appropriated by Mr. Lloyd George, owing to intensification for which the War Office was solely responsible taking place after the setting up of the Munitions Ministry, output only began really to sprout in the United States about sixteen months after the start. All, however (as already mentioned in the last chapter), was full of promise when the crash of the Revolution came to nullify what had been achieved.

Up to the date of that disastrous event, and even for a few weeks subsequently, one did one's best to accelerate the supply and the despatch of war material from this country to Archangel and, after the closing of that great port by ice, Murmansk, which was just beginning to serve as an avenue into the country owing to the completion—after a fashion—of its unstable railway. The Milner Mission had been as profuse in its pledges as it had been erratic in its anticipations, and had committed itself to somewhat comprehensive engagements in connection with the furnishing of further war material. So that, almost synchronizing with the downfall of the Romanoff dynasty and the setting up of a new regime, this country found itself let in for diverting munitions of all sorts, in addition to what had already been promised, to an Ally in whom trust could no longer be placed. On one occasion in the course of the winter I had defeated the combined forces of Sir W. Robertson and the Master-General of the Ordnance before the War Cabinet over the question of deflecting a few howitzers to Russia. But one's point of view underwent a transformation subsequent to the dire events of March in Petrograd. So far from pushing the claims of the revolutionary government for war material, it then seemed expedient to act as a drag on the wheel, and to take the side of the C.I.G.S. and General Furse when Lord Milner from time to time pressed the question of sending out armament. The War Office deprecated depriving our own troops of munitions for the sake of trying to bolster up armies that were disintegrating apace owing to the action of Kerensky and his like. It was very disappointing—apart from the threatening political situation, prospects had seemed so good in Russia. But all the endeavours that had been made to assist during the previous few months were evidently going to be to no purpose. Just when the despatch of what our Ally required had been got on a thoroughly sound footing, the organization was to prove of no avail.

Still, there was always Roumania to be thought of, even if the problem of getting goods through to that country in face of the chaos which was rapidly making way in Russia was almost becoming insoluble. The French, like ourselves, were most anxious to afford succour to that stricken kingdom. Amongst other things, they requested us to send off to Moldavia a certain consignment (thirty, I think it was) of 6-inch howitzers, which M. Thomas declared Mr. Lloyd George had promised him for the French army. But the worst of it was, there was a difference of opinion in regard to this reputed undertaking. The stories of these two eminent public servants clashed in a very important particular, for our man strenuously denied ever having committed himself to the alleged engagement. On only one point, indeed, were the pair in full agreement, and this was that the discussion in connection with the matter had taken place after luncheon.

Bearing in mind Mr. Lloyd George's irrepressible passion for pleasing, and taking the fact into account that generosity with what belongs to somebody else is in the United Kingdom recognized as the masterstroke of Radical statesmanship, there did seem to be just a last possibility of M. Thomas having right on his side. Still, expansiveness, fantasy and oblivion serve for epilogue to a grateful midday meal, and, when all is said and done, possession is nine points of the law—we had the howitzers, so it was for the other party to get them out of us. But we should, no doubt, have sent them out to our Roumanian friends in due course had it not become virtually impracticable to get such goods through from the North Russian ports by the date that the subject came up for final decision.

It has to be confessed that all of our Continental Allies were not quite so well disciplined in the matter of procuring goods in this country as were the Russians. As time went on and raw material and manufactured commodities began to run short in the United Kingdom, *tracasseries* would from time to time arise in connection with certain rules which had been laid down in the interests of us all. The delegations manifested a highly inconvenient bent for purchasing in the open market, which did not by any means suit our book, as such procedure tended to run up prices and to disturb equilibrium. The trade, moreover, was ready enough to meet them, and occasionally to let them have goods more quickly and even cheaper than they could be procured through the authorized channels. A firm attitude had to be taken up in regard to this, even if it led to some misunderstandings. In the case of one of our pals (who shall be nameless) it was like fly-fishing for oysters on the Horse Guards Parade to try to extract receipts for goods received ; an embargo had, indeed, to be placed on further issues until overdue receipts were handed in.

But the United States representatives were always particularly considerate and helpful. When they came to be dealing with us on at least as great a scale as any

x

other Ally, their delegates appreciated the position that this country was in, and they took full cognizance of the risks that we were incurring of running out of vital commodities altogether unless disposal of these was kept under rigid control. They always fell in readily with our requirements, inconvenient as some of these may have proved. Still, all our friends were alike in one respect—they were all of them intent upon getting their full money's worth. As a pillar of literary culture in khaki, indeed, remarked to me in this connection: " They must, like Fagin in the ' Merchant of Venice,' have their pound of flesh." Such difficulties as arose could generally be smoothed over by personal intercourse, and the head of the Commission Internationale de Ravitaillement could charm the most unruly member of his flock to eat out of his hand by dint of tact and kindness.

It was just at the time when I was acting as D.C.I.G.S. in the summer of 1917 that the French suddenly wired over to the War Office to request us to send representatives to Paris to discuss with them what we were prepared to let Greece have, now that the Hellenes had come down off the fence and were going to afford active assistance to the Allies in the Balkans, but stood in need of equipment and of supplies of all kinds. Had I been free at the time, I should have proposed to go even though our new friends wanted clothing, personal equipment, transport, animals and food—goods with which my branch had nothing to do—rather than munitions. As it was, a couple of senior officers went over who had no proper authority to act, and who hardly knew the ropes. The Commission Internationale de Ravitaillement was forgotten altogether, and as for the poor dear old Treasury, not only was that Department of State treated with scorn, but the Lords Commissioners were not even informed, when our delegates were retrieved from the Gay City, that a casual sort of agreement, which *inter alia* involved appreciable financial obligations, had been entered into with our friends on the other side of the Channel. No determinate Convention of any kind or sort was drawn up or signed, what had been provisionally promised remained for a long time in a condition of ambiguity, and the transaction as a whole cannot be claimed as one of the cardinal achievements of the War Office during the course of the four years' conflict.

The French undertook to find almost all the requisite armament ; that we did not mean to find any was about the only point that was clearly laid down during the Paris negotiations, although this was altered later. My branch was therefore little concerned in the business until, as has been mentioned on p. 216, the dilemma that various departments were in over the affair was thrust before the War Cabinet, and steps were taken to get something done. Even then, it took some weeks before we arrived at a clear understanding with the French and the Greeks as to what exactly we were going to provide, and before a proper Convention was tabled. Much time was therefore wasted, and time must not be wasted in time of war.

Then, when it had at last been established what goods this country was to provide, there was fresh and almost unaccountable dilatoriness in certain quarters in furnishing important commodities, although the military departments of the War Office grappled with their side of the problem and overcame serious difficulties with commendable despatch. General R. Reade had been sent out to Athens to look after things at that end, and he with his assistants kept us fully informed of requirements and of progress ; but he had to put up with a procrastination at this end which was unquestionably preventible. One has to face uphill jobs from time to time in the army; but in thirty-six years of active service I never wrestled with so uphill a job as that of trying, in the year of grace 1918, to get our share of the fitting out of the Hellenic forces fulfilled. The only thing to be said is that the French, who had easier problems to contend with and less to do than we had, were almost equally behind-hand. But the result of it all was that, of the 200,000 troops whom, entirely apart from reserves, the Greek Government were prepared to mass on the fighting front if only they could be fitted out, barely half were actually in the field when (fortunately for those who were responsible for mismanaging the despatch of the requisite supplies from this country and from France) the Bulgarians realized that the game of the Central Powers was up, and they virtually threw up the sponge.

In so far as Serbia was concerned, a detailed Convention had been drawn up with the French in 1916, clearly indicating what the two respective Governments were to furnish for the service of Prince Alexander's war-worn troops. Under the terms of this agreement, we were concerned chiefly with the question of food and forage; but we also, needless to say, provided the bulk of the shipping on which the Serbian contingents depended for their existence. They, as it happened, came to be none too well equipped, and it was a pity perhaps that we had not undertaken somewhat heavier obligations in connection with these sorely tried Allies of ours and thereby ensured their being properly clothed. A fresh Convention was drawn up in London in September 1918, under which we accepted somewhat increased responsibilities, and Brigadier-General the Hon. C. G. Fortescue was sent out to look after matters in Macedonia in the Serbian interest. The end came, however, before the arrangements made could exercise any appreciable effect during the actual fighting; but I believe that good work has been done since that date.

Considering the exceedingly burdensome character of our liabilities in connection with maintaining the associated forces of the Entente in Macedonia for the space of three years—for practical purposes we had to find pretty well all the food, and we had, moreover, to get the food (and almost everything else) to Salonika in our ships, which paid heavy toll to enemy submarines during the process—it was a faulty arrangement that the chief command out there was not reposed in British hands.

To press for it would have been awkward, seeing that the chief command in the Dardanelles operations that had proved so abortive had rested with us ; and it was, moreover, perfectly well known in Paris that the military authorities in this country looked askance at the whole business and that our Government entertained doubts on the subject. Had the operations been conducted by a British commander-in-chief they might not have been attended by greater success than they actually were, but, considering the strength of the mixed forces which remained locked up so long in this barren field of endeavour, they could hardly have proved less effective than they actually were for nearly three years.

CHAPTER XVII

THE PRESS

IT is inevitable, perhaps, that a rather time-honoured War Office hand—thirteen years of it, covering different periods between 1887 and 1918—should entertain somewhat mixed feelings with regard to the Press. As long as I can remember, practically, the War Office has provided a sort of Aunt Sally for the young men of Fleet Street to take cock-shies at when they can think of nothing else to edify their readers with, and uncommonly bad shots a good many of them have made. Assessment at the hands of the newspaper world confronts every public department. Nor can this in principle be objected to ; healthy, well - informed criticism is both helpful and stimulating. But although many of the attacks delivered upon the War Office by the Fourth Estate, in the course of that perpetual guerilla warfare which is carried on by journalism in general against the central administration of the army, have been fully warranted, the fact remains that no small proportion of them has been based upon misapprehension, and that a good many of them can be put down to pure ignorance. Never has this been more apparent than during the progress of the Great War. But a reason for this suggests itself at once ; many newspapers, no doubt, for the time being lost the services of members of their staff who possessed some qualification for expatiating upon military questions.

It has to be acknowledged that the Press was badly treated by the War Office and G.H.Q. at the outset. This circumstance may have contributed towards setting up relations during the contest between us in Whitehall and the world of journalism which were not always too cordial. The question of correspondents in the war zone naturally cropped up at a very early stage, and the decision arrived at, for better or for worse, was that none of them were to go. The wisdom of the attitude taken up by the military authorities in this matter is a question of opinion ; but my view was, and still is, that the newspapers were treated injudiciously and that the decision was wrong. I was, indeed, placed in the uncomfortable position of administering a policy which I disliked, and which I believed to be entirely mistaken. It, moreover, practically amounted to a breach of faith.

The General Staff had for some years prior to 1914 always intended that a reasonable number of correspondents should proceed to the front under official aegis on the outbreak of a European war. A regular organization for the purpose actually took shape automatically within the War Office, in concert with the Press, on mobilization. A small staff, under charge of a staff-officer who had been especially designated for the job two or three years before, with clerks, cars, and so on, came into being *pari passu* with G.H.Q. of the Expeditionary Force on the historic 5th of August.   The officer, Major A. G. Stuart, a man of attractive personality and forceful character, master of his profession and an ideal holder of the post, had been in control of the Press representatives at Army Manœuvres in 1912 and 1913, and he was therefore personally acquainted with the gentlemen chosen to take the field. (He was unfortunately killed while serving on the staff in France, in the winter of 1915–16.)   The General Staff had, moreover, gone out of their way to impress upon correspondents at manœuvres that they ought to regard the operations in the light of instruction for themselves in duties which they would be performing in the event of actual hostilities.   They were given confidential information with regard to the programme on the understanding that they would keep it to themselves, and they always played the game.

But when war came, all this went by the board.   Leave for correspondents to go to the front, whether under official auspices or any other way, was refused, and the staff and the clerks and the cars abode idle in London under my wing.   The Press world accepted this development philosophically for the opening two or three weeks, realizing that the moment when the Expeditionary Force was being spirited over to France was no time for visitors in the war zone.   But after that the Fourth Estate became decidedly restive.   Enterprising reporters proceeded to the theatre of war without permission, while experienced journalists, deluded by past promises, remained patiently behind hoping for the best.   The old hounds, in fact, were kept in the kennel, while the young entry ran riot with no hunt servants to rate them.   Some unauthorized representatives of the British Press were, it is true, arrested by the French, and had the French dealt with them in vertebrate fashion—decapitated them or sent them to the Devil's Island—we should have known where we were.

But as the culprits were simply dismissed with a caution the situation became ridiculous, because no newspaper man bothers about marching to a dungeon with gyves upon his wrists and tarrying there for some hours without sustenance. It is part of the game. So the military authorities were openly flouted.

One result of the abrupt change of policy also was that, instead of the supervision of messages emanating from the front falling upon officers at G.H.Q. who were in a position to wrestle with them to good purpose, this task devolved upon the Press Bureau in London, which naturally could not perform the office nearly so well and which was, moreover, smothered under folios of journalistic matter originating in quarters other than the theatre of war. Furthermore, editors and managers and proprietors of our more prominent organs considered that we had broken our engagements—as, indeed, we had. At the very fall of the flag, the Press of the country was in my opinion gratuitously fitted out with a legitimate grievance. This could not but react hurtfully from that time forward upon the relations between the military authorities and British journalism as a whole.

There was one direction in which the Fourth Estate did serious mischief in the early days of the war. As being behind the scenes during those strenuous, apprehensive months, when the process of transforming the United Kingdom into a great military nation at the very time when the enemy was in the gate was making none too rapid progress, I have no hesitation in asserting that one of the principal obstacles in the way was the excessive optimism of our Press. Every trifling success won by, or credited to, the Allies was hailed as a transcendent triumph and was placarded on misleading posters. When mishaps occurred—as they too often did—their seriousness was whittled down or ignored. The public took their cue only too readily from the newspapers, and the consequence was that a check was placed alike on recruiting and on the production of the war material which was urgently required for such troops as we could place in the field.

And yet, journalists could plead in excuse that they were in some measure following a lead set by the authorities. It has already been admitted in Chapter II. that a system of official secretiveness in connection with reverses was adopted, and that it did no good. This took the form of concealing, or at any rate minimizing, setsback when these occurred—an entirely new attitude for soldiers in this country to take up, and one which was to be deprecated. We should never have gathered together those swarms of volunteers in South Africa in 1900, volunteers drawn from the United Kingdom and from the Dominions and from the Colonies, had Stormberg and Magersfontein and Colenso been artistically camouflaged. The facts were blurted out. The Empire rose to the occasion. Hiding the truth in 1914–15 was a blunder from every point of view, because there never was the slightest fear of the people of this country losing heart. No doubt the incorporation of ordinances directed against the propagation of alarmist reports calculated to cause despondency, as part of the Defence of the Realm Act, was necessary. But one at times positively welcomed the appearance of well-informed jeremiads in the newspapers, as an antidote to the exultant cackle which was hindering a genuine, comprehensive, universal mobilization of our national resources in men and material.

This excessive optimism which did so much harm was, it should be observed, to some extent the handiwork of " experts " whose names carried a certain amount of weight, who turned out several columns of comment weekly, and whose opinions would have been well enough worth having had they been better acquainted with the actual facts. For one thing, they did not realize that the augmentation of our military forces was hampered by the virtual impossibility of synchronizing development in output of equipment and munitions with the expansion

THE PRESS

of numbers in the ranks. They were, moreover, entirely unaware of the unfortunate condition of the Russian armies in respect to war material; they imagined that those hosts were far larger numerically than the insufficiency of armament permitted, and they consequently greatly overrated the potentialities of our eastern Ally in the conflict. To such an extent, indeed, was one of them unintentionally deceiving his readers as to the position of affairs in that quarter that I wrote to him privately giving him an inkling of the situation; he gave that side of Europe a wide berth for a long time afterwards.

The mischief done in this matter rather influenced one against the Press, and perhaps made one all the more ready to take cognizance of its blunders and to accept its criticisms (when these were ill-informed) in bad part. Are we not, however, in any case rather disposed to take our journals too seriously, and is not one result of this that we have the Press that we deserve? Public men have to treat the journalistic world with respect, or it will undo them; but that does not apply to mere ordinary people. Yet we all bow the knee before it, submissively accept it at its own valuation, and consequently it fools us to the top of our bent. We believe what we see stated in our paper as a matter of course, unless we happen by some accident to know that the statement is totally contrary to the actual fact. The Fourth Estate is exalted into an acknowledged autocrat because it is allowed to have things all its own way; and your autocrat, whether he be a trade union official or he be a sceptred potentate or he be the President of a republic saddled with a paradoxical constitution, is an anachronism in principle and is apt to be a curse in practice.

Autocracy is particularly to be deprecated in the case of the Press, seeing that here we have what is in reality the most widespread trade union in the country. Journalism harbours its internal squabbles and jealousies, no doubt, just as is the case with most great associations; but, assail it from without, and it closes up its ranks as a nation

rent with faction will on threat from some foreign foe.
It is generally acknowledged that in political life a formidable opposition in the legislature renders the government
of the day all the more efficient. But the Press, in what
may be called its corporate capacity, is not disciplined
nor stimulated by any organized opposition at all, and
the consequence is that it has perhaps got just a little
too big for its boots. Judged by results in respect to its
handling of military questions during the Great War,
the Fourth Estate has not (taken as a whole, and lumping
together journals of the meaner class with the representative organs which have great financial resources to refresh
them) proved itself quite so efficient an institution as its
protagonists claim it to be.

Before the war, one was disposed to accept as gospel the
pontifical utterances of newspapers concerning matters
with which one was unacquainted — the law, say, or
economics, or art. But never again! Journalists on
occasion gave themselves away too badly during those
years over warlike operations, army organization, and so
forth, for one to let oneself be bluffed in future. Given
the leisure, the inclination, and the necessary access to a
large number of the organs of the Press, a libraryful of
scrap-books could have been got together, replete with
gaffes and absurdities seriously and solemnly set out in
print. One or two examples of such blunders may be
given for purposes of illustration.

After a shameful U-boat outrage committed on a
hospital ship, a London morning paper actually urged,
in its first leader, that half a dozen German officers should
be " sent to sea in every hospital ship *and in every transport* " (the italics are mine). Here was a case of an editor
(surely editors read through the leaders which are supposed
to give the considered opinion of the journal of which
they are in charge) deliberately proposing that this country
should play as dirty a trick as any Boche was ever guilty
of. A belligerent has a perfect right to sink a transport
in time of war, just as he has a perfect right to bomb a

train full of enemy troops. The Japanese sank a Chinese transport at the outbreak of the war of 1894 in the Far East, causing serious loss of life ; the vessel was conveying troops from Wei-hai-wei to the Korean coast. According to this newspaper, a hostile attack upon the flotilla of vessels of various sorts and kinds which conveyed our Expeditionary Force to France would have been as much an act of treachery and a breach of the customs of war, as would an attack upon the vessels covered by the Red Cross which brought the wounded back.

An Army Order in April 1918, again, laid down that promotion to the rank of general would in future be by selection, not by seniority. A number of newspapers of quite good standing thereupon promptly tumbled head over heels into a pitfall entirely of their own creation. They started an attack upon the War Office for not having recognized the principle of advancement in the higher grades of the army by merit sooner, having failed to notice that the Army Order concerned the question of promotion to the rank of full general. Of their own accord, and quite gratuitously, they exposed their ignorance of the fact that promotions to the ranks of brigadier-general, major-general and lieutenant-general had been effected by selection for several years previously ; and they also exposed their ignorance of the fact that, up till the time of the Great War, there had never been any special importance attached to the rank of full general. In the South African War, when we had a far larger military force on active service than ever previously in our history, only three general officers of higher rank than lieutenant-general were employed—Lord Roberts, Sir R. Buller, and Lord Kitchener—and, although all three were in the field together, Lord Roberts was a field-marshal ; when, later, Lord Kitchener was in supreme command he had no full general under him.

The Great War produced an entirely new condition of things, because we then came to have operating in the field, not merely one army but several armies, each consisting of several army corps, and each of those army corps commanded by a lieutenant-general. It was therefore convenient that the armies should be commanded by full generals, and the rank of full general suddenly assumed a real instead of merely a nominal importance. It thus became necessary to effect promotion to full general by selection instead of by seniority. Nobody expects editors to know details of this kind ; but it surely is their duty to investigate before starting on a crusade. In the case of people who knew the facts, this particular blunder merely made the newspapers that committed it look ridiculous ; but the majority of those who read the drivel in all probability had no idea of the facts, and were led to imagine that promotions to the various ranks of general officer had hitherto all been a matter of seniority. It is an example of the way in which the public have been misled about the War Office by the Press for years past.

A year or so after the Armistice, one of the London evening papers, when criticizing the disinclination of the War Office to adopt new ideas in respect to devices for use in the field (a fair enough subject of discussion in itself), gave itself away by complaining that " tanks were not adopted before the war " ! In that case the absurdity was so obvious that its effect upon most readers of the article probably was to make them regard the whole of it as rubbish, which was not correct. One wonders whether the following passage, which appeared in the very early days of the war in one of our foremost newspapers, may not have had something to do with that entirely unwarranted confidence in the " steam - roller " on the Eastern Front which prevailed in England between August 1914 and May 1915 · " I refer to General Sukhomlinoff, the Russian Kitchener, who is reorganizing the Russian armies. Thanks to him, the Tsar's armies are irreproachably equipped." Compare p. 283.

An article appeared in a leading Sunday newspaper in the spring of 1919, signalized by this amazing travesty of the actual facts.   In a reference to our land forces of the early days of the struggle, the writer spoke of " armies sent to war lacking almost every modern requisite." Now, the Press generally manages to avoid grossly false statements of that kind when referring to individuals ; if it does fall into such an error, the sequel is either an abject apology or else an uphill fight in the law courts followed by the payment of heavy damages.   It is quite conceivable that the author of this unpardonable mis-representation imagined himself to be telling the truth and that he erred out of sheer ignorance ; but, if so, that merely serves to indicate how badly informed jour-nalists often are of the matters which they are dealing with, when the question at issue happens to concern military subjects.

The expediency of affording greater opportunities to that great body of temporary officers who had joined up (many of them men of marked ability and advanced education), for occupying superior positions on the staff or for holding high command, was taken up warmly by a number of newspapers at the beginning of 1918.   It is not proposed to discuss the theme on its merits—there was a good deal to be said for the contention.   The matter is merely referred to because of the manner in which it was handled by the organs that were pressing it upon the notice of the public.   Reference was very properly made to brains.   But not one word was said about knowledge.   Now, brains without knowledge may make an efficient Pressman—one is sometimes tempted to assume that the battalions of journalism are to some extent recruited from this source of supply.   But brains without knowledge will no more make a superior staff officer who can be trusted, nor a commander of troops of all arms who will be able to make the most of them in face of the enemy, than will they make a successful physician or a proficient electrical engineer.   It was also completely overlooked by the propagandists of this particular stunt that the experience which on every front, other than the Mesopotamian, temporary officers had been gaining was for practical purposes confined to trench warfare, and that, if a decision was ever going to be reached at all, it would be brought about under profoundly different tactical conditions from those which had been prevailing. The whole question hinged upon whether the requisite knowledge could be acquired, and upon what steps would be necessary to bring that desirable result about. The writers who dealt with the point perhaps recognized that brains were merely a means to the end, and not the end. But if they did, why did they fail ever even to mention the pinion upon which the whole question in reality hinged ?

Journalists, when complaining of the censorship, have put forward the suggestion that this sort of thing ought to be left to the patriotism and honour of newspapers, that, if such a plan were adopted, the Press would of its own accord refrain from publishing any information that might be of value to the enemy in time of war, and that there would then be no need for any special official department dealing with this matter. That sounds plausible, but it will not stand examination for a moment. Granted that the great majority of editors and their staffs would never dream of wittingly disclosing information injurious to their country during hostilities, the fact remains that a chain is no stronger than its weakest link. If one journal, in its eagerness to attract, prints what ought to have been kept secret, the reticence of the remainder is of no avail. Nor is this merely a question of honour and patriotism. It is also a question of competence. Censorship responsibilities demand knowledge and call for certain qualifications which the personnel of the Press in general does not possess. A few editors, no doubt, could be trusted to do the work efficiently ; but that claim to omniscience which is unobtrusively, but none the less insistently, put forward by the Fourth Estate has no, solid foundation. One of the lessons of the Great War has been that censorship is ,an extremely difficult operation to carry out even when in the hands of individuals well versed in the conditions that arise in times of national emergency. The idea that the Press could censor itself is ridiculous. That such a theory should ever have been put forward argues a strange inability to understand the essentials of the subject, and sets up a doctrine of infallibility in the world of journalism for which there is no justification.

The Press Bureau which was established at the commencement of the war was a civil department, entirely independent of the Admiralty and the War Office although it was in close touch with those institutions, as also with the Foreign Office, the Board of Trade and other branches of the Government. In so far as the War Office was concerned, the Bureau dealt with the Operations Directorate, which was responsible for watching the censorship of newspapers in general, just as it was responsible for actually controlling the censorship of cables and foreign correspondence. As the primary *raison d'être* of newspapers is to provide their readers with news, it was inevitable that restrictions placed upon publication of information, however necessary they might be in the interest of the State, would hamper the activities of those in charge and be regarded as a nuisance. It was natural that the Press should chafe at the restraint and should be disposed to exaggerate the inconvenience to which it was put. But the public, it must be remembered, have heard only one side of the story. The country has derived its information concerning the Press censorship from the Press itself—in other words, from what is to all intents and purposes a tainted source. The nation has had to decide on a subject of general interest on one-sided evidence.

In so far as the military share of the Press censorship was concerned, some of the groans of its victims were, no doubt, well justified. Delays were inevitable. But cases of unnecessary delay no doubt occurred. Instances could be mentioned of one censor sanctioning the publication

Y

of a given item of news while another forbade mention thereof. It is human to err, and individual censors were guilty of errors of judgment on occasion. Examples of information, which might have been given to the world with perfect propriety, being withheld, could easily be brought to light. How the humorists of the Fourth Estate did gloat over " the Captains and the Kings "! There was at least one instance early in the conflict of an official *communiqué* that had been issued by the French military authorities in Paris being bowdlerized before publication on this side of the Channel.

Few of the detractors of the military Press Censorship, on the other hand, gave evidence of possessing more than a shadowy conception of the difficult and delicate nature of the duties which that institution was called upon to carry out. There is little evidence to indicate that the critics had the slightest idea of the value of the services which it performed. Nor would they appear to be aware that the blunders committed by the censors, such as they were, were by no means confined to malapert blue-pencilling of items of information that might have appeared without disclosing anything whatever to the enemy. As a matter of fact, cases occurred of intelligence slipping through the meshes which ought not on any account to have been made public property.

When, for example, one particular London newspaper twice over during the very critical opening weeks of the struggle divulged movements of troops in France, the peccant passage was, on each occasion, found on investigation to have been acquiesced in by a censor— lapses on the part of overworked and weary men poring over sheaves of proof-slips late at night. Nearly all our newspapers published a Reuter's message which stated the exact strength of the Third Belgian Division when it got back by sea to Ostend—not a very important piece of information, but one that obviously ought not to have been allowed to appear. At a somewhat later date, a journal, in reporting His Majesty's farewell visit to the troops, contrived to acquaint all whom it might concern that the Twenty-eighth Division, made up of regular battalions brought from overseas, was about to cross the Channel.

It will readily be understood that incidents of this kind—those quoted are merely samples—worried the officials charged with supervision, and tended to make them almost over-fastidious. Soldiers of experience, as the censors were, remembered Nelson's complaint that his plans were disclosed by a Gibraltar print, Wellington's remonstrances during the Peninsular War, the details as to the siege-works before Sebastopol that were given away to the enemy by *The Times*, and the information conveyed to the Germans by a Paris newspaper of Mac-Mahon's movement on Sedan. They were, moreover, aware that indignant representations with reference to the untoward communicativeness of certain of our prominent journals were being made by the French and Belgians. So the Press Bureau took to sending doubtful passages across for our decision—a procedure which necessarily created delay and caused inconvenience to editors. Publication, it may be mentioned, was approved in quite four cases out of five when such references were made. One rather wondered at times, indeed, where the difficulty came in.

But a verdict was called for in one case which imposed an uncomfortable responsibility upon me. This was when a telegram from the Military Correspondent of *The Times* from the front, revealing the shell shortage from which our troops were suffering, was submitted from Printing House Square to the Press Bureau in the middle of May 1915, and was transmitted by the Press Bureau to us for adjudication. It was about three weeks after Mr. Asquith's unfortunate reference to this subject in his Newcastle speech. Publication of the message could at the worst only be confirmatory to the enemy of information already fully known, and national interests did seem to demand that the people of the country should be made aware how this particular matter stood, seeing that the labour world had not yet fully risen to its responsibilities in connection with the prosecution of the war which depended to so great an extent upon our factories. Choice of three alternatives presented itself to me—leave might be refused, higher authority might be referred to, publication might be sanctioned then and there. The third alternative was adopted, although one or two minor details in regard to particular types of ordnance were excised. It seems to be generally acknowledged that publication of the truth about the shell shortage was of service to the cause ; but for some of the attacks upon the War Office to which the publication of the truth gave rise there was no justification whatever. The attacks, indeed, took the form of a conspiracy, which has only been exposed since mouths that had to remain closed during the war have been opened.

For the General Staff at the War Office to have formulated apposite, hard-and-fast regulations for the guidance of the Press Bureau covering all questions likely to arise, would, it may be observed, have been virtually impracticable, or at all events would not have really solved the problem. Sir S. Buckmaster, when in charge of the Bureau, pressed me as regards this subject more than once, but there were serious objections to hard-and-fast rules. Everything must necessarily depend upon the interpretation placed on such ordinances by the individuals who were to be guided by them. Thus a rigorous enactment governing any particular type of subject, if strictly interpreted by harassed censors, would prevent any tidings as to that subject leaking out at all ; while an indulgent enactment, if loosely interpreted by the staff of the Bureau, might well lead to most undesirable disclosures being made in the columns of the Press. Censors planted down in London could not, furthermore, be kept fully acquainted with the position of affairs at the front —a factor which greatly aggravated the perplexities of their task. We of the General Staff in Whitehall were

in this respect very differently situated from G.H.Q.
Over on the other side, where the situation of our own
troops and of the French and the Belgians was known
from hour to hour, newspaper representatives could
always have been instructed by the bear-leaders in charge
of them as to exactly what they might, and what they
might not, touch upon in reference to any operations in
progress.

Matters in connection with the air service and the
anti-aircraft service—the two things to a great extent
go together—are primarily problems for experts ; but it
seemed to me, as an outsider, that certain powerful organs
of the Press made themselves so great a nuisance over the
subject of air-raids at one time that they constituted an
actual danger. Ridicule was poured upon the plan of
darkening the streets of the metropolis until an attack
took place ; the first Zeppelin visit put an end to that.
Then, when the threat of raids became a serious reality,
the demand for retaliation was loudest from a combination
of journals which happens to be extremely well informed,
although it was almost a matter of common knowledge that
anything of the kind was impracticable at the time because
we had not got the requisite long-distance machines. It
was even contended that the physical difficulties to be
overcome in an attack upon the Westphalian cities were
far less than those which an enemy faced when flying to
London from the Belgian coast, although the distance
to be traversed over territory in the antagonist's hands
was three or four times as great in the former case as in
the latter. (Not one reader in fifty will look at the atlas
in a case like this and learn, at a glance, that he is being
made a fool of.) This Press campaign did grave mischief.
Dwellers in the East End, who were suffering seriously
from the raids and were almost in a condition of panic,
were induced to believe that pro-German influence in
high places was at the bottom of our failure to resort to
retaliatory counter-measures.

When the Prime Minister placed a newspaper proprietor in charge of the Air Service, he made in some respects a clever move. Press criticism practically ceased, and what there was of it mainly took the form of demands for a separate Ministry of Air. It would have been far better, however, if no decision had been arrived at on this subject until after the war was over, when the question could have been gone into carefully, and when a newspaper man would not have been actually in charge.

It may be remarked in conclusion that, had procedure within the War Office subsequent to mobilization more nearly followed the lines contemplated before the war, and which were only resumed some months later, there would probably have been less friction with the Press. The question of the war correspondents which has been mentioned above is a case in point. Then, again, a branch like mine which possessed an adequate staff, had it been given a freer hand, had it been allowed the requisite responsibility, and had it been kept better informed of what was actually going on in respect to operations, could have furnished newspapers with useful hints on many subjects. Take, for instance, that incessant outcry during the first two years or so of the war over the services of individual corps in action not being made known. As far as I am aware, journalists were never informed that the chief grounds for reticence in this matter arose from a simple sense of fairness. Everybody who has had to deal with history of military operations knows how hard it is to discover the actual facts in connection with any tactical event, and what careful weighing of different reports is necessary before the truth can be established. In these days of electric communications, official reports are sent off at very short notice and before details can possibly be known. If some unit is especially singled out for praise, injustice is likely to have been done; some other unit, or units, may in reality have done better without the full story having come to hand when the report was despatched.

In matters of this kind, the Press might advantageously have received greater assistance from the War Office. At all events that was so during the earlier portion of the time when the branch, which in pre-war days had been supposed to control such subjects, was under me, but only held restricted powers. The foregoing paragraphs have not been intended for one moment to suggest that British journalism did not, take it all round, behave admirably during the war. Newspapers almost always fell in readily with the wishes of the military authorities. On many occasions they were of the utmost assistance in making things known which it was desirable from the military point of view should be known. But there is no such thing as perfection in this world, and, even supposing the Press to be conscious of certain foibles of which it has been guilty, it can hardly be expected to advertise them itself. So an attempt has been made in this chapter to indicate certain directions in which it was occasionally at fault. The most important point of all, however, is that, when journalism and officialism happen to come into collision, the public in practice only hears the Fourth Estate's side of the story.

CHAPTER XVIII

SOME CRITICISMS, SUGGESTIONS, AND GENERALITIES

Post-war extravagance—The Office of Works lavish all through—The Treasury—Its unpopularity in the spending departments—The Finance Branch of the War Office—Suggestions—The change made with regard to saluting—Red tabs and red cap-bands—A Staff dandy in the West—The age of general-officers—Position of the General Staff in the War Office—The project of a Defence Ministry —No excuse for it except with regard to the air services, and that not a sufficient excuse—Confusion between the question of a Defence Ministry and that of the Imperial General Staff—The time which must elapse before newly constituted units can be fully depended upon, one of the most important lessons of the war for the public to realize—This proved to be the case in almost every theatre and in the military forces of almost every belligerent— Misapprehensions about South Africa—Improvised units could not have done what the " Old Contemptibles " did—Conclusion.

MY period of service on the active list closed a very few days before the Armistice of the 11th of November, so that no claim can be put forward to have formed one of that band of dug-outs who became dug-ins, and who continued to serve their country for extended periods with self-sacrificing devotion although the enemy was no longer in the gate.   But even in the disguises of private life a craftsman, fully initiated into the mysteries by long practice, could appraise the proceedings of the central administration of the Army from the standpoint of inner knowledge, could watch its post-war proceedings with detachment, and could note that amongst the numberless Government institutions which took " it's never too late to spend " for their motto after the conclusion of hostilities, the War Office was not absolutely the most backward. Only by such formidable competitors as the Munitions

Ministry, the Air Ministry, and, last but not least, the Office of Works did it apparently allow itself to be outpaced.

For relative prodigality during the course of the great emergency and after it was over, the Office of Works perhaps, upon the whole, took precedence over all rivals. Its prodigality was, to do it justice, tempered by extortion. Did the system of commandeering hotels and mammoth blocks of offices create new Departments of State ? Or did the creation of new Departments of State precede the commandeering of the hotels and blocks of offices ? Were the owners and occupiers of the blocks of offices paid for them, or were they bilked like the hotel proprietors ? We know that householders were not only paid, but that they were in many cases preposterously overpaid. And the worst of it was that the Office of Works was not one of those *parvenu* institutions, set on foot by Men of Business, which welled up so irrepressibly on all sides. It was not one of those *macédoines* of friends of Men of Business, and of fish-out-of-water swashbucklers in khaki, and of comatose messengers, and of incompletely dressed representatives of the fair sex perpetually engaged in absorbing sweets. It was an old-established portion of the structure of State. A nomad offshoot of the War Office, such as that I was in charge of for the last two years of the war, which after quitting the parent building shifted its home three times within the space of twelve months, enjoyed somewhat unusual opportunities for sizing up the Office of Works.

In the matter of numerical establishment· of its personnel, one Department of State with which I was brought a good deal into contact during the war, the Treasury, almost seemed to go into the opposite extreme from that which found favour in most limbs of the public service. If the guardians of the nation's purse-strings practically let the strings go during the early months of the contest, this may have been due to the effervescent personality of the then Chancellor of the Exchequer. But·they took an uncommonly long time to recover possession of the strings. Was this in any way attributable to insufficiency of staff in times of great pressure? There was none of that cheery bustle within the portals of Treasury Buildings such as prevailed in the caravanseries of Northumberland Avenue after the Munitions Ministry had seized them; typewriters were not to be heard clicking frantically, no bewitching flappers flitted about, the place always seemed as uninhabited as a railway terminus when the N.U.R. takes a holiday.

The Treasury has ever, rightly or wrongly, been ana-thema to the professional side of the War Office. The same sentiments would appear to prevail amongst the sea-dogs who lurk in the Admiralty; for after my having a slight difference of opinion with the Treasury representative at a meeting of the War Cabinet one day, an Admiral who happened to be present came up to me full of con-gratulations as we withdrew from the battlefield. " I don't know from Adam what it was all about," he declared, " but I longed to torpedo the blighter under the table." But when one had direct dealings with the Treasury its officials always were quite ready to see both sides of any question, to take a common-sense view, and to give way if a good case could be put to them; moreover, when they stuck their toes in and got their ears back, they generally had some right on their side. Such feeling of hostility as exists in the case of the War Office towards the controllers of national expenditure housed on the farther side of Whitehall is perhaps to some extent a result of unsatisfac-tory internal administration on its own side of the street.

It is the manifest duty of the Finance Branch of the War Office to keep down expenditure where possible, to examine any new proposal involving outlay with meticu-lous care and critically, and to intimate what the effect will be in terms of pounds, shillings and pence supposing that some new policy which is under consideration should come to be adopted. But, once a point has been decided by the Army Council (the Finance Branch having had its say), that branch should fight the War Office corner " all out," and should regard itself as the champion, not of the Treasury but of the Department of State of which it itself forms a part. The Treasury, it should be mentioned, is treated entirely differently as a matter of routine from other outside institutions. Letters to it have to emanate from the Finance Branch, while letters to other Departments of State—the Colonial Office, say, or the Board of Trade—can be drafted and, after signature by the Secretary, despatched by any branch of the War Office concerned. This rule might perhaps be modified. A regulation should also exist that the Finance Branch must not despatch a letter to the Treasury concerning some matter in which another branch is interested, without that branch having been given an opportunity of concurring in the terms of the draft.

But no officials in any State Department probably were set a harder and a more thankless task during the war than were the staff of the Finance Branch of the War Office, and in spite of this its members were always approachable and ready to meet one half-way in an amicable discussion. They are also entitled to sympathy, in that the close of hostilities in their case has probably brought them little or no relief in respect to length of office hours and to weight of work. To revert to normal conditions in their case will probably take years. The grievance of the military side is that under existing conditions the financial experts are too much in the position of autocrats, when they happen to be recalcitrant on any point.

Who can that caitiff have been who abolished the plan of the soldier saluting with the hand away from the individual saluted? Travelling on the Continent before the war one was struck with one point in which our methods were superior to those abroad—in many foreign countries private soldiers had to salute non-commissioned officers in the streets, which must have been an intolerable nuisance to all concerned, and in all of them the soldier always saluted with the right hand instead of adopting the obvious and convenient procedure of saluting with the outer hand. There at least we showed common sense. The Army Council were, no doubt, responsible in their corporate capacity for abolishing the left-hand salute, but there must have been some busybody who put them up to it. Whoever he was, I wish that he had had to walk daily along the Strand for months (as I had) constantly expecting to be hit in the face or to have his cap knocked off by some well-intentioned N.C.O. or private trying to salute with the hand next to him in a crowd. Their contortions were painful to see. Had the War Office been guilty of such *bêtises* when dealing with the things that really mattered during the struggle, they would have lost us the war. The reform was so inconvenient to all concerned that it may have helped to produce those untoward post-war conditions under which the men, if not belonging to the Guards, virtually abandoned the practice of saluting officers altogether in the streets of London.

Then, how about those red tabs? The expression " red tabs " is, however, employed rather as a shibboleth ; staff-officers must be distinguished somehow when they are not wearing armlets, and were the tabs less conspicuous there would be no special harm in them. It is the red band round the cap that is so utterly inappropriate when imposed upon service dress. It ought to have been abolished within six months of the beginning of the war. General-officers and staff-officers who came under fire had to adopt a khaki valance to conceal their cap-band ; they were to be seen going about in this get-up in the Metropolis when over on duty or on leave, and yet no steps were taken officially to assimilate their headgear to that of the ordinary officer. But for the red band and its distinctive effect, it is open to question whether officers performing every kind of special duty would have been so perpetually clamouring to be allowed to wear the red tabs. The practice of glorifying the staff-officer in his dress as compared with regimental officers is to be deprecated, although his turn-out should of course be, like Caesar's wife, above suspicion—to which I remember an exception when making first acquaintance with a staff I had come to join.

On reporting myself at headquarters at Devonport in the morning after arriving to take up an appointment a good many years ago, I learnt that there was to be no end of a pageant that afternoon.   The British Association, or some such body, had descended upon Plymouth for a palaver.   There was to be a review in Saltram Park on the farther side of the Three Towns so as to make sport for the visitors.   The general was very keen on mustering as many cocked hats around him for the performance as could be got together, and he pressed me to borrow a horse somehow and to put in an appearance, proposing that I should ride out with him and the A.D.C. as, being a stranger, I would not know the way.   So a crock was procured, saddlery was fished out of its case and polished up in frantic haste, and in due course we jogged out to the venue.   On arriving in the park we found the garrison, reinforced by a substantial Naval Brigade which had been extracted from H.M. ships in harbour, drawn up and looking very imposing, while people from round about had gathered in swarms and their best clothes to witness the spectacle.   As we rode on to the ground the Assistant-Adjutant-General came cantering up.   " The parade's all ready for you, sir," he reported, " and everything's all correct—except the Assistant-Quarter-master-General.   He, sir, is *in rags*."   He was.

There was one broad principle, the truth of which was brought out very clearly during the course of our British campaigns between 1914 and 1919—the principle that commanders of brigades and divisions require to be young and active men.   There were exceptions, no doubt ; but the exceptions only proved what came to be a generally accepted rule.   The old methods of promotion in the Army, methods which hinged partly on the purchase system and partly on the prizes of the service going by interest and by favour, were highly objectionable ; but those methods did have the advantage that commanders in the field, whether they turned out to be efficient or to be inefficient, were at least fairly young in years as a rule. Wellington himself, and all his principal subordinates other than Graham and Picton, were well under fifty years of age at the end of the Peninsular War ; Wellington was forty-five, Beresford was forty-six, Hill was forty-two, Lowry Cole was forty-two. Wolfe, again, and Clive, Amherst and Granby, the most distinguished British commanders of the eighteenth century except Marlborough, were all comparatively young men at the time when they made their mark. It was only in the course of the long peace that followed Waterloo that our general-officers as a body came to be well on in life—Lord Raglan at the beginning of the Crimean War was sixty-six, Brown was sixty-four, Cathcart was sixty—even if at a somewhat later date a prolonged course of small wars did produce a sufficiency of young commanders to go round for minor campaigns. It would seem advisable to reduce the limit of age for promotion to the grade of major-general from fifty-seven to fifty, and that for the grade of lieutenant-general from sixty-two to fifty-seven. The great obstacle in the way of a reform of this kind, as a rule, arises from the fact that the decision rests to a large extent in the hands of comparatively old officers, who do not always quite realize that they are past the age for work in the field. That is not so much the case now, so that it seems to be the right time to act.

The position of the General Staff within the War Office appears to be pretty well assured now. But it also appeared to be pretty well assured before the war ; and yet there were those incidents of the non-existence of the high-explosive shell for our field artillery which nearly all foreign field artilleries possessed, and of Colonel Swinton's Tank projects being dealt with by a technical branch and the General Staff never hearing of it, which have been mentioned in this volume. The military technicalist, be he an expert in ballistics or in explosives or in metallurgy or in electrical communications or in any other form of scientific knowledge, is a very valuable member of the martial community. But he is a little inclined to get into a groove. He stood in some need of being stirred up from outside during the Great War, and he must learn that he is subordinate to the General Staff.

The old project of instituting a Ministry of Defence has cropped up again, very largely owing to the importance that aeronautics have assumed in war and to the anomalous position of affairs which the creation of an Air Ministry has brought about. Could aviation in its various forms be left entirely out of consideration in connection with defence problems, no case whatever could be put forward for setting up such a central Department of State. The relations between the sea service and the land service are on a totally different basis now from what they were when Lord Randolph Churchill, thirty years ago, proposed the establishment of a Ministry which would link together the Admiralty and the War Office, each of which was under his plan to be controlled by a professional head. It was in many respects an attractive scheme in those days. The departments that were respectively administering the Royal Navy and the Army were not then in close touch, as they are now ; they badly required association in some form or other. But it has been found possible to secure the needed collaboration and concert between them without resorting to heroic measures such as Lord Randolph contemplated. The sea service and the land service generally worked in perfect harmony during the Great War—except in the one matter of their respective air departments. There was a certain amount of unwholesome competition between them over aeronautical material up to the time when one single air department was established late in 1917.

Aeronautics do unquestionably constitute a difficulty, and a difficulty which did not make itself apparent during the late conflict in quite the same form as it might in future wars. The Navy and the Army must both have air services absolutely under their control in peace and in war ; but there is also, no doubt, immense scope for independent aeronautical establishments, kept separate from the fighting forces on the sea and on land. Three more or less distinct air services, in fact, seem to be needed, and the question of equitable distribution of material between them at once crops up. Supposing all three to be administered, from the supply point of view, by an Air Ministry, this institution may show itself disposed to look better after its own child, the independent air service, than after its stepchildren, the naval and military air services. Were a Minister of Defence to be set up as overlord, he could act as impartial referee. But this one phase of our defence problems as a whole can surely be dealt with effectively without creating an entirely new Ministry, for the establishment of which no other good excuse can be put forward. The problem of preventing competition and rivalry in respect to material between the three branches of combatant aeronautics ought not to be an insuperable one, if firmly handled.

In this connection it may be observed that a certain confusion of ideas appears to exist in some quarters between a Defence Ministry co-ordinating naval, military and aeronautical questions, and an Imperial General Staff concerning itself with the sea, the land and the air. The two things are, and must always be, totally distinct. A Defence Ministry would in the nature of things be an executive institution. In the Empire as it is now constituted, an Imperial General Staff can only be a consultative institution. A General Staff in the ordinary meaning of the term is executive as well as consultative ; it issues orders with regard to certain matters, and it administers certain military departments and branches. But so long as the Empire comprises a number of self-governing Dominions and has no common budget for defence purposes, the Imperial General Staff can only make recommendations and tender advice ; it can order nothing.

Amóngst the innumerable professional lessons taught by the experiences of the Great War, there is one which professional soldiers had learnt before it began, but which the public require to learn. This is that newly organized troops or troops of the militia type such as our Territorials of pre-war days, who necessarily have undergone little training previous to the outbreak of hostilities, do not make really effective instruments in the hands of a commander for a considerable period after embodiment. The course of events proved, it is true, that the individual soldier and officer can be adequately prepared for the ordeal in a shorter space of time than had generally been believed necessary by military men, and that they can be incorporated in drafts for the front within a very few months of their joining the colours. But that does not hold good with individual units. Still less does it hold good with collections of individual units such as brigades and divisions.

The records of the New Army, of the Territorials, of the improvised formations sent to fight by the great Dominions oversea, all go to show that such troops need to be broken in gradually after they take the field before they can safely be regarded as fully equal to serious operations. Our Allies' and our enemies' experiences were similar. We know from enemy works that, although the German " Reserve Corps " fought gallantly during the early months, they achieved less and suffered more heavily in casualties than would have been the case had Regular Corps been given corresponding tasks to carry out. It was the same with the French Territorial Divisions. The American troops proved fine fighters from the outset, but owing to lack of experience and of cohesion they took a considerable time before they pulled their weight ; moreover, the larger the bodies in which they fought independently of French and British command, the more noticeable this was.

Certain regiments hastily got together on the spot from men who could shoot and ride and who knew the Boers and their ways, performed most distinguished service during the South African War, so much so, indeed, that an idea got abroad amongst civilians at that time that the need for the elaborate and prolonged training, which professional soldiers always insisted upon, was merely a question of prejudice. Happily those who were responsible for our Army organization and for its preparation for war knew better, and August 1914 proved that they were right. It was not merely due to the stubborn grit of their personnel that the " Old Contemptibles " carried out their retreat from Mons in face of greatly superior hostile forces with what was in reality comparatively small loss, and that they were ready to advance and fight again as soon as they got the word. It was also due to rank and file and regimental officers and staff knowing their business thoroughly. Had those five divisions been, say, New Army divisions just arrived at the front, or divisions such as landed under General Birdwood's orders at Anzac on the 25th of April, they would have been swept back in hopeless confusion. They would not have known enough about the niceties of the game to play it successfully under such adverse conditions. The framework would not have stood the strain.

The sedentary type of operations which for three years played so big a part in most theatres was, it must be remembered, particularly favourable to newly created formations. Mobile warfare imposes a much more violent test. When really active work is being carried on in the field by partially trained troops, the platoon may do capitally, the company fairly well, the battalion not altogether badly ; but the brigade will be all over the place, and the division will be in a state of chaos. Whatever conditions future campaigns may bring forth, trench warfare is unlikely to supervene immediately, nor to be brought about until something fairly important has happened ; and it will not continue to the end unless the result of the conflict is to be indecisive.   In 1918 there was nothing to choose between British divisions which had had no existence in August 1914 and those which had fought as the point of England's lance at Le Cateau, on the Marne and on the Aisne.   But wars will not always last four years.   Nor will the belligerent who has to create entirely new armies to carry on the struggle always prove victorious in the end.

THE END

Printed in Great Britain by R. & R. CLARK, LIMITED, *Edinburgh*,

Printed by BoD™in Norderstedt, Germany

9 781440 098826